Joseph Rowntree Foundation

Housing Finance Review 1995/96

Steve Wilcox

Contents

Acknowledgements	3
Lists of figures and tables	4
Introduction	8

Contemporary issues

1 The PSBR handicap — 9
John Hawksworth and Steve Wilcox

2 The rising number of households requiring homes - the national and regional picture — 16
Alan Holmans

3 What has happened to the North-South divide in house prices and the housing market? — 25
Alan Holmans

4 A shrinking safety net for a changing market — 32
Peter Williams

The Housing Finance Review 1995-96

1 Economic prospects and public expenditure — 38

2 Dwellings and households — 44

3 Private housing — 50

4 UK Housing expenditure plans — 56

5 Housing needs and homelessness — 66

6 Help with housing costs — 70

Acknowledgements

Drawing as it does on such a wide range of sources, this annual compilation of statistical data would not have been possible without the substantial help and guidance of a host of civil servants, at the Department of the Environment, the Treasury, the Scottish, Welsh and Northern Ireland Offices, the Department of Social Security and elsewhere.

Similar assistance was given from the Council of Mortgage Lenders, the Housing Corporation, Scottish Homes, Housing for Wales, the National Federation of Housing Associations and their Scottish and Welsh counterparts, the Association of District Councils, the Association of Metropolitan Authorities, the Convention of Scottish Local Authorities, the London Research Centre and others. The enormous help they have again provided in the compilation of this year's edition of the *Review* is most readily and gratefully acknowledged.

Much of the statistical data presented here is generally available in a variety of published statistical series and sources are comprehensively acknowledged against each Table in the Review. A particular debt must be acknowledged for the wide range of data and tables drawn or adapted from *Housing and Construction Statistics* (available from HMSO).

The author is also particularly grateful to the direct contributors to the *Review*, Alan Holmans, now retired from the Department of the Environment, Peter Williams at the Council of Mortgage Lenders, and John Hawksworth at Coopers & Lybrand.

A further vote of thanks is due to Alan Holmans this year for making many detailed suggestions for additions, amendments and re-organisation of the tables in the *Review*, and helping with the construction of the new tables.

The successful production of the *Review* continues to make heavy demands on the professionalism and patience of David Darton and his team at the Joseph Rowntree Foundation. The author remains ever grateful for their continuous support throughout all stages of the work in compiling and producing the Review.

For all the help provided, and despite every attempt that has been made to check and double-check all the figures included in the *Review*, and the construction put upon them, the final responsibility for any errors, omissions or misjudgements are entirely the responsibility of the author.

Steve Wilcox
September 1995
Centre for Housing Management and Development
Department of City and Regional Planning
University of Cardiff, Wales, Tel: 01823 323891

List of figures and tables

All the tables listed below contain UK-based figures unless otherwise indicated in the table title. Where English regional figures are shown, this is indicated in the title. Tables showing breakdowns between England, Wales, Scotland and/or Northern Ireland are shown with a single asterisk and those showing international comparisons with a double asterisk. Tables containing a historic time-series of several years are indicated by a †. Figures and tables labelled with a Roman numeral appear within the text part of the Review rather than within the main table section.

Economic prospects and public expenditure

Macro-economy

Table 1†	Key economic trends	77
Table 2†	Average male and female earnings in Great Britain	77
Table 3†	Personal disposable income, consumer spending and savings	78
Table 4*†	Regional unemployment rates	79
Figure IV	Unemployment rates	40
Table XX	Employment, unemployment and the labour force 1981-2001	41
Table XXI	Employment status of working age population	42
Figure V	Changes in employment status, 1993-2001	41

Housing

Table 5†	Personal housing wealth, borrowing and net equity	77
Table 6†	Equity withdrawal	80
Table XIX	Negative equity by region	39
Figure III	Net equity per home-owner	40
Table 7**†	Gross fixed investment in dwellings	80
Figure VI	Gross fixed investment in residential dwellings	43
Table I	European social housing: accounting and financial control	13

Public expenditure

Table 8**†	Growth of real Gross Domestic Product	81
Table 9**†	General Government Financial Balances as a percentage of Gross National Product	81
Figure I	Government deficit and public sector borrowing	12
Table 10	The Budget Economic Forecast	82
Table 11	General Government Expenditure, receipts and borrowing	83
Table 12†	General Government Expenditure, Gross Domestic Product and the PSBR	85
Table 13†	Public sector capital expenditure	86
Table 14†	General Government Expenditure by function	87
Table 15	Control total by department	89

Dwellings and households

Provision of dwellings

Table 16*†	Dwellings by tenure	92
Figure VII	Housing stock	45
Table 17†	Gross fixed capital formation in dwellings	96
Table 18*†	Housing starts and completions	97
Figure VIII	Housing completions in Great Britain	46
Table 19*†	Right to Buy	103
Table 20*	Changes in regional provision of social housing	104

Housing conditions

Table 21*	Households lacking amenities by tenure and territory	105
Table 22	English housing conditions 1986 and 1991	106
Table 23	Welsh housing conditions 1986 and 1993	107
Table 24	Scottish housing conditions 1991	108

List of figures and tables

Renovation grants

Table 25*†	Regional renovation grants paid to private owners in Great Britain	109
Table 26*†	Number of local authority, new town and housing association dwellings receiving renovation grants by region in Great Britain	111

Households

Table II	Past and projected increases in households in England	17
Table III	Projections of population by region	19
Table IV	Past and projected net increases in households by region	20
Table V	Distribution of increase in households between regions	20
Table VI	Projected increases in households in Metropolitan districts, London and Counties	21
Table VII	Differences between 1989-based and 1992-based households projections by type of area	23
Table XXII	Household projections for England	46
Table XXIII	Household projection for Wales	46
Table XXIV	Household projection for Scotland	47

Tenure profiles and characteristics

Table 27	Property characteristics by tenure in Great Britain	112
Table VIII	Type of accommodation occupied by one-person households under age 60	23
Table 28	Tenure profile of heads of household in Great Britain	113
Table 29	Race by tenure, dwelling type and bedroom standards in Great Britain	116
Table 30	Tenure and consumer durables in Great Britain	117
Table 31	Employment status of household heads by tenure	118
Table 32	Employment status of recently moving household heads by tenure	119
Table XIV	Employment status of home-buying household heads	34
Table 33	Average income of head of household by tenure in Great Britain	120
Table 34	Tenure and sources of income	120
Table 35	Tenure and gross weekly household income in Great Britain, 1993	121
Table XVIII	Tenure of households in the bottom income decile 1979 and 1991/92	37
Table XXV	Incomes by tenure and economic activity	48
Table XXVI*	Incomes by tenure and region	49
Figure IX	Incomes by tenure	48

Private housing

Level of market activity

Table 36†	Numbers of property transactions in England and Wales	123
Table 37†	Numbers of mortgage advances per year in Great Britain	123
Table IX	Regional distribution of house purchase transactions from SOPT	27
Table X	Regional distribution of house purchase advances from BSM	27
Table XI	SOPT-based estimates of house purchases in 'the South' and the rest of England and Wales	30
Table XII†	Private sector house building in 'the South' and 'the Midlands and the North'	30

Home lending in relation to incomes and wealth

Table 38†	Building societies advances	124
Table 39†	Advances to first-time buyers and former owner-occupiers	126
Table 40	Housing wealth, borrowing and equity	128
Figure XI	First-time buyers and all home-buyers average mortgage costs	51

Land and house prices

Table 41*†	Regional land prices	128
Table 42*†	Average regional house prices	129
Table XIII†	House prices and house starts for private owners in England and Scotland	31
Table XXVII*	Average regional house prices by size of dwelling in 1993	52
Figure II	Ratio of house prices in the South East to those in the North	26

Mortgage repayments, arrears and repossessions

Figure X	Building society interest rates	51
Table 43*†	Average regional mortgage repayments	131
Table 44†	Mortgage arrears and repossessions	132
Table XXVIII	Moving into and out of mortgage arrears 1991 - 1993	53
Table 45	Regional court orders for mortgage repossession in England and Wales	132
Table 46	Court actions for mortgage repossessions in England and Wales	133
Figure XII	Mortgage arrears and repossessions	52

Private renting

Table 47	Types of letting in the private rented sector	134
Table 48	Investment in Business Expansion Scheme Assured Tenancy Companies	134
Figure XIII	Private lettings	54

Housing expenditure plans

Housing expenditure and investment in the UK and Great Britain

Table 49*†	Territorial analysis of identifiable General Government Expenditure	136
Table 50*†	Gross social housing investment in Great Britain	137
Table 51*†	Local authority gross investment plans in Great Britain	138
Table 52*†	Housing associations' gross investment plans in Great Britain	139
Table 53†	UK local authority housing revenue accounts	140
Figure XIV	Council housing receipts and expenditure	58

Housing expenditure and investment in England

Table 54†	Housing capital investment in England	141
Table 55†	Housing capital provision in England	143
Table 56	Housing Corporation Approved Development Programme	144
Table 57	Housing Corporation planned revenue expenditure	144
Figure XV	Housing Corporation investment	59
Table 58†	Regional local authority housing capital expenditure in England	145
Table 59†	Estate Action Programme in England	146
Table 60	Large-scale voluntary transfers of council housing in England	147
Table 61	Local authority revenue accounts in England	149
Table 62	Rent 'surpluses', housing subsidy and housing benefit subsidy in England	150
Table 63†	Rents and earnings in England	151
Table 64	Regional housing association and private sector rents in England in 1993	152
Table XXIX	Average local authority rents by region, size and type of dwelling in England in 1993/94	61

Housing expenditure and investment in Wales

Table 65†	Welsh housing capital expenditure	153
Table 66†	Welsh housing capital plans and investment	154
Figure XVII	Gross social housing investment in Wales	62
Table 67†	Welsh local authority housing revenue accounts	155
Table 68	Housing subsidy and housing benefit subsidy in Wales	157
Table 69†	Rents and earnings in Wales	158

Housing expenditure and investment in Scotland

Table 70†	Scottish gross housing investment	159
Figure XVIII	Social housing investment in Scotland	64
Table 71†	Scottish housing investment by agency	159
Table 72†	Provision for local authority housing investment in Scotland	160
Table 73	Scottish Homes capital grants and private finance	161
Table 74†	Scottish local authorities consolidated housing revenue account	162
Table 75†	Average costs, rents and subsidies in Scottish housing revenue accounts	163
Table 76†	Rents and earnings in Scotland	163

Housing expenditure and investment in Northern Ireland

Table 77†	Financial provision for housing in Northern Ireland	164
Table 78†	Gross housing investment in Northern Ireland	165
Table 79†	Northern Ireland Housing Executive rents and average earnings	165

Housing needs and homelessness

Level of homelessness

Table 80†	Local authority homeless acceptances	167
Figure XIX	Homeless acceptances	67
Table 81†	Homeless households in temporary accommodation	167
Figure XX	Accommodation for homeless households	67
Table 82	Regional homelessness in England	168
Table XXX	Official estimate of housing needs in England	69

Nature of homelessness

Table 83	Reasons for homelessness	168
Table 84	Homelessness: categories of need	169
Table 85*	People sleeping rough in Great Britain in 1991	169

Lettings

Table 86†	Local authority dwelling stock, new dwellings and lettings in England	170
Table 87†	Regional lettings to homeless households and new tenants in England	171
Table 88	Regional lettings to new tenants by size of dwelling in England in 1993/4	172
Table 89†	Housing association lettings in England	172
Table 90	Projected output from the Housing Corporation's Approved Development Programme	173
Table 91†	Local authority and housing association lettings to new tenants	174
Table 92†	Welsh local authority lettings	175
Table 93†	Scottish local authority lettings	175
Table 94†	Northern Ireland Housing Executive lettings and homelessness in Northern Ireland	175

Help with housing costs

Mortgage interest tax relief

Table 95†	Mortgage interest tax relief	177
Table 96	Mortgage interest tax relief by income band	177
Table 97*†	Regional mortgage interest tax relief	177
Figure XXI	Financial assistance per home-buyer	71

Local authority housing subsidies

Table 98*†	Subsidies for local authority housing in Great Britain	179

Income support for home owners

Table 99†	Mortgage interest taken into account for income support	181
Table 100	Range of mortgage interest taken into account for income support	181
Table XXXI*	Average Mortgage interest taken into account for income support by region	72
Table XV	Time receiving income support for mortgage interest (ISMI) May 1993	35
Table XVI	Type of mortgage interest claimants by duration of current income support claim	35
Table XVII*	Regional increases in housing costs in 1995	36
Figure XXII	Housing assistance to households on income support	72

Housing benefit

Table 101†	Housing benefit - numbers of claimants and average claim in Great Britain	182
Table 102	Supplementary benefit assistance with housing costs in Great Britain	182
Table 103†	Housing benefits expenditure and plans for Great Britain	183
Table 104*	Average housing benefit per recipient in Great Britain	184
Table 105*	Numbers of housing benefit recipients in Great Britain	185
Table 106	Housing benefit for housing association and private tenants	186
Table XXXII*	Housing benefit caseload and payments by tenure and region	73
Table 107	Characteristics of housing benefit recipients in Great Britain in 1993	187
Table 108	Earnings and income levels at which housing benefit entitlement ceases	188
Table 109†	Income support and housing benefits	189
Figure XXIII	The costs to the government of increasing rents by 10%	74

Summary of assistance with housing costs by tenure

Table 110†	Assistance with housing costs for home-owners, local authority tenants and private tenants	190
Figure XVI	Rents and mortgage costs	62
Figure XXIV	Financial support for housing	75

Introduction

The primary objective of this, the fourth edition of the *Housing Finance Review*, remains simply to draw together key current financial data about both public and private housing in the United Kingdom and rapidly assemble them in a coherent and accessible format.

To that end the *Review* draws on a wide range of expenditure plans and departmental reports, as well as statistical volumes, survey reports, and other more occasional research reports. The *Review* also includes a number of tables constructed from databases that are not routinely published elsewhere.

In most cases the tables in the *Review* start at the beginning of the last decade, to provide a consistent context for the most recent year's figures. The precise starting-points for each table, however, vary for entirely practical reasons in the compilation of the *Review*.

The structure of the *Review*, and the sparse text, aim above all to provide a swift guide to that data, with detailed analysis confined to the articles on *Contemporary Issues* at the beginning of the *Review*.

The section of short chapters offers a brief introduction and commentary on the key developments in policy, financial provision and output that are reflected in the tables and figures in the main body of the *Review*.

Regional issues

This year the opportunity has also been taken to include a number of additional tables providing regional data on housing finance and related issues. These tables, to be found in the relevant chapters, complement the regional tables in the main body of the *Review*, and the detailed analyses of some key regional issues provided in two of the *Contemporary Issues* articles by Alan Holmans.

Getting better

The *Review* has welcomed the generally improved style and content of the departmental reports as a measure of developments in official culture that bode well for the Government's commitment to open government. It remains the case, however, that the Welsh Office Annual Report does not provide any detailed breakdown of its plans for housing expenditure more than one year ahead, rather than for the whole three-year period of the expenditure plans.

In previous years, the *Review* has particularly welcomed the improved official candour about the prospects for local authority capital receipts, and the willingness of the Department of the Environment, and subsequently the Welsh Office, to provide explicit projections about the contribution that council rent 'surpluses' are required to make towards the costs of housing benefits.

This year a special mention should be made of the official estimates of housing need published by the Department of the Environment, and submitted to the Environment Committee. It is now nearly two decades since any official estimates of this kind were last published, and, while the content of the estimates is critically examined in Chapter 6, here it is appropriate to welcome the fact of their publication.

Regrets

Sadly this year there is also one failure to publish that must be recorded. For reasons of economy, the Scottish Rent Officer Service has decided that it will no longer collect Scottish-wide statistics on rent officer decisions. Given the new housing benefit regulations due to be introduced in 1996, which will give rent officers even greater responsibilities, it is very much to be hoped that this decision will be rapidly reversed.

Contemporary issues 1

The PSBR handicap

John Hawksworth and Steve Wilcox

There must be some way out of here

Restrictions on permitted borrowing for council housing investment have been a constant frustration for councillors, managers and tenants over the last two decades. Those frustrations have been accentuated in recent years by the tighter controls imposed in England and Wales since 1990, and the contrast with the freedom of housing associations to raise private finance without government controls.

This financial freedom for housing associations follows from their status, in national accounts terms, as private non-profit corporations. Their borrowing is therefore private sector borrowing, and does not count as public spending.

Councils are, however, inescapably part of general government, and it logically follows that their borrowing must inevitably count as public expenditure. One way out of that logical conundrum has been established in the last six years as, by the end of March 1995, 40 English and one Scottish councils have transferred their total housing stock, comprising some 180,000 dwellings, in almost all cases into the ownership of newly created local housing associations (in schemes known as large-scale voluntary transfers or LSVT).[1]

The housing associations set up for these stock transfers have been able to raise some £2.65 billion in private finance, partly to purchase the stock from the councils but also to undertake substantial programmes of 'catch-up' repairs and improvements which are the envy of councils remaining within the grip of government capital spending controls. Under those controls council housing investment is now set to fall, in real terms, to below one-third of its 1979/80 level.[2]

The housing company option

While the initiative for stock transfers has come from local councils, it has been shaped and regulated by central government, through the powers of the Secretary of State to grant or withhold consent for the transfers to take place.

One constraint that has been imposed since the inception of the stock transfer programme is that local council representation on the committee of the new landlord body should not exceed 20%. A 1993 report showed how, even in terms of the Government's own legislation (Part V, Local Government and Housing Act 1989), it would be possible for local authorities to have a far greater involvement in the new landlord bodies than 20%.[3] As long as the council representation on the new landlord body remained in the minority, this would neither change its status from private sector corporation or trigger the requirement to count the borrowing by the new landlord against the local council's capital spending limit.

The other key finding of the earlier study was to show that there could be financial advantages for both local and central government if urban authorities with levels of outstanding debt greater than the current capital value of their stock could be persuaded to transfer their stock to a new landlord body. To date the LSVT initiative has been limited to councils where the value of the stock exceeded the outstanding debt.

These potential financial gains were best illustrated in the study by the examination of the financial position of Newcastle MBC. This showed how stock transfer to a new landlord body (or bodies) whose borrowing did not count against the government budget deficit could release some £85 million for additional housing investment, with the greater part of that 25% increase becoming available in the first five years following transfer.

Against that, under current rules, the council would incur housing benefit costs of some £30 million. If the stock remained in council ownership, the full costs of housing benefit would be met by central government or by tenants.

At the same time there would be very considerable savings for the Treasury. Following a Newcastle stock transfer there would be a reduction of almost £97 million in the PSBR. The costs of residual debt subsidy would be offset by the capital receipt from the stock transfer, the removal of the need to provide public sector borrowing consents for investment on the housing stock, and the receipts of VAT income arising from the works contracts put out by the new landlord body.[4]

Joint study

A joint local authority and Department of the Environment study has for some time now been examining in greater detail the construction of a stock transfer programme around similar ideas to those laid out in the earlier report, and should report in the autumn of 1995.

In agreeing to this study, the DoE implicitly accepted that it would be willing to contemplate the provision of residual debt subsidy to councils undertaking stock transfers where the transfer receipt is not sufficient to clear the whole of the outstanding debt on the stock. Subsequently the Treasury has confirmed that residual debt subsidy will be available to Manchester if it proceeds with a proposed transfer of an overspill estate to a new landlord in 1996. As shown above the costs to the Treasury of residual debt subsidy will be offset by future capital savings and by capital and VAT receipts.

It is now clear from the White Paper that the DoE are ready in principle to relax the current LSVT guidelines on the constitution of new landlord bodies and agree to councils having something like one-third membership of their committees. This broadly corresponds with the recent relaxation of controls on companies with a minority council influence, introduced as part of the Government's private finance initiative.[5]

As with existing housing associations, minority-influenced companies would still, in national accounts terms, be private not-for-profit institutions whose borrowing is outside any measure of government or public expenditure. This approach represents more or less the limits for a mixed public/private venture to restructure council housing — while the PSBR remains the principal UK budget deficit measure.

It might be possible for a future government to push the level of permitted local authority involvement a little higher, but the local authority would still need to have only a minority interest and influence, and could not have effective control (i.e. the right to appoint and dismiss the board of directors) if the company was to be properly classified under international conventions as being within the private sector and so fall outside the PSBR.

International horizons

A new perspective on these issues has now come from a study of the international conventions on measuring government financial deficits, and the ways in which they effect the borrowing of social housing landlords in other European countries.[6]

Four measures of government financial deficits are commonly in use:

- The General Government Financial Deficit (GGFD)
- The General Government Borrowing Requirement (GGBR)
- The Public Sector Financial Deficit (PSFD)
- The Public Sector Borrowing Requirement (PSBR)

The first of these is the primary measure of government financial deficits in the System of National Accounts (SNA). The SNA is jointly published by the UN, OECD, IMF, European Union and World Bank, so carries a fair amount of weight. The PSBR measure is recognised in the SNA as an alternative measure of financial deficits, but it is a measure that is very little used outside of the UK.

There are two critical differences between the GGFD and PSBR measures. The first is that GGFD measures the deficits of only two government sectors — central government and local government. The PSBR also includes the borrowing of public corporations. The second is that the PSBR is measured net of privatisation receipts, while the GGFD measure is of deficits before taking account of the income derived from privatisation measures.

The GGFD measure has also been adopted by the European Union (EU) for the purposes of the Maastricht Treaty economic convergence criteria for European Monetary Union. The requirement that member states should seek to restrict their deficits to below 3% of Gross Domestic Product (GDP) is measured in terms of GGFD, not PSBR. While the UK has not as yet signed up to the principle of monetary union, the Government has now started to give rather more prominence to the GGFD measure, and submits GGFD returns to the EU as required by the Maastricht Treaty.

In recent years in the UK, the financial deficit measured in terms of the GGFD has been higher than the PSBR, as shown in Figure I. Over the last five years the UK GGFD has been some 1% to 1.5% higher than the PSBR. This is because, following the programme of privatisations of the public utility companies over the last fifteen years, there are very few remaining public corporations. At the same time receipts from privatisation and from council house sales continue to reduce the level of the PSBR.

In the years ahead, however, the UK PSBR and GGFD measures are expected to converge. This is partly

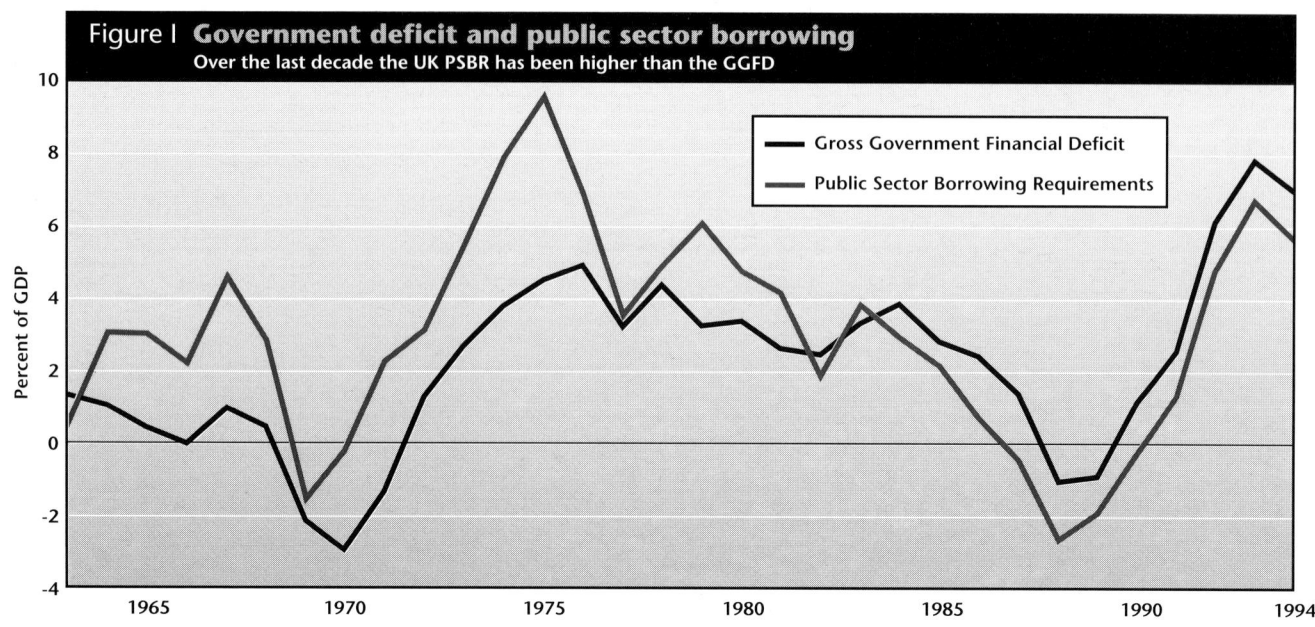

Figure I **Government deficit and public sector borrowing**
Over the last decade the UK PSBR has been higher than the GGFD

Source: Hawksworth & Wilcox (1995)

because privatisation measures now in the pipeline (British Rail) will further diminish the public corporate sector in the UK, and partly because thereafter no more privatisation measures are currently planned.

European social housing landlords

The adoption of government, rather than public sector, measures of budget deficits provides the basis for understanding why it is that social sector housing landlords in other European countries are free to raise private finance without the kind of government borrowing controls that apply uniquely to council housing in the UK.

Basically, in other countries the principal agencies providing social sector housing are either public or private corporations under the international accounting conventions, and in every case the borrowing of those agencies falls outside the primary measure of government financial deficits adopted by the country in question. Table I gives some examples of how these conventions and fiscal policies apply in a number of European countries.

In France, for example, the primary social housing landlord bodies are the *habitations à loyer modéré*. The HLM take various forms, from municipally sponsored *Offices publics* to non-profit-limited liability companies. Within those main forms the extent of public and private sector involvement varies, so that some are clearly in the public sector, while others are equally clearly in the private sector. In either case their borrowing is outside the key French budget deficit measure and is not subject to direct controls.

There is a similar diversity in the forms of social sector landlords in Germany, and again the non-profit-limited liability companies clearly divide between the public and private sectors. In 1986, municipalities had a controlling interest in over a half of such companies, while others had been sponsored by trade unions, employers and churches.

In Germany, tenure boundaries are further blurred by the direct participation of commercial private sector landlords in the provision of subsidised housing. As in France, the non-profit companies, in all their forms, fall in the corporate sector and their borrowing is outside the general government budget deficit adopted by the German government.

In the Netherlands the primary social housing agencies are housing associations, although local authorities do have a continuing minority role as direct landlord bodies in some areas. The housing associations, like their UK equivalents, are private sector non-profit institutions, that fall wholly outside the public sector. In consequence their borrowing would escape the comprehensive public sector measure adopted by the UK, let alone the central or general government measures adopted by the Dutch government.

The Swedish model

The primary social housing agencies in Sweden are closest in form to UK council housing. In Sweden local housing companies are predominantly wholly owned

Table 1 **European social housing: accounting and financial control**

Country	Primary agency	Financial sector	Key budget deficit measures
France	Habitations à loyer modéré	Private & public corporations	Central government
Germany	Non-profit companies	Private & public corporations	General government
Netherlands	Housing associations	Private corporations	Central/general government
Sweden	Local housing companies	Public corporations	Central/general government
United Kingdom	Local authorities	Local government	Public sector

Source: John Hawksworth and Steve Wilcox, *Challenging the Conventions*

by local authorities. They are, however, established as quite separate non-profit foundations or companies.[7] Under the SNA conventions they therefore constitute not-for-profit trading bodies and consequently fall into the public corporate sector. As a result, their borrowing is outside both the central government budget deficit measure adopted by the current Swedish government, as well as the general government measure favoured by international conventions and used in the Maastricht Treaty.

Council housing in the UK stands alone as the only case where a government body is itself the direct provider of the majority of social sector housing. In both legal and financial terms the affairs of council housing are inextricably bound up with the wider organisation and finances of local authorities. Borrowing for council housing investment is therefore inescapably part of overall local government borrowing and as such would fall within a general government measure of budget deficits, as well as the comprehensive public sector deficit measure adopted by all UK governments since the mid-1970s.

Two changes would be needed to transform UK council housing into Swedish-style housing companies, whose borrowing for investment would fall outside the scope of budget deficit measures, and the inevitable constraints that implies. The first step would be to restructure council housing so that it would qualify as a public corporation, rather than as part of local government. The second step would be for the UK government to adopt GGFD, or some general government-based measure, rather than the PSBR, as its primary fiscal deficit measure.

Council housing as a public corporation

To be accounted for as within the public corporate sector, council housing would need to be restructured to meet three criteria:

- charging economically significant prices
- operating and being managed in a similar way to a corporation; and
- maintaining a complete set of accounts that enabled its operating surpluses, savings, assets and liabilities to be separately identified and measured.[8]

The SNA criteria for accounting for council housing as a local public corporation would be even more clearly met if the housing was transferred into the ownership of a wholly separate company, albeit one wholly- or majority-controlled by the local authority.

While not insignificant, the institutional changes required are clearly less radical than those involved in stock transfers to housing associations, or even minority-influenced local housing companies. There is little to be gained from such a transformation, however, while the UK government holds to the PSBR as its primary measure of budget deficits.

The case against the PSBR

There are several arguments for removing the PSBR from the primary position it has held in government fiscal policy since 1976. Decisions on such an issue will, however, obviously be taken on the basis of broad economic and political considerations, rather than in terms of the ramifications for housing policy. At best, the potential housing example gives an indication of some of the advantages of such a change.

The main case for a change is that publicly owned trading bodies, such as post offices and national railways, should be free to undertake commercial borrowing against their trading incomes and that direct government borrowing controls for such trading bodies are unnecessary.

Where any payments of subsidy are involved the government would have a continuing legitimate concern that any borrowing should not add to those subsidy costs. It need not, however, adopt a budget deficit measure that results in decisions being taken about commercially self-financing investment by public corporations, in order to comply with self-imposed limits on overall government budget deficits.

If council housing was transferred to local public housing corporations on the same financial basis as applies for LSVT, this would rule out the need for any subsidy payments to the new landlord body. As with existing LSVT housing association landlords, they would be borrowing against their future rent streams, and the extent of the borrowing that they could undertake would have to be balanced both against decisions on rent levels, and their efficiency in containing their routine operating costs.

Housing benefits

In the case of rented housing, however, much of the rental income received by landlords is underpinned by housing benefit payments to the tenant. Gross housing benefit expenditure is currently running at around £11 billion per annum in Great Britain, of which almost £6 billion relates to council housing and the remainder to private housing including housing associations.

If local housing corporations were to be established, it would clearly be legitimate for central government to ensure that they had incentives to limit rents, and that they would not, without limit, rely on housing benefits to meet any rent they chose to levy.

Without some such restriction, it could be argued that the rents charged by the local housing corporations would not be economically significant. They would not in that case be classified as a trading body, and instead would be accounted for as part of general government, even if they were established as separate legal entities.

As with housing associations, it may not be considered sufficient to rely on the measures restricting private sector rents, as most council rents are currently far lower than housing association, let alone private rents. One possible approach would be to relate the eligible rent limits for housing companies to the rent levels assumed in their stock valuation and financial restructuring.

Such a measure would ensure that central government was insulated both directly and indirectly from the consequences of the corporations' choices about investment levels, and the relative efficiency of their overall operations. Great care would be needed, however, in defining any such measure, as an unduly restrictive limit would make it more difficult to attract private finance.

Critical choices

There are now clear indications that following the next election a large number of urban and district councils will pursue whatever stock transfer options the government of the day makes available, if this is what it takes to obtain the investment resources they require.

The White Paper and the detailed report from the joint study will set the framework for decisions on many of the practical issues that will have to be dealt with if transfers of stock by urban authorities to local housing companies are to move from theory to practice. Critical issues to consider are:

- the need to provide a regulatory body for the new companies; the White Paper proposes extending the current regulatory functions of the Housing Corporation to cover all forms of stock transfer landlord;

- the need to satisfy funders about the underlying financial security of lending against urban estates with limited potential for vacant possession sales and where the rent streams are effectively the only real security for the loan; and

- dealing with the element of housing benefit costs that would fall onto the General Fund for councils undertaking stock transfers where there would be no offsetting General Fund financial benefits.

Beyond these essential practical considerations there remain some key government policy decisions that will shape the scope of the future options available to councils and their tenants.

If the government of the day chooses to maintain the PSBR as its primary budget deficit measure, then the future options for council housing will almost certainly include, in one form or another, minority-influenced housing companies. The outcome of the next election might result in some important changes to the details of policies on minority-influenced companies; but not to the basic principles.

If, and only if, a future UK government makes the wider decision to switch from the PSBR to a general government deficit measure, will the option of Swedish-style council housing companies also move onto the agenda.

The UK tradition of council housing has built up a substantial housing stock, and still has an asset base far greater than that of existing housing associations. This council house inheritance will be passed on to successor bodies in the years ahead. We have yet to see the form (or forms) that those successor bodies will take. Predictably, however, the inheritors of the council housing asset base will be among the most powerful players in the UK social housing sector in the new millennium.

References

1. For further background on the emergence of the large-scale voluntary transfer (LSVT) initiative see the third Contemporary Issue article in the 1994/95 edition of the Review. For the up-to-date statistics on stock transfers in England see Table 60.
2. See Tables 54 and 55 and Chapter 4.
3. *Local Housing Companies: New opportunities for council housing,* Steve Wilcox, Glen Bramley, Alan Ferguson, John Perry and Clive Woods, Joseph Rowntree Foundation in association with the Chartered Institute of Housing 1993.
4. All the Newcastle figures quoted are in the summary form of 'Net Present Values' of thirty years income and expenditure streams, calculated using an annual 6% discount rate in line with Treasury convention.
5. *Our Future Homes,* Department of the Environment and Welsh Office, June 1995; *New Private Finance Rules for Local Authorities,* Department of the Environment Private Finance Unit, March 1995.
6. *Challenging the Conventions,* John Hawksworth and Steve Wilcox, Chartered Institute of Housing 1995.
7. For a detailed account of Swedish housing companies see *Housing Policy and Tenure in Sweden,* L J Lundqvist, Avebury 1994.
8. Para 4.107, *System of National Accounts,* United Nations 1993.

Contemporary issues 2

The rising number of households requiring homes - the national and regional picture

Alan Holmans

A serious housing policy dilemma has now become apparent. The Department of the Environment has published new projections of how many households there will be in England over the period to 2011. In England as a whole and in most individual areas these new (1992-based) projections show substantially larger increases in the number of households in the two decades from 1991 than did the previous (1989-based) projections which they supersede. This article examines the projections at national and regional level and concludes that northern conurbations (especially Greater Manchester) and London probably cannot house the new households now projected without a serious decline in housing conditions.

The total increase in households in England over the two decades is now put at about 3.5 million, nearly three-quarters of a million more than shown previously. This upward revision has important implications for demand and the need for housing, and equally far-reaching implications for land-use policy and planning.

The land-use implications will follow from the increases in households at regional and sub-regional level rather than from the national increase. But in considering these implications, it is essential to recall that the regional and sub-regional projections of population and households are derived from national projections and not vice versa. A different pattern of internal migration, however caused, that resulted in smaller increases in population and households in one area would necessarily result in balancing larger increases in other areas.

The national projections and the assumptions from which they are derived therefore have to be looked at first, since these are all-important both for explaining why the regional and sub-regional projections show the increases that they do, and also for what changes, including policy changes, might cause some of the increases to turn out differently.

National projections

A brief outline of the methods and sources used for the national projections is given here, with a fuller description being available in the DoE report, *Projections of Households in England to 2016*.

The starting-point is the official projection of the population, analysed by sex and age and then further cross-analysed by marital status. (In the 1992-based projections, 'marital status' includes whether or not cohabiting.) Within each population category defined by sex, age, and marital status, the proportions

Table II Past and projected increases in households in England
Thousands

	Change due to population	Change due to other causes	Total change
1971-81	1,363	825	538
1981-91	1,910	1,300	610
1991-2001	1,831	1,222	609
2001-11	1,724	1,136	587

Source: Department of the Environment, *Projections of Households in England to 2016*, Table II

heading households (headship rates or, in the terminology and method introduced for the 1992-based projections, 'household representative rates') are projected from past trends.

The relative importance of different factors leading to the projections is highly relevant to considering what could cause the actual increase in the number of households to turn out differently from the projection. The most important distinction is between increases in the number of households due to the growth of the population (and changes in its age structure) and all other causes. This distinction is drawn in Table II, with the corresponding figures for 1971-81 and 1981-91 for comparison.

Both in 1991-2001 and 2001-11 some two-thirds of the projected increase in the number of households is due to population change. The increase due to 'other causes' foreseen in the two decades is very similar to the increases in the previous decades; but the increase due to population growth and change is very different. Projected population growth is also the main reason for the sharp upward revision in the projections. (Further details of the population directors can be found in the OPCS Monitors.)

The change in the total and age structure of the population up to 2011 and 2016 will be determined primarily by: the ageing of the population already alive in 1991; mortality; and migration. Future births will not have a significant effect on the population of household-forming age during the period. The key points are:

- Ageing will contribute to the growth of the adult population as the rest of the 'baby-boom' generation reaches adulthood, and will add further to the number of households as that generation reaches ages where household headship is highest.

- Falling death rates are also having a substantial effect. Death rates fell by about 10% during the 1980s, and similar falls in the next two decades are assumed in the projection. The fall in death rates that is projected adds about 800,000, in round terms, to the population in 2011 compared with what would happen if death rates remained unaltered.

- Migration is also expected to result in substantial increases in the population. Net inward migration to the United Kingdom is put at 50,000 a year in the medium term, with inward migrants to the United Kingdom exceeding outward migrants by around 900,000 between 1991 and 2011. This is a powerful influence on the projected increase in the population, and accounts for two-thirds of the upward revision to the projection of the adult population in 2011. Reference to the OPCS report on migration (OPCS, 1993) is essential for any consideration of whether changes of policy on immigration could bring about lower figures for net inward migration than currently assumed in the population projections.

In the 1989-based populations, and hence the 1989-based household projections, net inward migration to the United Kingdom in the medium term was assumed to be zero. The difference between this and net inward migration at 50,000 a year is fundamentally important for the differences between the present (1992-based) projections and those that they supercede.

Internal migration

The population projections for local government areas — i.e. counties, metropolitan districts, and London boroughs — are derived from the national projections. Observed differences in death rates are assumed to persist during the projection period. The key assumptions are about the places of origin of outward migrants from the United Kingdom and the destination of inward migrants; and about internal migration within the United Kingdom:

- The international migration flows are assigned between areas mainly on the evidence of the International Passenger Survey, and the Census for inward migrants.

- Assumptions about internal migration are based on the 1991 Census migration data and the National Health Service Central Register. The base period for the assumptions about internal migration was one when North-South migration was at a low level owing to the economic recession being more severe in the South of England. A regional summary of the projection of population is shown in Table III, together with sub-totals for the metropolitan districts and London.

Two features of Table III warrant particular comment: the regional distribution of the increase in the projected population; and the turn-round, compared with the 1970s and to a lesser extent the 1980s in the population of the metropolitan districts of the North of England and still more so in London:

- Both are to a degree the outcome of the assumption about inward migration. Inward migrants from outside the United Kingdom go for the most part to the cities, especially London, but also to the cities of the Midlands and North of England.

- Migration from the Northern cities to the South of England was depressed by the economic recession in the South of England; and movement to the suburbs is also slow in depressed housing market conditions. In these circumstances, increases in population in the Northern metropolitan districts in total (though not in each individually) are foreseen, after a long period of falling population.

- These features are to be seen in a more pronounced way in Greater London. At regional level, the high proportion of inward migrants from overseas that come to London more than offsets the reduction in North to South migration, with the result that some 69% of the projected increase in the population of England between 1991 and 2011 is shown as being in the three regions of the South of England, where 51% of the population lived in 1991.

The migration assumptions are trend-based, so question may be raised about whether the

The rising number of households requiring homes - the national and regional picture

Table III Projections of population by region
Thousands

	1971	1981	1991	2001	2011
North	3,152	3,117	3,092	3,113	3,103
Yorkshire & Humberside	4,902	4,918	4,983	5,116	5,205
North West	6,634	6,459	6,396	6,489	6,564
North sub-total	**14,688**	**14,494**	**14,471**	**14,718**	**14,872**
East Midlands	3,652	3,853	4,035	4,270	4,459
West Midlands	5,146	5,187	5,266	5,375	5,453
Midlands sub-total	**8,798**	**9,040**	**9,301**	**9,645**	**9,912**
East Anglia	1,688	1,894	2,082	2,245	2,395
South East	17,125	17,011	17,637	18,408	19,032
South West	4,112	4,381	4,718	5,006	5,248
South sub-total	**22,925**	**23,286**	**24,437**	**25,659**	**26,675**
England	**46,412**	**46,821**	**48,208**	**50,022**	**51,458**
Metropolitan districts					
North	9,051	8,680	8,537	8,624	8,677
Midlands	2,811	2,673	2,629	2,617	2,593
Greater London	7,529	6,806	6,890	7,170	7,407

Source: OPCS Monitor pp3 94/1, Table 1: Population Trends No. 78 Table 3

consequences of these trends being continued twenty or twenty-five years into the future would force a change of trend. London is the extreme case; the implications of the projected increase in population in London are commented on when the regional and sub-regional household projections are discussed, but the same question would be raised elswhere if the actual increase in population in London were held below the projection by more outward migration to the Home Counties, East Anglia, and the South West.

Regional household projections

Regional and sub-regional projections of households are made in the same way as the national household projections, to which they are constrained by a controlling procedure. They are derived from the population projections for local authority areas. The national projected changes in headship rates are taken to apply sub-nationally, though with different starting points.

A summary of the regional household projections is shown in Table IV, similar in form to the summary of population projections in Table III. That the table refers only to England and does not include Scotland, Wales and Northern Ireland is due to there being no comparable household projections for Scotland or Northern Ireland. Projections for Wales are produced along with those for England by the Department of the Environment, for technical reasons, but household projections for Scotland are the responsibility of the Scottish Office. Table IV shows net increases in households rather than the projected totals, because the net increases are the starting point for assessment of the needed increase in the housing stock, both in terms of housing policy and of land-use.

Comment on the projected increases in 1991-2001 and 2001-16, and how they compare with the 'estimated increases in 1971-81 and 1981-91' is in terms of the aggregates of regions in Table IV, as it would be beyond the scope of this article to discuss (for example) the reasons for differences in the rates of increase in households between the North and Yorkshire/Humberside, or between East Anglia and the South West.

The expression 'estimated increases in 1971-81 and 1981-91' is used advisedly, especially about 1981-91. No one has suggested an alternative procedure to that used by OPCS to apportion the 'missing' population in 1991 (i.e. the difference between the Census population and the official population estimate) between local authority areas. That such a procedure had to be used, however, necessarily imparts uncertainty to the 1991

Contemporary issues

Table IV Past and projected net increases in households by region
Thousands

	1971-81	1981-91	1991-2001	2001-16
North	83	90	86	114
Yorkshire and Humberside	125	166	163	204
North West	109	151	157	272
North sub-total	**317**	**407**	**406**	**610**
East Midland	165	187	179	239
West Midland	163	182	175	211
Midlands Sub-total	**328**	**369**	**354**	**450**
East Anglia	116	131	115	170
South East	379	739	728	1.004
South West	211	265	226	319
South Sub-total	**706**	**1,135**	**1,069**	**1,493**
England	**1,351**	**1,909**	**1,831**	**2,552**

Source: Department of the Environment, *Projections of Households to 2016, Table 12; 1971 DoE unpublished*

Table V: Distribution of increase in households between regional aggregates
Percent

	North	Midlands	South	England ('000)
1971-81	23.5	24.3	52.3	1,351
1981-91	21.3	19.3	59.4	1,909
1991-2001	22.2	19.4	58.4	1,831
2001-16	23.9	17.6	58.5	2,052
Total households	30.9	18.9	51.1	19,215

Source: Department of the Environment, *Projections of Households in England to 2016*

population based on them, and hence to the 1991 household estimates derived from them. The household estimates for 1991 are subject to additional uncertainty owing to the assumptions that had to be made to translate the population under-count into households. These uncertainties affect the levels in 1991 and therefore in subsequent years, but have much less effect on the increases. The composition of the increase in the national total of households in terms of regional aggregates is shown in Table V.

The proportion of the projected increase in the number of households that is in the South of England after 1991 is smaller than the proportion of the population (Table III) because the changing age structure of the population and rising headship rates result in an increase in the number of households, even if the population is static or even falling slowly. That apart, the regional distribution of the projected increase in the number of households is very similar to the distribution of the population increase — as household projections are so closely related to the population projections.

Before considering the implications of the household projections, it is necessary to look in slightly more detail at the increases in the number of households in the metropolitan districts, including differences from the previous (1989-based) increases in the metropolitan districts, London and the counties (see Table VI).

The 1989-based projections put the increase in households in London and the metropolitan districts at only 10% of the national total, whereas in the 1992-based projections the proportion is 30%. The projected increase in households in the counties is only about 200,000 higher than in the previous projections, but in London and the metropolitan counties it is over half a million higher.

In the 1992-based projections, in none of the 36 metropolitan districts is there a fall in the number of households between 1991 and 2011. In only two is the projected increase less than 5%; in another 8 it is between 5 and 10%; in the other 26 it is over 10%. The previous projections showed steep falls in households in the same period in some of the districts. Liverpool was the extreme example; the 1989-based

Table VI Projected increases in households in Metropolitan districts, London and Counties
Thousands

	London	Metropolitan districts	Counties	England
Households in 1991	2,842	4,428	11,945	19,215
Net increase 1991-2001				
1989-based	228	281	2,308	2,817
1992-based	526	527	2,501	3,554
Difference	298	246	193	737

Source: Department of the Environment, *Household Projections England 1989-2011*; and *Projections of Households in England to 2016*

projections showed a fall of 24,000 households between 1991 and 2011; the present projections, in contrast, show an increase of 19,000 households there.

That substantial increases in the number of households are foreseen in so much of the urban areas and the North has important implications. If the projections for these areas are borne out, houses left empty through falling demand stemming from a decline in the number of households cannot be more than a very localised phenomenon.

Implications for the housing system and housing policy

When considering the implications of the household projections outlined in this article, whether for housing demand and need in England as a whole or for provision of land for housing regionally or sub-regionally, an important issue is the distinction between a projection and a forecast. The official household projections are explicitly trend-based and not policy-based forecasts of intended outcomes.

The question therefore arises of whether constraints imposed by policy could force a change of trend. Examples of such constraints are subsidised building for letting being held for public expenditure reasons to levels well below the difference between the increase in households and the increase in the stock of owner-occupied dwellings and dwellings let at market rents; and provision of land for house-building well below what would be needed for increases in the housing stock commensurate with the increase in the number of households. Both are clearly very likely to come up for discussion when the implications of the new projections are considered.

Whether constraints of the kind just discussed, or policy changes, could cause changes of trend must be considered separately at national and at regional level. At national level there is no reason to think that constraining the housing stock could affect the growth of the population and changes in its age structure. Given the sources of inward migration, there is no reason to think that any feasible changes of policy could make anything more than a very small difference to net inward migration.

The national population increase therefore has to be taken as independent and unaffected by constraints on the size of the housing stock. The question is whether, and if so in what ways, constraints on the size of the housing stock could affect the proportions of the population that live as separate households (headship rates).

Concealed households at the national level

The definition of a separate household is all-important. In the projections standard British statistical practice is followed in defining a household either as an 'individual catering for him or herself and not sharing a sitting-room with someone else' or 'two or more people with a common housekeeping or sharing a sitting-room'.

Households defined in this way do not necessarily occupy a house or flat by themselves. Two or more households can live in one dwelling; so one consequence of constraining the increase in the stock of separate dwellings could be an increase in the number of dwellings occupied by two or more households, i.e. more households having to share instead of having a house or flat to themselves. A second possible consequence is more couples and lone-parent families having to live as part of someone else's household. Although colloquially couples are said to 'share' with in-laws, in household estimates and projections they are termed 'concealed families' and not counted as households.

Housing shortages could obviously force more couples to live in this way, as was the case in the post-war years. By this route, housing constraints could hold the number of separate households below what would otherwise have happened, though the sum of separate households and concealed families would be no different. Another route is to force would-be couples to live apart, far from rare in the post-war years. The post-war years provide direct evidence about the effect of housing shortages on household formation. There is ample evidence of sharing and of living as concealed families, and some indications of split couples, but no sign of household formation being held down in other ways.

In recent years, the increase in households from causes other than population change was very similar in the 1970s and the 1980s (Table II above) even though in the 1980s the housing stock just kept pace with the total households whereas in the 1970s the housing stock had increased much more than the total households (in England by 1.85 million, compared with an increase of 1.36 million households). The balance of evidence is thus against constraints on the increase in the housing stock holding down household formation except through more couples having to live as concealed couples or split couples.

These are housing shortage phenomena, as are involuntary sharing and living in bed-and-breakfast hotels and hostels. A greater prevalence of these phenomena would be the probable result of constraining the increase in the housing stock below the projected increase in households.

Impact at the local level of constraining house-building

At local level, in contrast to the national level, constraining the number of houses built can have some effect on migration flows. Particularly within the hinterlands of major employment centres, locations in different districts — and to some extent different counties — are substitutes for each other. Limits to the supply in one location can therefore divert the demand to other localities. Substitutability by this means appears to be less than complete; and the larger the area on the whole the less substitutability.

Limits to building in individual counties in the South of England are likely to have much more effect on moves within the South than on North to South migration. The effects of house price differences on North to South migration have been the subject of investigation and controversy, but with no evidence of modest changes in price differences, as distinct from the difference at the height of the boom in 1987 and 1988, having significant effects.

Given how widespread is the projected increase in households, including places where declines were previously expected, changes in internal migration could not reduce the total of dwellings needed by bringing back into use dwellings that would otherwise have been left empty as the number of households declined. Internal migration could thus affect the location of the dwellings needed to provide for the increase in households, but not the total.

Constraints, conflicts and costs

From this follow far-reaching implications. If trend rates of migration for an individual county cannot continue for the whole of the projection period because there is not enough land left, more inward migration has to be provided for elsewhere. In Surrey, for instance, most of the land not already built on is either Green Belt land or in an Area of Outstanding Natural Beauty (AONB), so the house-building required to provide for the projected increase in households, almost 20% (77,000) between 1991 and 2016, is unlikely to take place. The projected households that will not be accommodated in Surrey will, however, have to be accommodated somewhere else where they want to live.

In all regions, but especially in the South, the question posed by the new projections is how far the projected increases in households in the conurbations can be accommodated there, and how far they will have to be accommodated in the surrounding counties. Counties' land-use planning has for the most part taken on board the increases in households shown by the 1989-based household projections. In the South-East they were the basis in total, though not county by county, for the housing element of the Regional Guidance issued in 1994 (RPG 9).

The questions posed by the new projections are thus elucidated more clearly by examining the difference between the new projections and the previous projections and this is shown region by region in Table VII, separately for the metropolitan districts and counties. The counties of the South West and East

Table VII Difference between 1989-based and 1992-based household projections by type of area
Thousands

	Conurbations	Counties	Total
North	+38	+44	+81
Yorkshire and Humberside	+49	+12	+62
North West	+126	+14	+141
East Midland	...	+10	+10
West Midland	+32	+20	+51
South	+298	+90	+389
England	+534	+193	+737

Source: Department of the Environment, *Household Projections England 1989-2011*, Table 6; *Projections of Households in England to 2016*, Tables 6 and 12
Note: Detail does not always add to totals owing to rounding

Anglia are grouped with those of the South East region, since the projected increase in the number of households in London has implications for the counties in all three regions.

In the South there is clearly a very serious question about whether so large an increase in the number of households could be accommodated in London without a severe worsening of housing conditions; and a similar question, though on a smaller scale, about the conurbations of the North of England, especially Greater Manchester. More outward migration is clearly one possibility, with questions raised about whether spontaneous migration will suffice or whether new towns or planned expansions will have to come back onto the agenda.

But plainly there is a prospect of conflict or worsening housing conditions. If what is explicitly or implicitly done is to rely on increases in house prices and rents in the South of England stemming from limits to the supply of new housing there, to curb inward migration, the financial implications (including Housing Association Grant and housing benefit) will be substantial.

One-person households

One further comment on the implications of the projections needs to be made, and this is the high proportion of the increase that consists of one-person households (2.76 million between 1991 and 2011, out of a total of 3.55 million). The view is sometimes expressed that one-person households do not really need separate dwellings, or if they do, then small converted flats will suffice, so that the land that will be needed for housing will be determined by the number of one-person households willing or able to live in shared accommodation or in converted flats.

Table VIII shows some details from the *Survey of English Housing* for 1993/94. The table is restricted to

Table VIII Type of accommodation occupied by one-person households under age 60
Thousands

	Owner-occupiers	LA and HA Tenants	Other Tenants	Total
Self-contained				
Houses				
1 or 2 bedrooms	484	72	89	645
3 bedrooms or more	626	69	43	738
Purpose-built flats				
1 bedroom	91	232	32	355
2 bedrooms or more	105	105	25	235
Converted flats				
1 bedroom	60	38	100	198
2 bedrooms or more	56	7	39	102
Other	-	1	15	16
Not self-contained	15	26	138	179
Total[1]	1,437	548	480	2,465

Source: Department of the Environment from Survey of English Housing
Notes: 1. Excludes households where whether or not self-contained was not known. Detail does not always add to rounding.

men and women under age 60 in order to exclude the special case of the widowed survivor from a multi-person household who continues to live in a family-sized house. Also excluded is accommodation that goes with the job, because the occupier often has no choice in the matter.

93% of one-person households lived in self-contained housing; only 12% lived in converted flats; and 24% in purpose-built flats. In the owner-occupied sector, where arguably there is a wider range of choice (for those with the financial means to exercise it) than in the other tenures, 44% of one-person households lived in houses with three bedrooms or more, and a further 34% in small houses.

Only 8% lived in converted flats, and a further 6% in small (one-bedroom) purpose-built flats. It is in the local authority and housing association sectors that 50% of one-person households live in one-bedroom flats. Where one-person households are in a position to choose, rather than decide whether or not to accept accommodation allocated to them, only rarely do they choose small flats. There is no reason to expect that voluntary sharing or preference for small flats by one-person households will materially reduce the provision required to accommodate the increase in households that is in prospect.

Key reading

Projections of Households in England to 2016, Department of the Environment, HMSO 1995.

OPCS Occasional Paper No.42, *National Population Projections: A new methodology for determining migration assumptions,* HMSO 1993

Contemporary issues 3

What has happened to the North-South divide in house prices and the housing market?

Alan Holmans

Inter-regional differences in house prices attracted a great deal of attention in the 1980s, for the first time. Hitherto little attention had been paid to the subject, but in the 1960s regional disparities in house prices had widened substantially (see Figure II).

Differences in house prices were not among the economic indicators used by commentators in the early 1960s to describe the emergence of 'two nations' between the South of England and parts of the North, Wales and Scotland. Employment totals and unemployment rates were far more prominent when regional economic policy then took centre stage. With hindsight, it can be seen that inter-regional house price differences widened substantially at this time (see Figure II).

At the peak of the boom in 1988, the difference in house prices between South East England and the North was wider than at any time for which evidence is available. When the boom collapsed, house prices fell faster and further in the South of England than elsewhere. The first part of this article examines whether the result was simply a reversal of the widening of inter-regional differences which had also occurred after the end of the boom of the early 1970s or whether there are signs of a more profound change having occurred.

Such a change could well have occurred, given how severe, in comparison with the rest of the country, was the general economic recession in the South of England. After nearly seven decades of unemployment rates well below the national average, by 1992 unemployment rates in the South East were as high or higher. House prices in the South fell significantly in cash terms, not just relative to the general price level. How far these falls were accompanied by correspondingly greater than average falls in housing market activity, including new house-building for private owners, is considered in subsequent parts of the article.

The final part of the article discusses Scotland, which went its own way. The different Scottish experience of house prices and house-building in much of the 1980s and early 1990s contributed materially to the perception that the market for owner-occupied housing in Britain was breaking up into separate regional markets. This article argues against that hypothesis except for Scotland.

Changing differences in house prices between South and North

To answer the questions just posed about the changes in the inter-regional structure of house prices since the end of the 1980s boom, those changes must be set in a long-term context, long enough to see whether any of the widening of difference that occurred in the early 1960s has been reversed.

The history of inter-regional differences in house prices from 1968 to the mid-1980s could be summarised as differentials between the South East and the North, Wales and Scotland widening during housing market booms and narrowing during recessions, but with no long-term change. This is necessarily a somewhat simplified summary that does not bring in the rise in house prices in East Anglia and

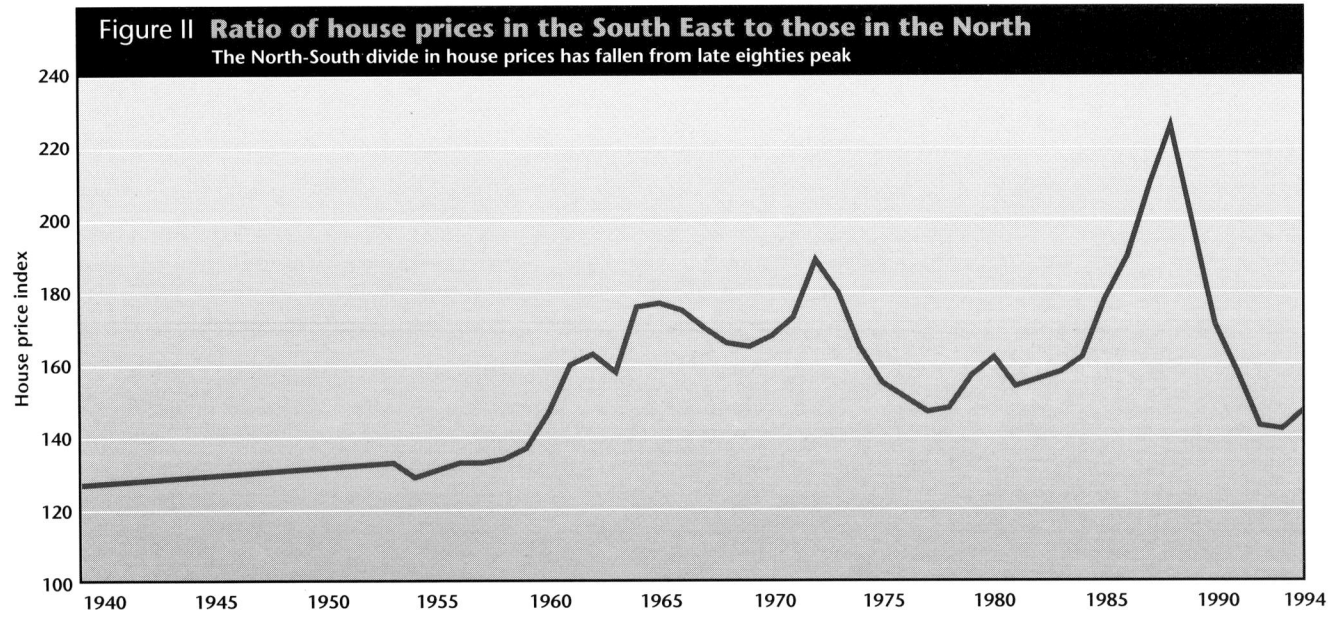

Figure II Ratio of house prices in the South East to those in the North
The North-South divide in house prices has fallen from late eighties peak

Source: Holmans, 1990, Housing and Construction Statistics

Box A: Regional house price and house purchase data sources

House prices

The history of inter-regional differences in house prices is most commonly described in terms of ratios of regional average house prices year by year to the United Kingdom average as calculated from data from the Building Societies Mortgage Survey (BSM). Regional average house prices from this source begin with the second quarter of 1968, so 1968 has of necessity to be the starting year for a time-series from this source.

This is longer than available from other sources. The Halifax index begins with 1983, and so cannot be used for any comparison between prices in the 1980s boom and the early 1970s, or between the fall in house prices in real terms when that boom collapsed and the early 1990s. The history of house prices since 1968 is therefore recounted in terms of the BSM data, though with reference to how far the Halifax indexes tell a different story about the boom of the 1980s and the subsequent slump.

To go back before 1968 it is necessary to use the indexes published by the Co-operative Permanent Building Society (subsequently re-named Nationwide). Indexes derived from the business of one building society are more at risk to distortion caused by shifts in market shares than average houses prices calculated from BSM which drew its sample from all the large building societies.

Comment about changes before 1968 must therefore be more tentative, but there is no reason to doubt the validity in general terms of the picture presented. The first year for which regional house price indexes were published by the Co-operative Permanent was 1953, but since the indexes were on base 1939 a comparison could be made between 1939 and the mid-1950s. These indexes have been used to estimate changes in inter-regional house price differences, by projecting back from prices in 1969 and 1970 (from BSM) and calculating ratios.[1]

For long-term comparison of inter-regional differences in house prices in the present context, the measure used is the ratio of average prices year by year in South East England (including London) to average prices in the North of England (the North, Yorkshire and Humberside, and North West standard regions aggregated). This measure is used for three reasons:

- ratios of all regional averages to the national average year by year are unwieldy for comparisons over a long run of years;
- the South East (as defined above) contributed on average about 30% of the national total of transactions, so comparing the South East with the national average is to a considerable degree comparing the South East with itself;
- a grouping of the society's regions which corresponds approximately to the North as defined above and to the South East is possible, but not for other regions.

This is the basis for Figure II.

House purchases

Two sets of data are available with which to delineate changes in the regional distribution of house purchases: the Building Societies Mortgage Survey (BSM) and, from 1992, the Survey of Mortgage Lending (SML); and the Inland Revenue's Survey of Property Transactions (SOPT). SOPT is a sample survey of particulars delivered in England and Wales by conveyancers.

SOPT has the advantage of a sample drawn from all transactions irrespective of the source of finance, very important in the mid-1980s when the 'new lenders' and foreign banks entered the mortgage market and severely reduced the building societies' market share. But residential property transactions in SOPT include a significant number of transactions which are not house purchases for owner-occupation.[2]

Moreover, the first full year of the survey was 1986, so it cannot be used for comparisons with the recession of the early 1980s or earlier. The BSM data are available back to 1968. Their disadvantage is that in the 1980s there were large shifts in the building societies' share of the mortgage market, which introduces substantial uncertainty about how closely shifts in the regional mix of lending by building societies reflect changes in the distribution of all house purchases between regions. Both are used, but neither is entirely secure for present purposes. Scotland and Northern Ireland are not included in SOPT, so they are excluded from the table derived from BSM. Table IX shows the shares of residential property transactions in grouped regions, as derived from SOPT.

Before commenting on the distribution of transactions shown by Table IX, a comparison may be made with the distribution shown by BSM, set out in Table X. Abbey National became a plc in 1989 and therefore a bank, but continued to contribute to BSM.

Table IX Regional distribution of house purchase transactions from SOPT
Percentages

	South	Midlands	North	Wales
1986	55.5	16.2	23.6	4.7
1987	55.4	16.9	23.0	4.6
1988	55.7	15.4	23.9	5.0
1989	44.7	16.6	33.2	5.6
1990	50.1	16.5	28.7	4.8
1991	52.2	16.8	26.5	4.5
1992	53.5	16.1	24.9	5.5
1993	56.2	15.5	24.3	3.9

Source: *Inland Revenue Statistics 1994*, Table 16.2; and comparable tables in earlier years

Table X Regional distribution of house purchase advances from BSM
Percentages

	South	Midlands	North	Wales
1986	51.3	18.5	26.1	4.2
1987	46.3	18.8	30.4	4.5
1988	46.3	17.5	31.5	4.7
1989	41.4	17.8	35.2	5.3
1990	48.3	17.9	29.5	4.3
1991	49.7	17.2	28.7	4.4
1992	49.3	17.4	29.0	4.4
1993	49.3	15.5	27.5	4.6

Source: Building Societies Mortgage Survey

the South West as the South Eastern housing market extended its sway beyond the regional boundaries, and the fall, relative to other regions, in the West Midlands as the prosperity of its industries declined.

The widening of inter-regional differences during the boom arose through prices rising sooner and faster in the South during the upswing, and the subsequent narrowing of inter-regional differences through their decelerating sooner and more rapidly when the boom was over. The sequence of prices turning upwards sooner and faster in the South East with prices in other regions following after varying lags gave rise to a perception that increases in house prices 'rippled out' from the South East. Up to 1986 the course of house prices during the boom fitted this picture.

To assess whether the further widening of inter-regional disparities in average house prices in 1987 and 1988 was without precedent one needs to look back to before the 1960s. In the 1950s house prices in the South East were about one-third higher than in the North of England, a margin probably not materially different, given the source, from what it had been in 1939. Between the end of the 1950s and the mid-1960s the difference in average house prices in the South East and the North widened very sharply. In the mid-1960s, a time of economic boom, house prices in the South East were about two-thirds higher than in the North.

The widening of the disparity came about through house prices rising slowly in the North, approximately in line with the general price level, but much more rapidly in the South East. As mentioned above, this was a time when there were growing concerns about more unemployment in the North (and in Scotland and Wales) than in the South of England. These concerns had a substantial basis of fact, even though at times there was a degree of exaggeration and in absolute terms the differences in unemployment rates between the less prosperous regions were small by the standards of the 1980s.

The difference between average house prices in the South East and the North reached in the mid-1960s persisted, with small fluctuations, for the next two decades. In 1966-85 the ratio averaged 165, with a range of 189 (in 1972) to 147 (in 1977). This relationship came to be regarded as normal, or even as a norm to which the ratio would inexorably return if pushed away from it. The house-price history in the 1950s and the first half of the 1960s would have shown differently; but because it was outside the period covered by the BSM data (see Box A) it was not widely known.

On the hypothesis of the differences observed in the two decades from the mid-1960s being the product of deep-seated forces, a narrowing would have been due after 1986; but instead house prices in the South East rose even faster in 1987 and 1988. The most likely explanation is that house prices were driven by expectations of still further increases to come, which produced a rush of attempts to buy before the expected price increases occurred.

Such expectations and behaviour are characteristic of a speculative 'bubble' and are inherently unstable because the demand to buy will fail if something dispels the expectation of strong future price increases. The 'something' was the steep increases in interest rates in the second half of 1988 and in 1989. At this time the economy, North and South, was still expanding. The cyclical turning point, if dated by unemployment, did not come until the second quarter of 1990.

What happened to the difference between house prices in the South East and the North after 1988 is shown in Figure II. The key question is whether the pronounced narrowing of the disparity is best explained as a repeat performance of what happened after the end of the boom of the early 1970s or whether the severe general economic recession in the South of England brought about a more fundamental change.

For the first time in sixty years (at least) a cyclical downswing in the British economy was more severe in the South of England than in the North. For a time the unemployment percentage was as high in the South East as in Scotland, something that had never been seen all the time that unemployment rates have been calculated (since 1923).

If greater prosperity and growth had caused the house-price differential between the South East and North to widen in the early 1960s and arguably also in the later years of the boom of the 1980s, the disappearance of the South's greater prosperity could bring about a fall in house prices in the South East relative to the North greater than could be accounted for by the greater cyclical volatility of house prices in the South East.

Clearly the exceptional widening of the North-South difference in house prices that took place at the height of the 1980s boom was reversed. But whether anything more than that has happened is uncertain. The ratios in 1992 and 1993 (Figure II) were only fractionally lower than that in 1977. Ratios in individual years are subject to chance effects in differences in the mix of dwellings since the average prices are simple averages. The difference is not great enough to give certainty that the widening of the difference that took place in the early 1960s has begun to be reversed.

This inference is drawn from the Building Societies Mortgage Survey (from 1992 the building societies' component of the Survey of Mortgage Lending). The Halifax Building Society's house-price data, though, showed a steeper fall in house prices in the South of England than did the BSM.

If the recent house-price history is taken from the Halifax, even though its data do not go back far enough for comparisons with the boom of the early 1970s, let alone the 1960s, it would point to a partial reversal of the widening of the difference that occurred in the first half of the 1960s. There would be nothing implausible about this, given how severely the recession affected the economy of the South of England.

This is not the place for an extended discussion of differences between the DoE and Halifax house-price measures. The former has the advantage of being based on data from a representative sample of building societies and so is less at risk of distortion from shifts of market shares and mix of business; the latter has the advantage of being calculated from a much larger number of mortgages, so that regional average prices are less subject to sampling variation.

That Figure II shows a widening of the differences in 1994, when there was a modest recovery from the recession, is of interest. Chance changes in the mix of dwellings from which the averages were calculated appear to have over-stated the widening, but clearly there was no further narrowing. The economy of the South of England has come out of the recession in the same way as the rest of the country, so a further narrowing of the house-price difference between North and South due to a worsening in economic conditions relative to the North does not seem in prospect.

Whether the difference will return to something close to the long-term average since the mid-1960s is another matter. The expectation is that the national increase in house prices in cash terms will be fairly slow owing to anti-inflation policy commitments. Without falls in house prices in cash terms in the North at a time of economic growth, increases in house prices in the South could only be slow, by past standards, as a matter of arithmetic. Whether the differentially severe recession in the economy of the South of England really did produce a long-lasting shift in the regional structure of house prices could therefore only emerge fairly gradually.

House purchases

There are similarities between regional house purchases shown by two data sources, SOPT (Table IX) and BSM (Table X), but sufficient differences to make exactly what changes occurred uncertain (see Box A for a description of each data source). SOPT consistently shows a higher proportion of transactions in the South of England. Part of the difference is probably due to a high proportion of outright purchases being by people moving to retirement areas, which are disproportionately in the South; also possible is that lending by the 'new lenders' and foreign banks (excluded in the BSA figures) was concentrated in the South.

Both sources show a steep fall in 1989 in the proportion of purchases that were in the South. After that, the two sources tell rather different stories. Owing to changes in building societies' share of the mortgage market, the proportions from SOPT are used to divide estimated house purchases in 1986 and after between the South of England and the rest of England and Wales. The estimates of the total of purchases in England and Wales were derived from estimates for the United Kingdom with a deduction, derived from BSM, for Scotland and Northern Ireland.[3]

Precision cannot be claimed for the figures in Table XI, but in outline the picture is probably fairly accurate. The fall in purchases in 1989 was heavily concentrated in the South of England, which tallies with the increase in house prices halting there at the end of 1988 and the beginning of 1989, even though they continued to rise elsewhere.

Such a quicker and larger fall in purchases in the South than in the rest of the country could be explained by the increases in interest rates producing much larger increases in net mortgage outgoings relative to income. House prices and hence mortgages were much higher relative to incomes; and owing to the £30,000 limit for mortgage interest relief a much higher proportion of debt attracted additional interest at the gross rate.

The fall in activity then spread to the rest of the country, as did the slow-down in house prices. The greater increase in the number of purchases in the South that Table XI shows does not fit the picture, however, since house prices in the South fell more than in the North, year on year. Nor did house-building for private owners (see Table XII) increase more in the South than in the rest of the country.

Table XI SOPT-based estimates of house purchases in 'the South' and 'the rest of England and Wales'
Thousands

	South	Rest of England and Wales	Total
1986	741	594	1,335
1987	823	662	1,485
1988	956	761	1,717
1989	524	649	1,173
1990	515	512	1,027
1991	526	482	1,008
1992	431	375	806
1993	506	395	901

Source: see text for method of estimation

House-building for private owners

The slump in house purchases that began in 1989 brought about a steep decline in house-building for private owners. Between 1988 and 1992 the number of houses started in England for private owners almost halved, from 196,000 to 100,000. The reduction in the number completed was smaller, from 176,000 to 120,000 (115,000 in 1993) but was substantial

Table XII Private sector house-building in 'the South' and 'the Midlands and the North'
Thousands

	Starts		Completions	
	South	Midlands and North	South	Midlands and North
1978	72.0	61.6	68.0	59.5
1979	65.2	55.9	64.6	53.8
1980	46.7	37.4	59.9	50.3
1981	56.5	45.4	55.5	43.4
1982	69.9	53.4	60.6	48.1
1983	88.9	62.1	75.0	54.5
1984	81.6	56.7	80.0	59.0
1985	88.6	55.7	79.7	55.8
1986	96.7	62.2	89.3	59.6
1987	108.3	66.6	96.1	65.6
1988	118.6	77.4	103.9	72.1
1989	74.9	67.0	90.7	63.3
1990	55.1	57.6	77.3	58.6
1991	60.0	54.3	71.7	59.5
1992	49.5	50.1	63.5	56.1
1993	58.6	58.1	58.7	56.7
1994	67.5	64.0	60.9	58.1

Source: *Housing and Construction Statistics 1978-1988; 1980-1990;* and *1983-1993*, Table 6.4; and *Housing Construction Statistics December quarter 1994*, Table 1.3

nevertheless. Starts and completions for private owners in the South and in the rest of England are compared in Table XII. It goes back to 1978 so that comparisons can be made between the recessions (or slump) of the early 1990s with that of the early 1980s.

In house-building for private owners, as in house prices, the boom of the 1980s was much stronger in the South of England than in the Midlands and North; and the slump was deeper. Between 1982, a year of recovery though hardly of boom, and 1988 starts increased by 49,000 (70%) in the South and 24,000 (45%) in the Midlands and North. The increases in completions in the same period were 43,000 (71%) and 24,000 (50%).

In the slump, starts in the South more than halved, by 69,000 (58%), between 1988 and 1992, compared with only 27,000 (35%). The much greater falls in private house-building in the South after 1988 were in contrast with what happened in the early 1980s when the slump in both starts and completions was proportionally greater in the Midlands and North than in the South. Starts in the South in 1992 were close to what they had been in 1980, the low point (in terms of starts) of the slump of the early 1980s; but in the Midlands and North they were nearly 13,000 higher. The less severe impact of the general economic recession on the Midlands and North in the early 1990s, in contrast to the early 1980s, is the probable explanation.

Scotland

Although the timing of the housing boom and slump in the Midlands and North of England was different from in the South and the amplitude was smaller, the housing-market cycle in the Midlands and North and in the South were clearly part of the same cycle. In these terms England in the 1980s and 1990s was still one housing market, of which Wales was also part. This was much less true of Scotland, where the market for owner-occupied housing in the 1980s and early 1990s to a considerable extent went its own way, on a different course from England. Table XIII illustrates the different courses in house prices, and house-building for the private sector (measured by starts).

Table XIII **House prices and house starts for private owners in England and Scotland**

	House prices (1990 = 100)		House starts (thousand)	
	England	Scotland	England	Scotland
1978	21.6	30.8	133.6	16.6
1979	28.0	36.9	121.1	15.2
1980	34.0	42.2	84.1	9.7
1981	36.0	46.0	101.9	11.0
1982	37.0	49.1	123.2	12.1
1983	40.9	55.6	151.0	15.2
1984	45.0	58.9	138.3	14.6
1985	49.1	62.3	144.3	14.1
1986	56.6	65.7	158.9	14.6
1987	66.4	70.4	174.9	13.1
1988	84.6	76.1	196.0	15.0
1989	101.8	89.8	141.9	18.1
1990	100.0	100.0	112.7	16.6
1991	97.9	108.4	114.3	15.9
1992	93.4	113.1	99.6	14.7
1993	90.4	117.3	116.7	17.2
1994	91.9	117.6	131.5	21.3

Source: *Housing and Construction Statistics 1978-1988, 1980-1990, and 1983-1993*, Tables 6.1 and 10.8

The course of house prices in Scotland was quite different from that in England. In the English boom years from 1983 to 1989, house prices in Scotland rose by 62% (19% in real terms relative to the Retail Prices Index), compared with 149% (84% in real terms) in England. When house prices fell in England, by 11% between 1989 and 1993, they continued to rise in Scotland.

In Scotland house-building for private owners was far more stable than in England. There was only a small increase in what in England were the boom years. But for the single year's high figure in 1989, a boom and recession would be hard to detect in the run of the figures from 1983 to 1992, whereas in England a severe oscillation is plain for all to see.

Scotland was much less affected by the general economic recession of the early 1990s than was Wales or any of the English regions, including the North. But whether that can provide the whole of the explanation for the differences between Scotland and England discussed above is too complex a question to investigate here. In the house-price boom of the late 1970s and the housing-market slump of the early 1980s, in contrast, there was very little difference between Scotland and England.

Concluding observations

The economic 'North-South divide' in England was much reduced in the early 1990s by a deep recession that, in contrast to the previous sixty years, had a heavier impact on the South than on the North. This was fully reflected in house prices and in house-building for private owners. Future prospects turn on what happens as the British economy comes out of the recession. Thus far, recovery in the South appears not to have lagged behind the Midlands and North, except perhaps in London, with no further widening of differences in house prices and house-building. Scottish experience in both the boom and the recession was different. But Scotland apart, house prices and house-building have moved in ways that show there to be a national housing market no less than before.

References

1 For further details, see *House Prices: Changes through time at national and sub-national level*, Alan Holmans, Government Economic Service Working Paper No. 110, Department of the Environment, 1990.

2 'Number of property transactions in England and Wales', P Heggs and A Holmans, *Economic Trends*, June 1991.

3 See Table 1, *House Prices: Changes through time at national and sub-national level*, Alan Holmans, Department of the Environment 1995.

Key reading

House Prices: Changes through time at national and sub-national level, Alan Holmans, Government Economic Service Working Paper No.110, Department of the Environment, 1990.

'Where have all the first-time purchasers gone?', Alan Holmans, *Housing Finance No.25,* February 1995.

Contemporary issues 4

A shrinking safety net for a changing market

Peter Williams

Introduction

1995 will herald an unfortunate conjunction. First, final recognition of fundamental change in the housing market and second a major restructuring of the state's safety net, which has been an important underpinning for this changing market. Income support for mortgage interest payments has been a feature of state support for the housing market since 1948. In the event of unemployment or sickness a household without any significant earned income and with savings of less than £8,000 can expect the state to pay the interest on their mortgage (up to the first £100,000 of a mortgage). In 1994, some 700,000 households will have claimed income support for mortgage interest (ISMI).

Following the 1994 Budget Statement the Secretary of State for Social Security announced proposals for changing ISMI. Despite all the arguments and evidence in favour of a substantial restructuring of the proposals, the Government is proceeding with only minor changes. In essence, the Government has proposed making the basis of ISMI payments a government-defined standard rate of interest rather than the actual rate of interest, removing immediate entitlement to ISMI and replacing this with a period of up to nine months when no payment will be received, and excluding improvements from the list of eligible housing costs. The Government hopes that by reducing entitlement it will encourage home owners to take out private insurance and thus transfer the cost to individuals.

In this short article, trends in income support are examined along with the current pattern of private insurance provision. Attention is then given to likely take-up of private provision and the implications of the planned changes in ISMI. Finally, the article concludes with brief consideration of how these changes may interact with a fundamentally restructured housing market.

Changing housing market

The issue of a safety net for home-owners must be viewed against the backcloth of the housing market of the late 1990s and beyond. The housing market is seen by many to have undergone fundamental change reflecting low levels of inflation, a changing job market, reduced government assistance and the experience and the consequences of the housing market recession. The housing market of the late 1990s and beyond is likely to be characterised by the following:

- narrower access to home-ownership as lenders take a more cautious and selective view of the risks involved in individual lending decisions;
- lower levels of transactions and a smaller market;
- lower inflation which will spread the real burden of the costs of home-ownership further into the purchasing period. This will increase the risk of default, particularly if house prices remain subdued;
- an increasing sense of vulnerability for existing owners as reductions in assistance occur and there is greater exposure to market forces;
- a reduction in the cushion provided by mortgage interest tax relief and income support for mortgage interest payments which will leave lenders with less room to manoeuvre if housing costs rise;
- a historically high level of arrears and repossessions;
- greater caution reflecting higher risk and the overhang of debt;
- entry to home-ownership delayed and possibly postponed indefinitely;
- housing becoming a consumption good rather than an investment good;
- increased demand for rented housing in both the public and private sectors.

ISMI: who gets it, what does it cost?

In 1994, it was estimated that, at any single point in time, there were approximately 550,000 borrowers in receipt of ISMI, which equates to about 5% of mortgages outstanding at the end of the first half of 1993. There is a significant turnover of claimants and the DSS expects there to be 380,000 new claims in 1994/95.

As Table 99 in the main body of tables shows, the number of claimants of income support has risen rapidly since 1988 reflecting the onset of the recession, but has recently begun to decline. Nonetheless in May 1994 there were 529,000 claimants receiving ISMI, compared to 300,000 in May 1988.

The amount claimed has also risen, from £286 million in 1988 to a peak of £1,270 million (at an annual rate) in February 1993 before falling to £1,222 million in May 1993 and £1,057 million in May 1994. The decline in interest rates has also resulted in the average amount per claimant falling from £46.34 in 1991 to £44.31 per week in 1993 and £38.42 in 1994.

Contemporary issues

> **Box B: Changing employment status of home-owners**
>
> In 1981, only 8% of heads of household who were home-owners with a mortgage were not in full-time employment. By 1991, 14% were not in full-time employment and by 1994 this had risen to 19% (see Table XIV).
>
> Overall 13% of the workforce are now self-employed, up from 10% in 1984 and the pattern of self-employment is highest in areas where home-ownership is also high, suggesting that if there are difficulties with the proposed arrangements there may be regional effects. In 1993/94, there were 1.4 million people in temporary jobs, 54% of whom were on fixed-term contracts and over half of these had contracts for 1 year or less.
>
> Recent research for the Joseph Rowntree Foundation by the Institute of Employment Research points to the rise in 'blue-collar' home-ownership and the concomitant rise in unemployed home-owners, while the DoE's own *Survey of English Housing* notes that 55% of unemployed heads either had difficulties meeting payments or were in arrears (17% of employed heads of households were in the same position).[1]
>
> **Table XIV Employment status of home-buying heads of household**
> Percent
>
> | | Home-buyers in | | | | |
> |---|---|---|---|---|---|
> | Employment status of household head | 1981 | 1984 | 1988 | 1991 | 1993 |
> | Full-time employment | 92 | 90 | 88 | 86 | 82 |
> | Part-time employment | 1 | 2 | 2 | 3 | 4 |
> | Unemployed[1] | 3 | 3 | 3 | 4 | 5 |
> | Retired | 2 | 2 | 3 | 4 | 4 |
> | Disabled or sick[2] | 1 | 1 | 1 | 2 | 2 |
> | Economically inactive | 1 | 2 | 2 | 2 | 2 |
> | Total | 100 | 100 | 100 | 100 | 100 |
>
> Source: Housing trailers to the 1981, 1984, 1988 and 1991 Labour Force Surveys; 1993/94 Survey of English Housing
> Notes: 1. Unemployed includes households that believe no work is available.
> 2. Disabled or sick includes only permanently sick.

It is important to recognise that the figures given only indicate the number of claimants at a point in time. The total number of claimants who actually receive ISMI in a 12-month period is considerably greater than the figures shown. The DSS has had difficulty producing this information but a crude estimate would suggest that, in 1994, there were probably 640,000 claimants in total (and it could be as high as 720,000). This contrasts with the snapshot figure of 529,000 in May 1994. The problem relates to whether one is counting the total number of claimants (some of whom will appear more than once in the same year) or the total number of loans subject to claims (some claimants will have more than one loan). The absence of a full data-set does not aid the policy evaluation process.

Characteristics of claimants

According to DSS income support statistics, about 17% of claimants are over 60 years old, 12% are disabled, 21% are lone parents and 43% are unemployed. Whilst unemployed home-owners are therefore the largest category of claimant, as these figures suggest, the majority of claimants are not the unemployed. It follows that introducing private insurance for unemployed home-owners will only partially address the situation because most beneficiaries of ISMI are outside this group.

It is also important to look at the length of time different categories of claimant have been in receipt of ISMI. Table XV shows that over 60% of pensioners who have been claiming have been doing so for over two years and this is true of 46% of disabled claimants and 42% of lone parents. This compares to 17% of

Table XV Time receiving income support for mortgage interest (ISMI) by type of household, May 1993

Length of time on ISMI	Thousands					Percentages				
	All cases	Unemployed	Aged 60+	Lone-parent	Disabled	All cases	Unemployed	Aged 60+	Lone-parent	Disabled
Up to 6 months	116	74	8	17	7	21	32	9	14	10
6 months to 1 year	111	58	8	18	10	18	24	9	15	15
1-2 years	151	65	21	34	19	27	27	22	29	28
2+ years	188	40	56	50	31	34	17	60	42	46
All cases	555	237	94	119	68	100	100	100	100	100

Source: Department of Social Security

unemployed recipients (although as of May 1993 44% had been on income support for more than one year). It is thus the elderly, disabled and lone parents who are more likely to be long-term income support recipients. They are also most likely to be unable to obtain private insurance to cover their inability to meet their mortgage repayments in the event of unemployment or sickness.

The data reveal very clearly that it is the unemployed who understandably move into and out of ISMI most quickly. Further recent information from the DSS makes this even more evident. Table XVI gives duration of claims in 1994 by type of claimant and breaks it down in a more detailed way. 65% of those on ISMI for two months or less and 62% of those on ISMI for two to six months are in the unemployed category. 42% of ISMI claimants who are unemployed move off ISMI within nine months. This is in complete contrast to the other categories. Only 26% of lone parents and 11% of pensioners cease being claimants within this period.

Looking to the future it would be reasonable to assume the numbers of unemployed claimants will continue to fall. However, regardless of any changes which may be brought in (or whether insurance has been taken out) the numbers of lone parents, pensioners and disabled claimants are likely to increase. For example, in England, the number of lone-parent households is projected by the Department of the Environment to rise to 1,257,000 by 2016, a 28% increase on the 1991 figure of 981,000. Similarly there is expected to be a 14% increase in couples aged 65 and over. Given that these groups are strongly represented amongst the long-term ISMI claimants, that many will not be able to get insurance and that both groups are growing in size, this will further diminish the prospects of significant reductions in ISMI expenditure.

Housing market impacts

The proposed changes in ISMI have already had an adverse impact on confidence in the housing market and on market activity. The currently fragile first-time buyer market will be acutely aware of the cuts in assistance to home-owners. Taking into account the rising trend in interest rates, the reduction in mortgage interest tax relief to 15% and the potential costs of mortgage payment protection insurance, many potential borrowers may be persuaded not to enter the owner-occupier market.

These costs will, of course, also affect existing borrowers. A family buying an average priced house at £64,000 with an 80% loan and an 8.35% mortgage rate faces increased costs of £33.00 a month (£400.00 a year) — the equivalent to an increase of 10.5% (this relates to creditor insurance and reduced tax relief, but ignoring any changes in interest rates). In Greater

Table XVI Type of mortgage interest claimants by duration of current income support claim
Thousands

	Less than 2 months	2-6 months	6-9 months	9 months or more
Pensioner	2	5	3	87
Sick/disabled	2	6	5	64
Lone parent	5	11	9	96
Unemployed	20	47	23	126
Other	3	7	3	27
All cases	31	76	42	399

Source: Department of Social Security

London the increased costs will average £43.00 a month. Table XVII below provides a more detailed regional breakdown.

In the second quarter of 1994 some 63% of all mortgages granted were to former owners. Of these only 46% were for new mortgages for house purchase. 25% were for remortgages on an existing property. The Government's revised plan to exclude such activity if the loan is for the same or a lesser amount as a basis for defining new borrowers is thus very significant. Recent research related to the British Household Panel Survey (BHPS) shows that, contrary to some claims, most additional loans were used for home improvements.

These will be treated as new borrowing and thus households could have mixed ISMI entitlements, as parts of their overall borrowing fall under different sets of regulations. The new system will thus be more complex and open to considerable confusion.

Increased costs of insurance will be a deterrent to some households entering home-ownership and the changes proposed by the DSS combine in impact with the reduction in MIRAS. Equally serious, the planned definition of a 'new borrower' may have a significant impact upon some major aspects of market activity in that different loans and groups of households are treated in different ways.

In addition, Box C describes how the proportion of home-owners who have low incomes has risen. Housing costs have increased significantly in real terms and relative to average incomes, thus placing even greater pressure on household budgets. Although the fall in interest rates since 1991/92 will have relieved some of that pressure, the figures on low-income home-owners give some indication of the strains of sustaining home-ownership and point towards the continuing importance of ISMI provision.

A private safety net?

The Housing and Savings Survey conducted in 1993 for the Building Societies Association gave a small amount of data on mortgage payment protection insurance. This showed that 12% of borrowers had unemployment insurance. Take-up was greatest amongst the younger age groups and those in the lower social grades. It was also stronger in certain regions (notably the East Midlands, Scotland, the North, the South West and Wales). First-time buyers were more likely to have it than existing borrowers.

Overall, the evidence suggested that households were beginning to take out insurance and that this was particularly true for those most exposed to the risk of unemployment. Recent research for the DoE confirms these figures. However, that same research suggests that fewer than one-in-ten of borrowers in arrears or repossession would succeed in claiming (on a private insurance policy) and in most cases they would not avoid falling into arrears because the terms of the insurance offer inadequate cover.[2]

Table XVII Regional increases in housing costs in 1995[1]

Region	Annual mortgage repayment Jan 1995 (A)	Mortgage repayment + insurance Oct 1995 (B)	Increase due to insurance + MIRAS (B)-(A)	Per cent increase
	£	£	£	%
Northern	2,741	3,067	326	11.9
Yorkshire & Humberside	2,972	3,314	342	11.5
East Midlands	3,205	3,563	358	11.2
East Anglia	3,481	3,859	378	10.9
Greater London	5,491	6,009	518	9.4
South East	4,713	5,177	464	9.8
South West	3,752	4,148	396	10.6
West Midlands	3,470	3,847	377	10.9
North West	3,354	3,723	369	11.0
Wales	3,253	3,615	362	11.1
Scotland	3,130	3,483	353	11.3
Northern Ireland	2,161	2,446	285	13.2
United Kingdom	3,800	4,200	400	10.5

Notes: 1. Excludes interest rate changes
Assumptions: (a) Average regional house price (b) Mortgage at 80% of house price (c) Mortgage rate 8.35% (d) Insurance at £7 per £100 repayment
Source: Constructed by author

> **Box C: Homeowners with low incomes**
>
> Over the last decade or more there has been a significant growth in home-owners with low incomes. Partly this reflects the growth in outright owners, many of whom are retired, but it is also a product of a range of government policies and programmes designed to draw households into home-ownership. The outcome has been a substantial rise in the number of home-owners at the bottom of the income distribution.
>
> As Table XVIII shows, the proportion of purchasing owners in the bottom decile in terms of income groups rose from 11% or 600,000 households (before housing costs) in 1979 to 28% or 1,600,000 households in 1991/92.[3]
>
> **Table XVIIIa Tenure of households in the bottom income decile**
> Thousands
>
> | | Owned with mortgage | Owned outright | Rented | Total |
> |---|---|---|---|---|
> | **Before housing costs** | | | | |
> | 1979 | 600 | 1540 | 3270 | 5410 |
> | 1991/2 | 1600 | 1370 | 2700 | 5670 |
> | **After housing costs** | | | | |
> | 1979 | 690 | 940 | 3780 | 5410 |
> | 1991/2 | 2010 | 560 | 3090 | 5670 |
>
> **Table XVIIIb Proportion of households in the bottom income decile who are in each tenure**
> Percentages
>
> | | Owned with mortgage | Owned outright | Rented | Total |
> |---|---|---|---|---|
> | **Before housing costs** | | | | |
> | 1979 | 11 | 28 | 60 | 100 |
> | 1991/2 | 28 | 24 | 48 | 100 |
> | **After housing costs** | | | | |
> | 1979 | 13 | 17 | 70 | 100 |
> | 1991/2 | 35 | 10 | 55 | 100 |

The emerging reality of private insurance provision is that, although the current market can be expanded, it will be no substitute for ISMI. The insurance industry estimates total take-up may rise from the current 1 million policy-holders to around 3.5 million. This would mean 6.5 million home-buyers have either opted not to take out insurance, were not eligible or could not afford it.

Current estimates suggest that at least 2.5 million households will find it difficult to take out insurance because of the type of employment they are in (self-employed, part-time or contract work), health (a pre-existing condition which would bar them from a claim), age (over 55) and reason for leaving work (for example, to become a carer). These constraints have now been recognised by the Government and it has conceded that such 'excluded' groups should be treated as existing borrowers where they become claimants; ie they will get ISMI at 80% after 2 months, and at the full rate after 6 months. New borrowers will have to wait 9 months to become entitled to ISMI (assuming they are eligible). At the same time, although the Government has now conceded that income from policies will not be taxed, it is a new cost for borrowers and some will not be able to afford it. Premiums are likely to reflect potential risk. Thus the more risky the case the higher the premiums.

Conclusions

Given continuing difficulties in the housing market there is a strong case for allowing a steady evolution of the private insurance market within the current policy framework. There is no evidence to suggest that the presence of ISMI has detracted from that market. Indeed under current arrangements there is already a potential market of say 7 million home-owners. The risk is that ISMI will be restricted but for some at least there will be no access to private insurance.

Lenders estimate that one effect of the proposals will be that the number of repossession cases will cease to decline as they have been doing for the last two years and indeed that they might rise. The Government is gambling on lenders offering forbearance for the nine months when a household could be without ISMI (or private insurance). Such risk-taking hardly seems the basis for policy development.

References

1. *House Tenure and Economic Activity in the Housing Market*, Terence Hogarth, Peter Elias and Janet Ford, Institute for Employment Research 1994. *Housing in England 1993/94*, Hazel Green and Jacqui Hansbro, OPCS/HMSO 1995.
2. *Mortgage Arrears and Possessions: Perspectives from borrowers, lenders and the courts*, Janet Ford, Elaine Kempson and Marilyn Wilson, Department of the Environment, HMSO 1995.
3. *Households below average income; a statistical analysis 1979-1991/92*, DSS, 1994.

chapter 1
Economic prospects and public expenditure

Housing market blues

The significance of the housing market for the wider economy is now widely recognised and is routinely considered in the assessment of economic prospects by the Treasury. In the 'Red Book' for 1995/96, the Treasury recognises negative equity (the excess of mortgage loans over house value), repossessions and the reductions in mortgage interest tax relief (or MIRAS) as factors that both limited the extent of the recovery in the home-ownership market in 1994 and will continue to do so in 1995.

While the UK mix-adjusted house price index rose in 1994 for the first time in five years, prices remained some 7% below 1989 levels (Table 42). As a result negative equity also eased but, as Table XIX shows, continued to affect some 1.2 million home-owners at the end of the first quarter of 1995. The average level of negative equity for those affected stood at £4,700.

While two-thirds of the households in negative equity were located in London or the South, Table XIX also shows that the phenomenon has a considerable impact on all regions, apart from Scotland and Northern Ireland.

More generally, net housing equity for all home-owners also continued to fall in 1994 and in real terms the average net equity for each owner-occupied dwelling was some one-third lower than in 1988 (see Figure III). The average net equity per owner-occupied dwelling nonetheless stood at close to £40,000 in 1994.

The Treasury expectation for 1995 is that — given relatively low interest rates and house price to income ratios — "continued economic growth, which increases the personal sector's resources and reduces uncertainty about the future, should lead to modest increases in both turnover and house prices".[1]

Halfway into 1995 it is already clear that the Treasury's assessment has, not for the first time, underestimated the extent of the difficulties confronting the housing market and, more particularly, the damaging impact of the proposed restrictions on income support help with mortgage interest costs that were announced in the November 1994 Budget.

Rather than continuing the process of modest recovery underway in 1994, 1995 is now more likely to see a stagnating private housing market, with repossessions rising again in the second half of the year and into 1996. Repossessions and persistent negative equity will continue to have a depressing influence on the market.

Uncertain prospects

The proposed income support changes are analysed in detail in the fourth *Contemporary Issues* article, but it is relevant here to acknowledge again the wider impact they are likely to have both on the housing market and

Table XIX Negative equity by region
Thousands

Region	Number of Households:							Average value in 1995 £
	1989	1990	1991	1992	1993	1994	1995[1]	
South East	108	241	361	661	536	491	434	6,100
Greater London	35	85	121	251	241	198	185	6,600
South West	43	81	121	225	206	157	159	4,800
East Midlands	11	45	54	145	101	86	99	2,100
East Anglia	23	50	59	100	84	83	71	6,000
West Midlands	6	38	10	115	102	73	63	1,100
North West	-	1	8	81	53	56	51	800
North	-	1	2	30	11	27	27	700
Yorkshire & Humberside	-	12	21	83	20	21	27	600
Wales	3	9	13	55	33	60	42	800
Scotland	-	-	6	19	-	14	3	100
Northern Ireland	1	1	-	3	1	2	2	1,100
United Kingdom	230	564	776	1,768	1,388	1,267	1,163	4,700

Sources: Rob Thomas, UBS Global Research, November 1994, January and April 1995.
Note: 1. All figures for fourth quarter of the year except 1995, which is for the first quarter.

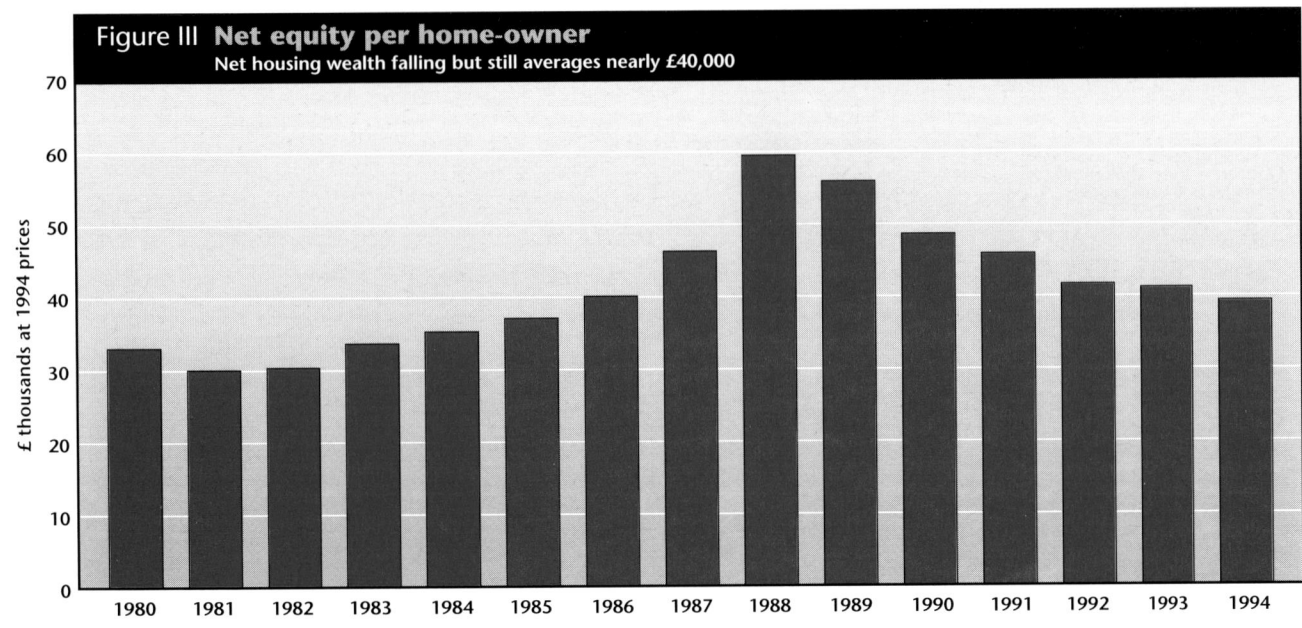

Figure III **Net equity per home-owner**
Net housing wealth falling but still averages nearly £40,000

Note: To calculate 1994 prices the gross domestic capital formation deflator was used

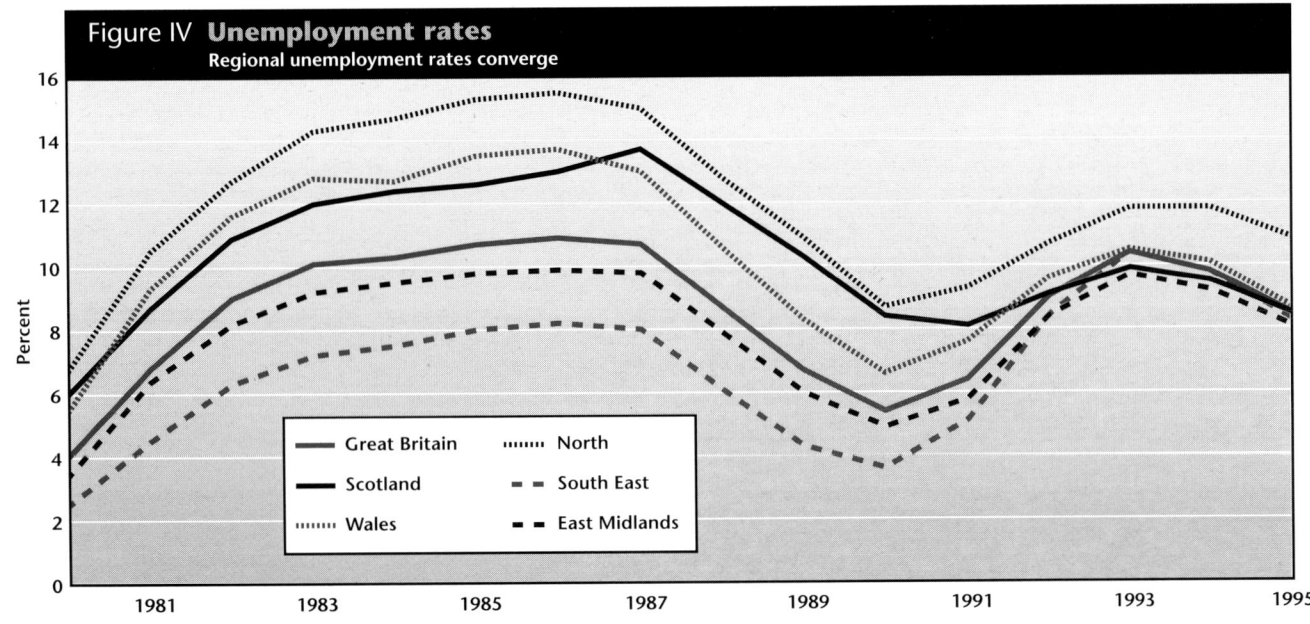

Figure IV **Unemployment rates**
Regional unemployment rates converge

Source: Table 4

the economy as a whole. The proposed greater limits on the availability of income support help for home-buyers will compound the uncertainties in a housing market still in the process of adjusting to a low inflation economy.

There is some irony that the proposed restrictions have also been announced at a time when there has been a growing awareness of the increasing uncertainties in the labour market and of the inherent and problematic significance of those changes for the future of the housing market. The proposals, and the controversy that they have provoked, have in turn accentuated that awareness.

The current trends of modest economic growth and declining unemployment are evidently not sufficient, in themselves, to reduce uncertainties about the future. The housing market shocks of the last recession are still reverberating and, while nationally unemployment has fallen back quite sharply since the beginning of 1993, in the South East unemployment rates remain as high as they were in 1986 (Figure IV).

At the national level, unemployment rates are projected to remain very close to 1995 levels through to the end of the decade (Table XX). There are also continuing qualitative changes in the labour market, with part-time and self-employment growing, while full-time male employment continues to fall (Figure V).

The decline in the proportions of full-time employees in 'secure' jobs over the last two decades has already been dramatic. In 1975, 56% of all working age people were in such jobs. By 1993 only 36% had such jobs. Several factors have contributed to that reduction

(Table XXI). These in part reflect economic and labour market trends, but the most significant individual factor has been the changes in employment legislation that have extended the period before workers qualify for employment protection.

These statistics do not, of course, reflect the uncertainties facing people in theoretically secure full-time employment, whether as a result of market restructuring or government policy. Housing professionals working for local authorities are, for example, very aware of the uncertainties that will shortly arise with the advent of compulsory competitive tendering for professional services in local government.

All these dimensions of labour market change connect with the housing market. One in five heads of home-buying household are, for example, either self-employed (15%), or in part-time or fixed-term employment.[2] The regional dimension to these connections is explored in the third *Contemporary Issues* article.

Perils of economic forecasts

These uncertainties are not only very likely to result in a stagnant private housing market in 1995, they also raise doubts about the rates of economic growth that will be achieved in the years up to and after the next general election. This is not because the Treasury is looking for housing market and domestic consumption led economic growth.

In its Budget forecast, the Treasury anticipated just 0.75% growth in private investment in dwellings and land. Consumer spending growth was forecast to run at just 2.5%, running slightly below both earnings (Table 2) and growth in gross domestic product (GDP). This forecast was linked to that for a relatively subdued recovery in the housing market. The Treasury is still quite deliberately restraining the housing market for fear of a repetition of the inflationary boom led by the housing market in the late 1980s. The failure to appreciate the market impact of its proposed income support policies, however, means that in 1995 we are more likely to see stagnation than modest recovery.

A potential consequence is that housing market 'equity withdrawal' — the villain of the late 1980s

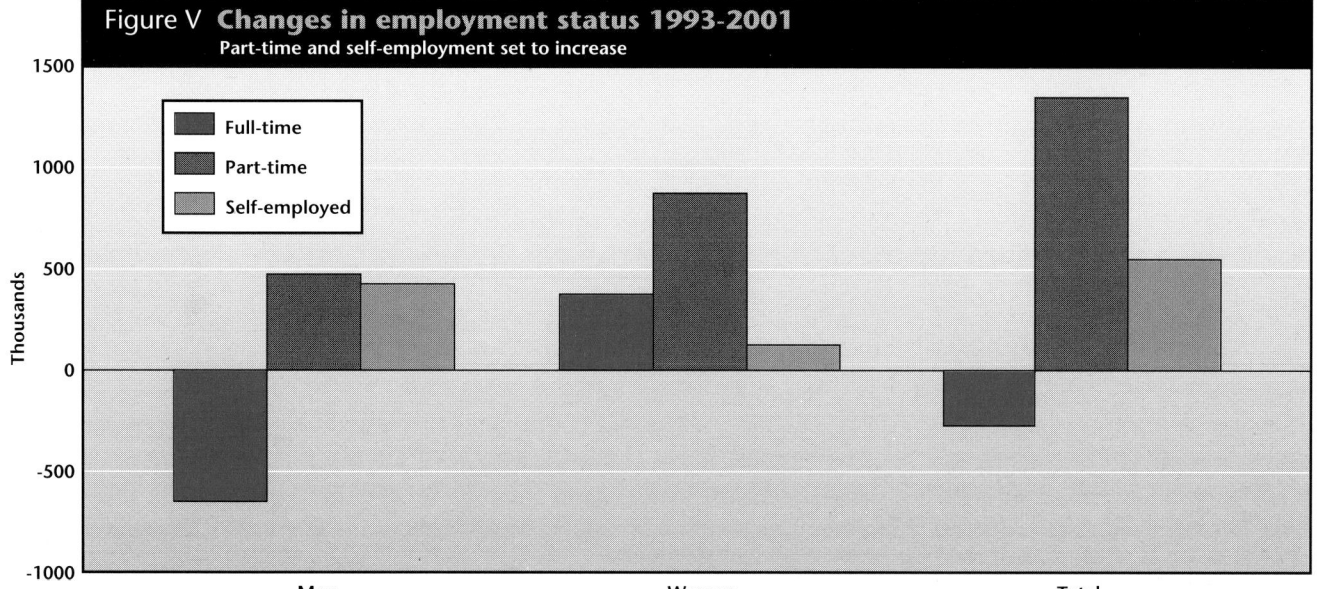

Figure V **Changes in employment status 1993-2001**
Part-time and self-employment set to increase

Source: Institute for Employment Research

Table XX Employment, unemployment and the labour force 1981 - 2001
Millions

	1981	1991	1993	1997	2001
Employees in employment	21.9	22.2	21.3	21.8	22.5
of which:					
Men	12.6	11.5	10.8	10.8	10.8
Women	9.3	10.7	10.5	11.0	11.7
H.M. Forces	0.3	0.3	0.3	0.2	0.2
Self-employment	2.1	3.1	3.0	3.2	3.5
Total employment	24.3	25.7	24.6	25.2	26.2
Labour force	27.2	28.2	28.0	28.5	29.2
of which :					
Men	16.3	16.3	16.0	15.8	15.9
Women	10.9	12.0	12.0	12.6	13.4
Claimant unemployment	2.8	2.3	2.9	2.4	2.3
Unemployment rate (%)	10.3	8.0	10.5	8.8	8.1
Male rate (%)	12.6	12.2	16.6	13.4	12.6
Female rate (%)	6.7	4.8	6.0	5.1	4.7

Source: Institute for Employment Research (1994)

Table XXI **Employment status of working age population**
Percentages

Employment Status	1975	1985	1993
Full-time employee (with tenure)	55.5	42.1	35.9
Full-time employee (no tenure)	3.6	7.8	12.8
Full-time employee (temporary)	-	1.3	1.9
Full-time self-employed	5.5	6.8	7.6
Part-time	11.6	12.9	14.7
Government schemes	-	1.3	1.1
Unemployed	4.6	8.7	8.1
Inactive	19.2	20.4	19.8

Source: 'A short history of labour turnover, job tenure, and job security, 1975-93', P Gregg and J Wadsworth, *Oxford Review of Economic Policy*, Vol 11, No 1, Spring 1995.

Notes: Part-time work is based on hours in 1975, but on self assessed part-time status afterwards. Full-time posts without tenure cover those with less than 6 months duration in 1975, 1 year in 1985 and 2 years in 1993. This follows from the changes in the qualifying period for employment rights between those years.

inflationary boom — will go negative in 1995 just as it did in 1993, and reduce the income available for consumer spending (Table 6). Such a change would be reflected in a reversal of the recent declining trend in the savings ratio (Table 3). The Treasury view is that there will be a further decline in savings as households seek to maintain their consumption expenditure, reducing savings to offset the effect of higher taxes.

Part way into the year the stagnation in the housing market is already apparent, while the indicators for the wider economy are providing mixed signals. The danger for the Treasury is not just that consumer spending will fall below their modest Budget forecast for growth, but that this will damage business confidence and restrain the hoped-for rapid growth in business investment. A key growth element for 1995 is anticipated to be the increased level of business investment that occurs, after some delay, during the up-swing of economic cycles. The Treasury Budget forecast was for 10.75% growth in 1995, compared to just 2% in 1994. This would counterbalance the slow growth in dwelling and land investment to give the projected 5.75% growth in overall fixed investment (Table 10).

Both the Treasury and the OECD forecast further strong growth in world trade, but with UK exports slightly down from 8.25% in 1994 to 7% in 1995. North Sea oil output in 1995 is not expected to see any further significant growth.

In its *Summer Economic Forecast* the Treasury scaled down its forecasts for economic growth, in view of what it considers 'surprising' weakness in the housing market. It now expects only 3% growth in GDP in 1995 (as opposed to 3.25% in the Budget forecast), and only 2% growth in consumer spending (down from 2.5%). The damage to business confidence is also recognised, with the forecast for growth in business investment slashed from 10.75% to 4.75%.

This brief description of some of the economic factors and processes involved in making economic forecasts makes abundantly plain the inherent limitations of all forecasts, however sophisticated the modelling techniques available. Past relationships can only provide a partial guide to the likely outcome of future situations which always include unique and original elements. For 1995, and 1996, the proposed income support changes remain the joker in the pack.

Public spending

The out-turn economic performance in 1995 will have a direct impact on the scope for public spending and taxation decisions in the next few years. The Treasury forecasts that economic growth will by 1997/98 lead to a positive 'current balance', so that public borrowing will then be lower than the level of net public sector investment. This anticipated compliance with the so-called 'golden rule' that net government borrowing should only be for investment purposes is clearly important for the Chancellor as he balances the objectives for prudent government finances against the desire to reduce taxation ahead of the general election.

With the economic recovery slower than anticipated, and the Public Sector Borrowing Requirement (PSBR) not falling as rapidly as forecast in the 1994 Budget, lower future public expenditure is the only alternative to foregoing either tax cuts or the Chancellor's reputation for financial prudence.

The PSBR was forecast in the Budget to fall to just £13 billion in 1996/97, down from the peak level of £45 billion in 1993/94 (Table 12). However, as a result of slower economic growth, the Summer Economic Forecast has revised the PSBR forecast for 1995/96 to £23.5 billion (up £2 billion) and the forecast for 1996/97 to £16 billion.

On target for monetary union

Even at that level the PSBR would represent just 2% GDP and the UK economy would be one of the few in the European Union that meets the 3% deficit criteria for monetary union (Table 9). Given the continuing political controversy in the UK about monetary union, this is, of course, rather ironic.

The key economic measure for monetary union under the Maastricht Treaty is not, however, measured in terms of the PSBR (which is a unique creation of the Treasury), but the General Government Financial Deficit (GGFD). The differences between these measures and their potential implications for the future of council housing are discussed further in the fourth *Contemporary issues* article.

Tight controls

The plans for public spending in the years to 1997/98 are already very tight, if not as tight as in 1995/96. In real terms the 'control total' for public spending in the years 1996/97 and 1997/98 provides for growth of 0.5% and 1% respectively (Table 15b). This compares with provision for a reduction in real terms of 0.8% in 1995/96.

These provisions for the control total include unallocated reserves of £3, £6 and £9 billion respectively for each of the years from 1995/96 to 1997/98. If those reserves are not, in the event, applied to increase the control totals for individual government departments, this will lead to further reductions in public expenditure in real terms in the years ahead.

Bottom of the league

This context offers little comfort for the future prospects for public expenditure provision for housing, which already holds the unenviable record as the function whose expenditure has suffered the greatest cutbacks over the last fifteen years (Table 14b).

Another league table where UK housing has an unenviable position is for gross fixed investment in residential dwellings, as a percentage of GDP. Compared with a range of OECD nations, the UK and Belgium share the honours for the lowest average level of investment over the period 1980-92 (Table 7 and Figure VI).

References

1 Page 24, *Financial Statement and Budget Report 1995/96*, HM Treasury November 1994, House of Commons No 12, HMSO 1994.
2 Answer to Parliamentary Question, 8/12/94, Hansard. Data from 1994 Labour Force Survey.

Key reading

Financial Statement and Budget Report 1995/96, HM Treasury November 1994, House of Commons No 12, HMSO 1994.

Public Expenditure, Cm 2821, HM Treasury, HMSO 1995.

OECD Economic Outlook 56, OECD 1994.

Summer Economic Forecast 1995, HM Treasury, HMSO 1995.

Inquiry into Income and Wealth, Volumes 1 & 2, Sir Peter Barclay (Volume 1) and John Hills (Volume 2), Joseph Rowntree Foundation 1995.

Challenging the Conventions, John Hawksworth and Steve Wilcox, Chartered Institute of Housing 1995.

Building Homes, Building Jobs, David Clapham, Geoff Meen, Stephen Thake, Steve Wilcox and Richard Walker, National Housing Forum 1995.

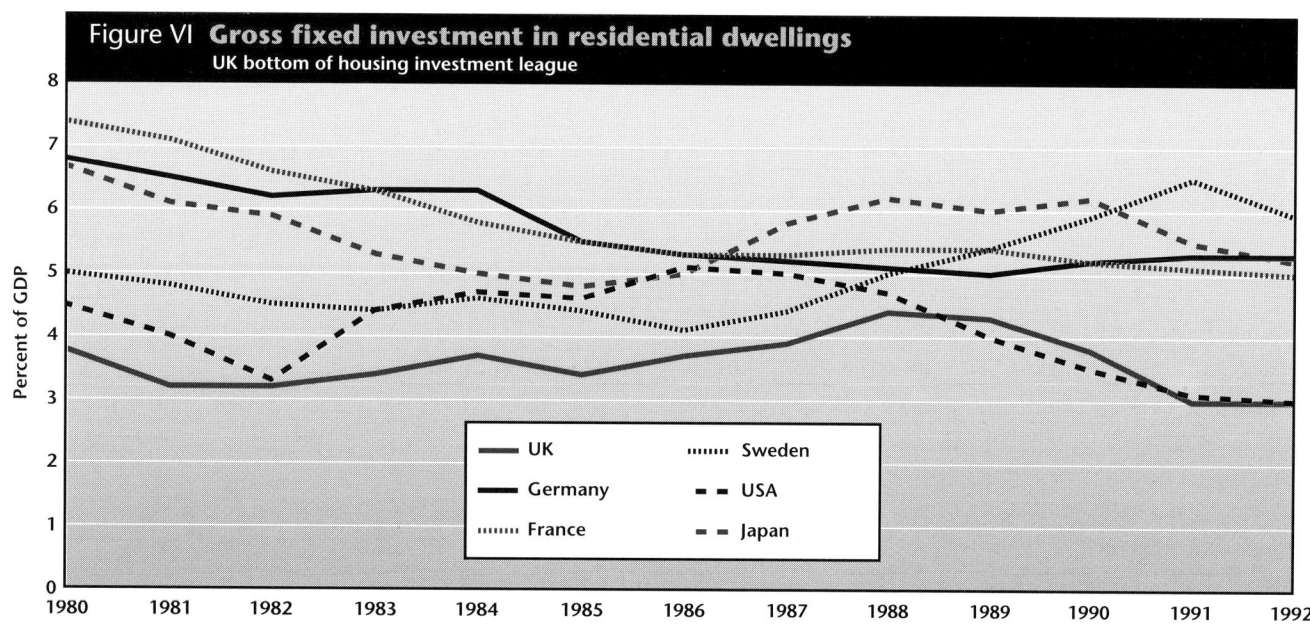

Figure VI **Gross fixed investment in residential dwellings** — UK bottom of housing investment league. Source: Table 7

chapter 2
Dwellings and households

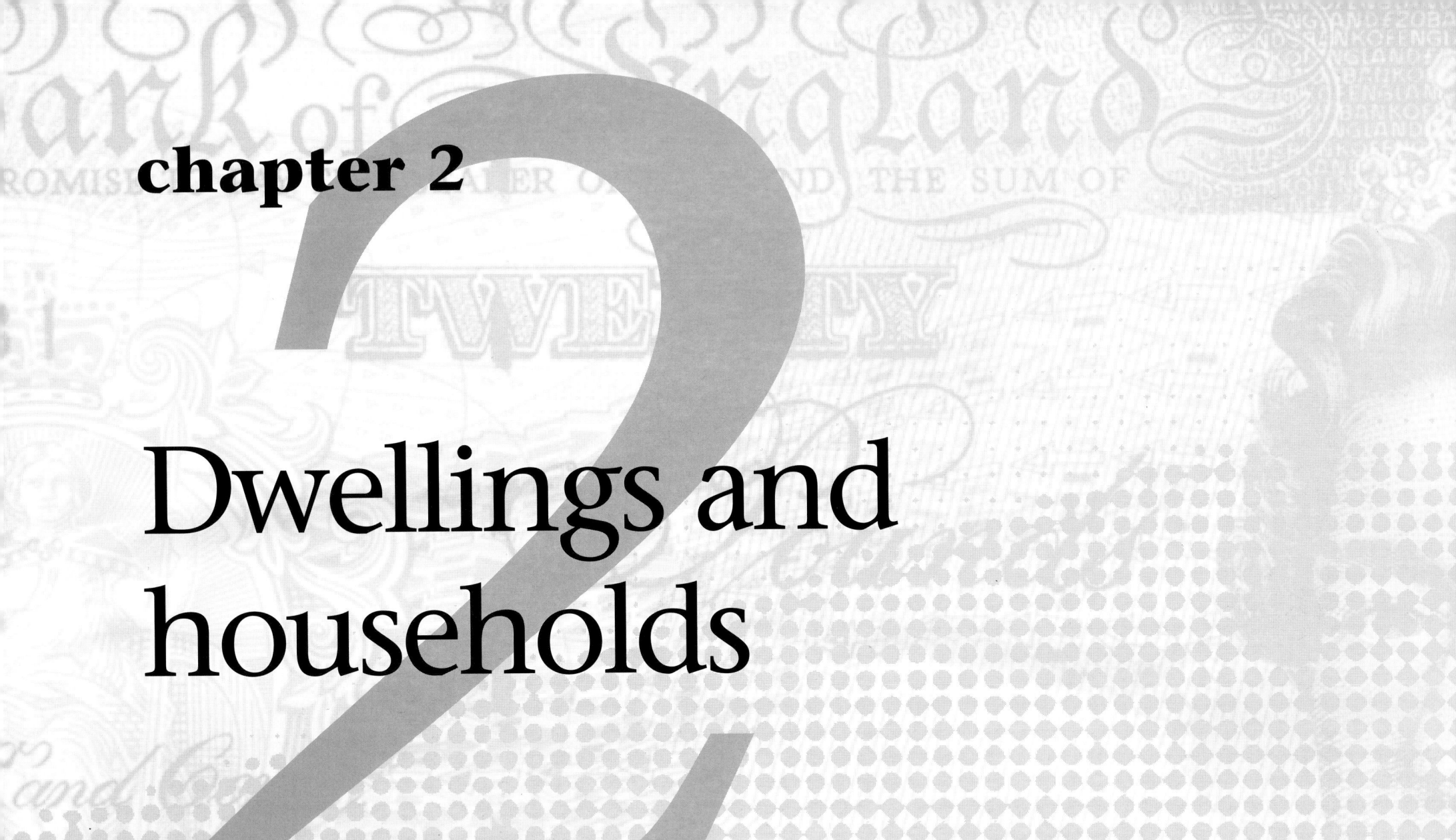

Ownership on hold

The housing market recession has continued to limit the growth in home-ownership severely; virtually the only proportionate growth in home-ownership over the last six years has been the result of the Right-to-Buy (Figure VII). It is also notable that the numbers of younger home-owners as a proportion of the sector have declined (Table 28a).

This is not just a result of the growth in the numbers and proportions of older home-buyers, that is itself a lagged result of earlier decades of growth in the proportions of new owners entering the sector. It is due to more younger households choosing to rent. In 1991, 35% of heads of household under the age of 25 were home-owners; by 1993 this had fallen to just 26%. There were also falls, albeit less sharp, in the proportions of heads of household aged 25-29 and 30-44 who were home-owners.

These falls were matched by growth in the proportions of younger households entering the private rented sector. Even so, by the end of 1994 the five-year resurgence of the private rented sector had also slowed to a trickle. The various factors involved in the market for private rented housing are discussed further in Chapter 3.

While Right-to-Buy sales picked up marginally in 1994 from the low point of 1993, overall sales in Great Britain remained below half the average annual level for the 1980s. Right-to-Buy sales for Scotland in recent years, however, are only a little below the average for the last decade, reflecting the marked differences in the tenure patterns and housing market trends in Scotland compared to England and Wales (see the third *Contemporary Issues* article).

The new 'rents to mortgage' variation on the Right-to-Buy scheme has made very little impact, as the narrowed gap between the costs of renting and owning and the continuing housing market doldrums have virtually wiped out the intended market niche for the scheme. It now looks set to follow its predecessor, the 'right to shared ownership', into the annals of British housing policy failures. Nonetheless, it should also be recorded that 1994 saw Right-to-Buy sales of council housing in Great Britain, in all its forms, pass the 1.5 million mark.

Million milestones

While the fortunes of housing associations have waned somewhat since they were moved centre stage in 1989 with the freedom to raise private finance, they should nonetheless pass some major milestones during the course of 1995. By the end of 1994 there were 944,000 housing association homes in Great Britain, and just over 956,000 in the UK (Table 16).

Following on from the Budget cuts, new housing association completions will now decline, reversing the welcome growth over the last few years (Figure VIII). However, local authority stock transfers to housing associations in England are continuing apace. By mid-1995 housing associations will have passed the millionth home mark in the UK, and by the autumn they will pass the same milestone just for Great Britain.

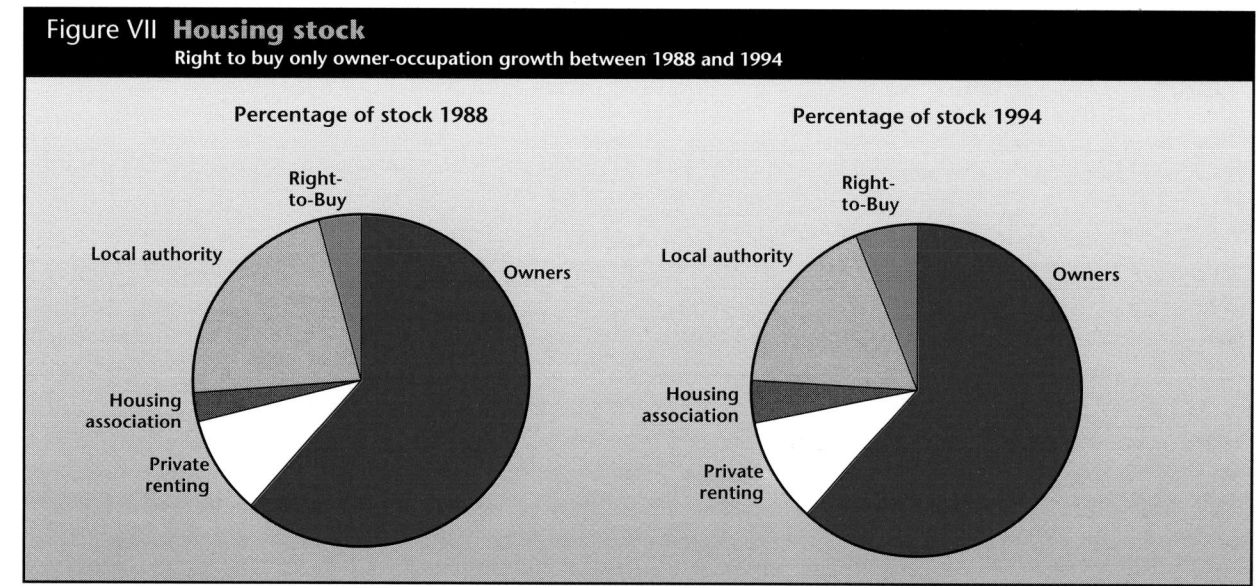

Figure VII **Housing stock**
Right to buy only owner-occupation growth between 1988 and 1994

Source: Tables 16 & 19

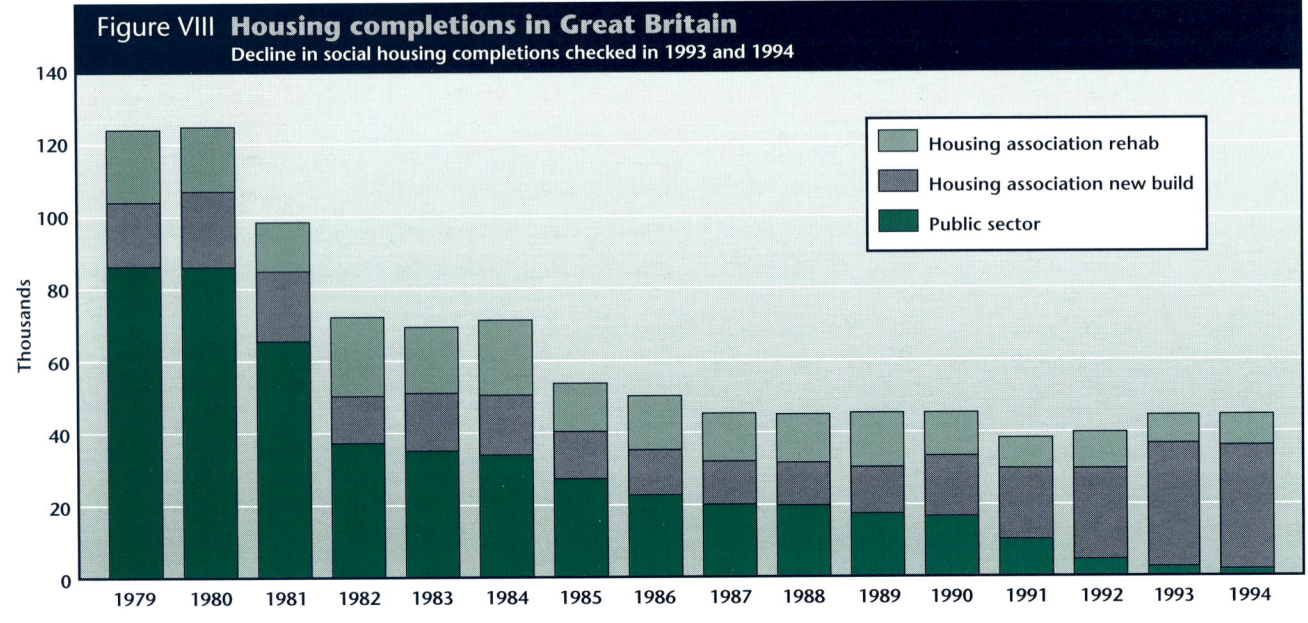

Figure VIII **Housing completions in Great Britain**
Decline in social housing completions checked in 1993 and 1994

Note: Tables 18 & 26

The housing association sector will have doubled in size in just over 12 years. This is quite an acheivement for a movement that took some 750 years to reach their first half million![1] How rapidly the sector grows in the future will depend in no little measure on the outcome of the debates around the ideas for local housing companies, rather than housing associations, as successor bodies for council housing (see the fourth *Contemporary Issues* article).

Household projections

During the course of the year new household projections have been published, separately, for England, Wales and Scotland. The main results are shown in Tables XXII, XXIII and XXIV. The projections for England and Wales share a similar format but, as can be seen, the approach taken by the Scottish Office is rather different.

Table XXII Household projections for England
Thousands

Household type	1971	1981	1991	1996	2001	2006	2011	2016
Married couple	11,249	11,012	10,547	10,341	10,217	10,118	10,037	9,945
+Cohabiting couple	204	500	1,222	1,377	1,447	1,499	1,549	1,579
+Lone parent	378	626	981	1,122	1,202	1,243	1,259	1,257
+Other multi-person	1,168	1,235	1,350	1,512	1,671	1,852	2,051	2,240
+One person	2,944	3,932	5,115	5,824	6,509	7,185	7,875	8,577
=Total	15,942	17,306	19,215	20,177	21,046	21,897	22,769	23,598
Concealed families:								
Couple	127	83	74	67	62	60	60	60
Lone parent	108	83	89	86	82	83	84	83

Source: *Projections of Households in England to 2016*, Department of the Environment

Table XXIII Household projections for Wales
Thousands

Household type	1992	1996	2001	2006	2011	2016
Married couple	650	640	630	621	612	600
+Cohabiting couple	56	61	64	67	69	70
+Lone parent	60	67	70	72	72	72
+Other multi-person	82	88	98	109	121	130
+One person	289	321	359	395	430	463
=Total	1,138	1,177	1,221	1,264	1,304	1,335
Concealed families:						
Couple	4	4	4	4	4	4
Lone parent	8	7	8	8	8	8

Source: *1992-Based Household Projections for Wales*, Welsh Office

Table XXIV **Household projections for Scotland**
Thousands

Marital status	Persons in household	1992	1998	2006
Married couple	1	45	53	62
	2+	1,161	1,157	1,131
Widowed/divorced	1	337	379	436
	2+	168	164	150
Single	1	214	258	313
	2+	142	171	202
Totals:	1	596	690	810
	2+	1,471	1,492	1,483
	All	2,067	2,183	2,293

Source: *1992-based household projections for Scotland, Scottish Office Statistical Bulletin*

A central feature of the new household projections for England and Wales is that they make the distinction between married couples, cohabiting couples and lone parents. As a result it becomes clear that a substantial part of the projected growth in lone parenthood shown in earlier projections can now be more properly identified as growth in cohabiting. Beyond 1996, the new projections suggest only a very limited growth for lone-parent households. By far the largest component of the overall projected future growth in households — in England, Wales and Scotland — is the growth of single-person households.

A detailed analysis of the English projections, and the methodology on which they are based, can be found in the second *Contemporary Issues* article. The article also examines in detail the regional projections and some of their implications for planning and housing policy. An official assessment of the future requirements for social rented housing based on the new projections is critically reviewed in Chapter 5.

Renovation and stock condition

The results of the 1993 *Welsh House Condition Survey* were published towards the end of 1994; the main findings are set out in Tables 23a, 23b and 23c. Unfitness rates in Wales remain far higher than for England (Table 22b), but have fallen by a third when compared to 1986. The Welsh Office target is to achieve a further 25% reduction between 1992/93 and 1996/97, and to that end financial support for renovation grants was increased by more than 50% in 1992/93.

The numbers of private sector renovation grant payments made in Wales fell in 1994, however (Table 25b). In contrast grant payments in England rose in 1994, but AMA/ADC expenditure estimates suggest that they too will fall back in 1995. Renovation grants, including mandatory grants, are quite explicitly being rationed in line with available resources. By 1995/96 an estimated one in five English councils are only awarding mandatory grants; for another quarter of all councils expenditure on mandatory grants will exceed 90% of all grant spending.[2]

Tenure, economic activity and incomes

Data from the recently published 1993 *Survey of English Housing* shows that there has been a further small decline in the proportions of heads of household who have recently moved house who are in employment, within both the council and housing association sectors (Table 32). Even so, excluding retired heads of household, some 45% of all heads of household in the social rented sector were in full- or part-time employment (Table 31).

The proportion of recent movers in the housing association sector in employment remained very slightly higher than for council tenants. This suggests that the evidence of new high rent housing association estates, that are almost exclusively occupied by economically inactive households, relates to particular cases, rather than necessarily being part of a more widespread trend.

The impact of the recent recession on home-owners is reflected in the increase (from 6% in 1984 to 10% in 1993) in the proportion of new home-buying heads of household not in full-time employment. Similarly in 1993 social security provided 5% of the total gross

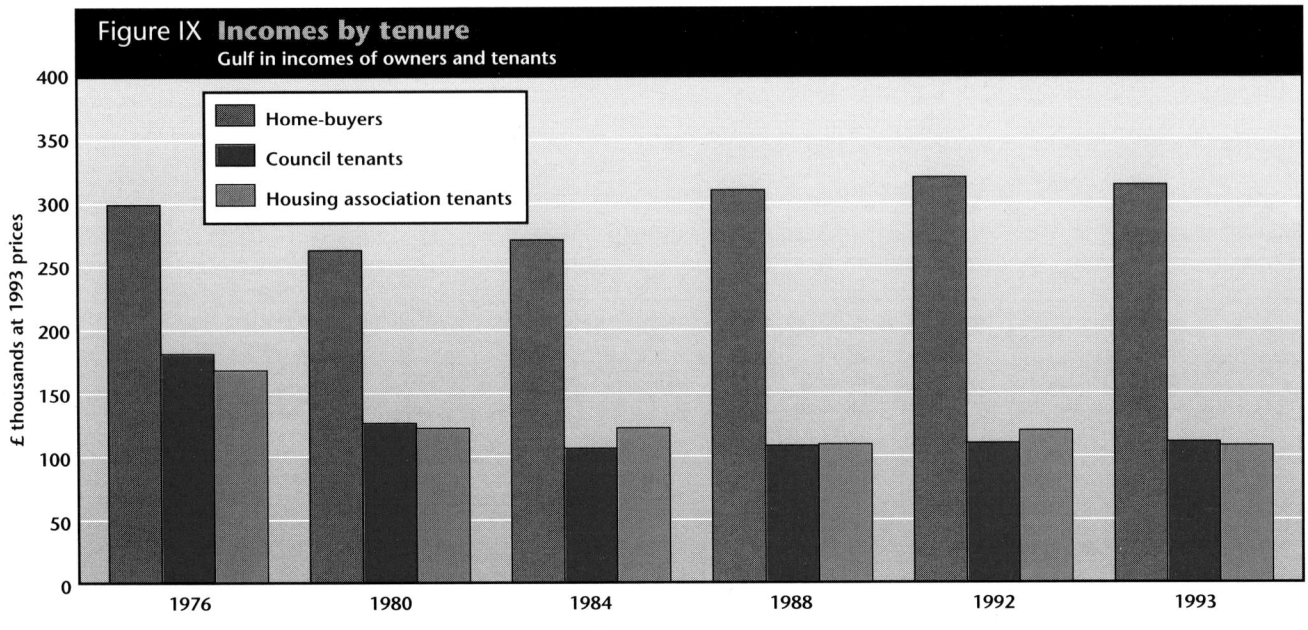

Figure IX **Incomes by tenure**
Gulf in incomes of owners and tenants

Source: Table 33

household weekly income of all home-buying households (Table 34), compared with just 3.6% in 1988.

While the average incomes of home-buying heads of household are still almost three times those of social rented sector tenants, the gulf between them slightly narrowed in 1993 (Figure IX).

New analyses from the Family Expenditure Survey

The 1993 *Family Expenditure Survey* provides an analysis of income distribution within tenures by deciles of households. This analysis (Table 35) replaces earlier analyses by given income bands, and will make it easier in future to undertake comparisons of changing patterns over time.

The table nonetheless shows a now familiar pattern, with social housing sector tenants concentrated in the lowest income deciles, and an overwhelming preponderance of home-owners within the upper income deciles. However, there is also a large proportion of owner-occupiers, principally outright owners, in the lowest income deciles. Indeed there are more outright owners, 58% of whom are retired (Table 31), in the lower half of the income range, than in the upper half.

Results from some specially commissioned analyses from the *Family Expenditure Survey* database are also set out in Tables XXV and XXVI. These show that the income differences between the tenures hold across households in various categories of economic activity,

Table XXV **Gross household incomes by tenure and economic activity**
£ per week

Tenure	Economically active:			Economically inactive:		
	Manual	Non-manual	Self-employed	Unemployed	Unoccupied	Retired
Home-buyer	430	625	494	304	305	238
Outright owner	372	558	441	220	274	224
Private renting	285	500	358	156	160	137
Social renting	296	317	242	131	136	114

Source: *Family Expenditure Survey 1993*; analysis commissioned by The Guinness Trust
Notes: Social renting comprises local authority and housing association tenants.
Private renting comprises furnished and unfurnished tenants, and excludes tenants of rent-free accommodation. These composite tenure groupings are used because of the small sample sizes for some categories.

both in and out of work (Table XXV). The income differences between tenures also holds across regions (Table XXVI), although there are some variations in the regional differentials in incomes within tenures.

The lower levels of income shown for working tenants in social housing includes some 12%-15% of income from social security benefits. The income differentials across tenures based just on earned incomes are rather higher.

References

1. Page 142, 'Housing associations: 1890-1990', Richard Best, in *A New Century of Social Housing*, ed. Stuart Lowe and David Hughes, Leicester University Press 1991.
2. Page 17, *ADC/AMA Housing Finance Survey 1995/96*, AMA/ADC 1995.

Key reading

General Household Survey 1993, OPCS, HMSO 1995.

Family Expenditure Survey 1993, Central Statistical Office, HMSO 1994.

Housing in England 1993/94, H Green & J Hansbro, Office of Population Censuses & Surveys, HMSO 1995.

1993 Welsh House Condition Survey, Welsh Office 1994.

Projections of Households in England to 2016, Department of the Environment, HMSO 1995.

1992 Based Household Projections for Wales, Welsh Office 1995.

1992 Based Household Projections for Scotland, Scottish Office Statistical Bulletin, Hsg/1995/3, 1995.

Table XXVI **Gross household incomes by tenure and region**
£ per week

Region	Home-buyers	Outright owners	Private renting	Social renting
North	421	264	245	165
Yorkshire and Humberside	455	262	207	178
North West	496	259	200	152
West Midlands	447	272	233	146
East Midlands	447	292	287	188
East Anglia	527	273	265	142
Greater London	620	430	366	210
Rest of South East	589	311	297	186
South West	461	286	245	161
England	513	298	276	173
Wales	426	277	202	165
Scotland	507	333	299	173
Northern Ireland	517	245	220	140
United Kingdom	508	297	274	172

Source and Notes: As Table XXV

chapter 3
Private housing

Private housing

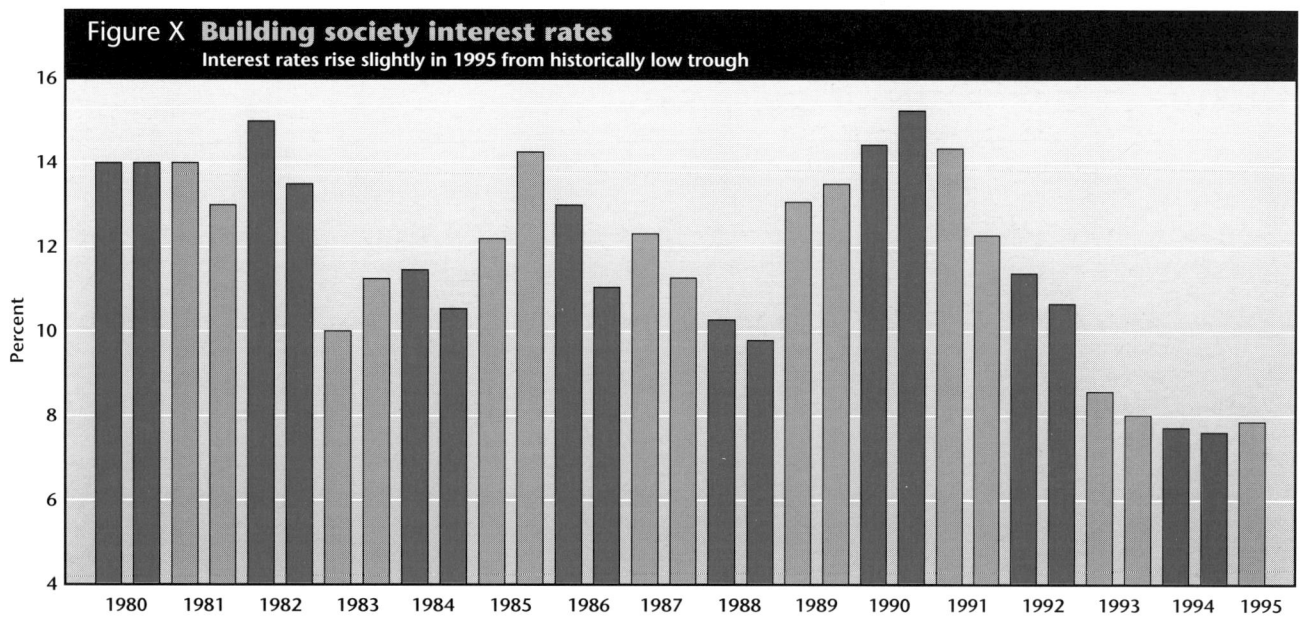

Figure X Building society interest rates
Interest rates rise slightly in 1995 from historically low trough

Note: Figures for January & July of each year
Sources: Housing Finance & Financial Statistics

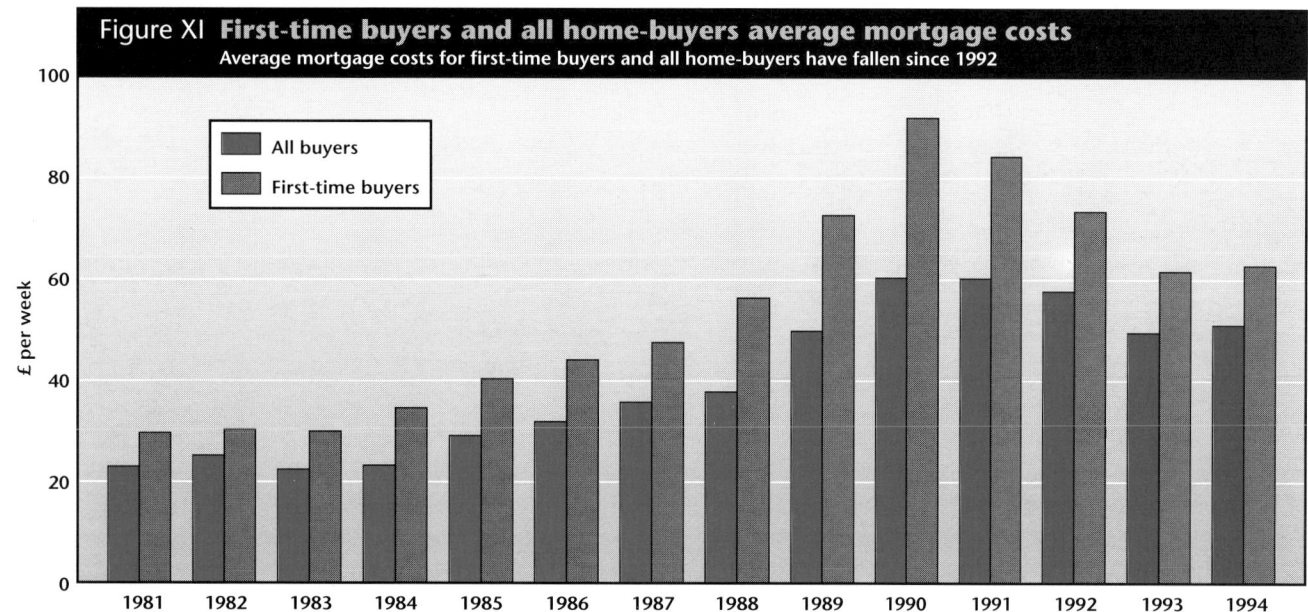

Figure XI First-time buyers and all home-buyers average mortgage costs
Average mortgage costs for first-time buyers and all home-buyers have fallen since 1992

Note: First-time buyer mortgage costs in the first year of mortgage
Sources: Tables 39a & 43

Housing market blues (continued)

The continuing difficulties in the home-ownership market have already been discussed in Chapter 1 in terms of their potential wider implications for the economy. In this chapter the discussion is confined to some of the key trends and issues within the private housing market. Although undoubtedly the most important issue facing the market in 1995 is the proposed restrictions on income support help for home-buyers, this is analysed in detail in the first *Contemporary Issues* article.

One measure of the stagnation in the housing market is provided by the numbers of property transactions. These picked up slightly in 1993 and 1994 as a whole, although they fell back in the second half of the year (Table 36a). Transaction levels remained flat into the first quarter of 1995, while the figures for April (100,000) and May (98,000) showed a further decline.

Quite apart from the impact of the income support proposals, this reflects the slight upturn in interest rates since mid-1994 (Figure X), compounded by the further reduction in MIRAS relief to 15% from April 1995. Even so, average mortgage costs for first-time buyers, and for home-buyers as a whole, are far lower than in 1992 (Figure XI).

For first-time buyers, basic mortgage costs (excluding insurances) represented 18% of incomes in 1994. Excluding the boom years (1989 to 1992) this is in line with the experience of the early 1980s, when the corresponding figures ranged from 17% to 21% (Table 39a). Given the post-recession increases in all

Table XXVII Average regional house prices by size of dwelling in 1993
£

Region	2 rooms or less	3 rooms	4 rooms	5 rooms	6 rooms	7 rooms or more
North	42,500	28,460	35,361	41,387	49,583	85,652
Yorkshire and Humberside	26,282	33,339	38,864	44,588	51,937	90,660
North West	29,460	35,853	39,032	45,814	53,598	94,412
West Midlands	34,497	33,967	41,245	46,729	54,590	93,689
East Midlands	33,360	31,915	39,566	42,142	50,707	86,905
East Anglia	28,989	30,190	41,712	46,862	55,333	84,767
Greater London	48,650	55,287	65,293	69,752	85,686	132,348
Rest of South East	38,980	39,864	51,214	60,580	72,877	116,720
South West	30,948	35,097	45,095	52,383	61,086	95,197
Wales	31,788	34,235	39,370	42,552	47,127	77,286
Scotland	31,557	33,387	36,572	43,260	64,531	103,591
Northern Ireland	20,725	26,748	25,714	29,335	38,170	61,867

Source: Analysis commissioned from DoE/CML 5% Sample Survey

Notes: Figures for two room dwellings should be treated with caution due to small sample sizes. Rooms include kitchens, but not bathrooms..

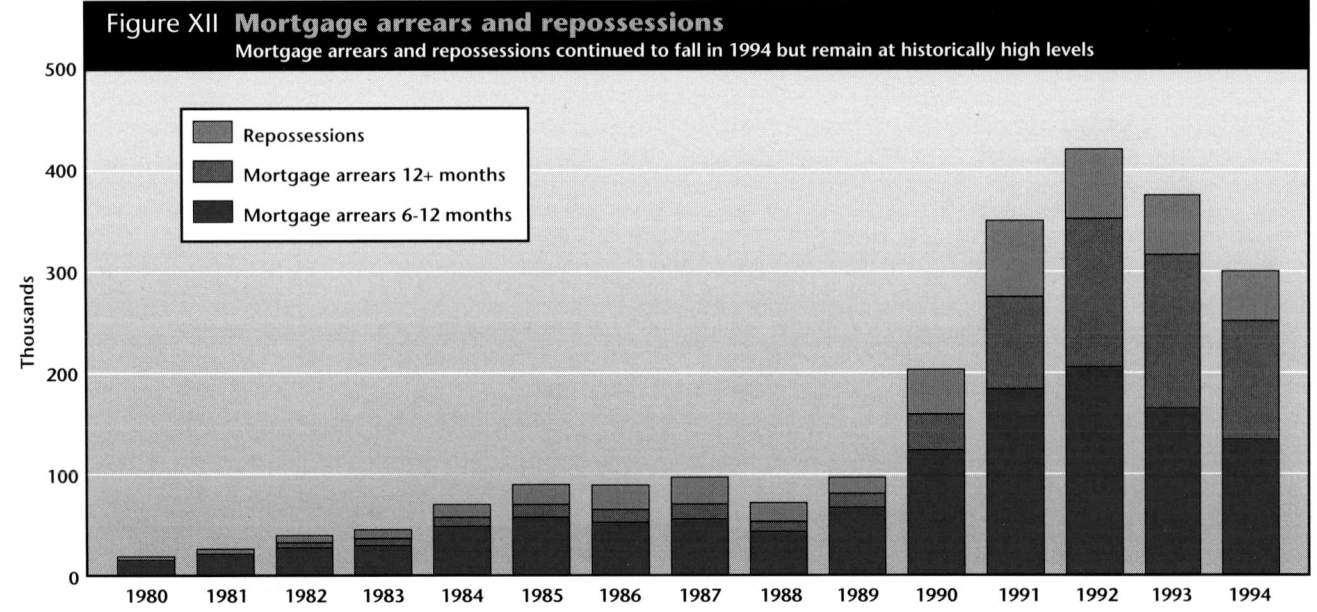

Figure XII **Mortgage arrears and repossessions**
Mortgage arrears and repossessions continued to fall in 1994 but remain at historically high levels

Source: Table 44

mortgage insurances costs, let alone the question of unemployment insurances, it would be surprising to see any increase in this ratio in 1995. With net mortgage interest costs in 1995 having already risen compared to 1994, and future interest rates expected to rise further, the forecasts for stagnant or falling house prices in 1995 look more credible than those for modest increases.

International and regional perspectives

One effect of the recent falls in house prices is that the overall levels of net housing equity held by home-owners in the UK are now far more in line with the experience in France, Germany and the USA (Table 40). The remaining difference, however, is that home-owner debt levels, as a percentage of national GDP, are far higher in the UK.

The characteristics of regional house markets within the UK and movements in regional house prices are analysed in the third *Contemporary Issues* article. A further breakdown of regional house prices by size of dwelling is provided in Table XXVII. This specially commissioned analysis has a number of uses. Together with data on mortgage costs, for example, it allows housing associations to compare their rents against the costs of purchasing properties of an equivalent size.

Down and out

Both mortgage arrears and repossession levels fell in 1994, compared to 1993 (Figure XII). However, repossessions remained higher than in 1990, the year in which the Government thought it necessary to launch the 'mortgage rescue' package. In the five years

1990-94 a total of almost 300,000 home-owners have been repossessed, more than twice as many as during the whole decade of the 1980s.

The Bradford and Bingley Building Society, and to a lesser extent the much larger Halifax Building Society, stand alone as the only building societies to have made a significant impact with the 'mortgage to rent' schemes[1] that were supposed to have been at the heart of the mortgage rescue package. To the extent that repossessions have been lower than they might have been over the last few years, this is rather the result of lender 'forbearance' in seeking repossessions, underpinned by the payment of income support monies for mortgage interest direct to lenders.

The recent downturn in long-term mortgage arrears is, however, little more than a reflection of the numbers of home-buyers repossessed during the course of the year. The results of a valuable new survey of households in mortgage arrears, commissioned by the Department of the Environment, show one in five home-buyers either having been in arrears at some point during the period 1991-93, or having experienced difficulties in finding payments in order to stay out of arrears (Table XXVIII).

While the survey found that as many home-owners recover from mortgage arrears as those that do not, this is before taking account of those home-buyers repossessed as a result of arrears during the period. When these are taken into account the survey suggests that only a minority of households in arrears have a realistic prospect of recovering and avoiding eventual repossession. This is a sombre finding given the quarter of a million home-buyers remaining in long-term arrears at the end of 1994.

The DoE survey also found only just over one in five home-buyers in arrears have entered into arrangements with their lenders to make reduced or interest-only payments.[2] Over a quarter had arrangements to make their monthly payments plus an additional payment to reduce their arrears, and almost one in eight had arrangements simply to maintain their normal monthly payments.

The survey adds to the evidence of both the extent, and the limitations and unevenness, of 'lender forbearance'. Clearly not all mortgage lenders have followed guidelines from the Council of Mortgage Lenders or made the same efforts to minimise repossessions. An extreme case is The Mortgage Corporation, which is being prosecuted by Surrey trading standards officials, accused of harassing home-owners with very minor levels of mortgage arrears and has also been threatened by the Office of Fair Trading with revocation of their consumer credit license.

The planned restriction of income support payments to average rates of mortgage interest will also see mortgage arrears increasing for home-buyers with mortgages with lenders, like The Mortgage Corporation, that now have mortgage rates some way above the industry average.

Limited protection

The most reported findings of the DoE survey relate to the limitations of existing mortgage protection plans intended to provide financial cover when home-buyers become unemployed. The survey identified a number of limitations to those policies, including the somewhat startling finding that two-thirds of all claims for assistance under those policies had failed. Not surprisingly, the researchers concluded that very little could be achieved by attempting to extend the role of such policies.[3]

Court actions related to mortgage arrears showed no signs of slowing in the first quarter of 1995 (Table 46) and, with mortgage lenders arguing that the new income support restrictions will bring an end to their commitment to the Government not to repossess

Table XXVIII Moving into and out of mortgage arrears, 1991 to 1993

	Percentage of all mortgagors
Arrears during 1991-1993, cleared and no current payment difficulties	3
Arrears during 1991-1993, cleared but currently some difficulty finding payments	3
Arrears during 1991-1993, cleared but currently in arrears again	1
In arrears for the whole of 1991-1993	1
Fallen into arrears for the first time during 1991-1993	3
Total percentage of mortgagors experiencing arrears at some point during 1991-1993	11
Currently having some difficulty finding payments, but with no current or past arrears	9

Source: *Mortgage Arrears and Possessions: Perspectives from borrowers, lenders and the courts*, Ford, Kempson and Wilson, Department of the Environment, HMSO

home-buyers where they receive direct payments of income support, the prospects for any easing in repossession levels in 1995 do not look good. Indeed, repossession figures for the first half of 1995 are slightly up from 1994 levels (Table 44).

In 1996, we will see the direct impact of the new income support restrictions. While these have been modified in the face of wide-ranging criticism from every quarter (apart, of course, from the Association of British Insurers) the substantive core of the proposals remains.

While the nine-month restriction on income support claims by new borrowers and the limited benefits of mortgage insurance policies will only have a gradual direct impact on arrears and repossession levels, the predictable downturn in the housing market as many self-employed and other mortgage applicants without secure employment are excluded or deterred from entering the market could well trigger an upturn in possession actions against existing long-term arrears cases.

Private renting

The slowdown in the recent resurgence of the private rented sector was noted in Chapter 2. One factor is likely to have been the gradual outflow of properties that had been rented out temporarily because of the housing market recession. A survey (supported by the Joseph Rowntree Foundation) undertaken at the end of 1993 identified one in ten lettings as being owned "by landlords who were only in the sector because of the property slump".[4]

An important related finding from a Government survey of private rented housing is that the growth in the private rented sector between 1988 and 1993 was almost entirely the result of increases in the numbers of lettings by private individual landlords.[5]

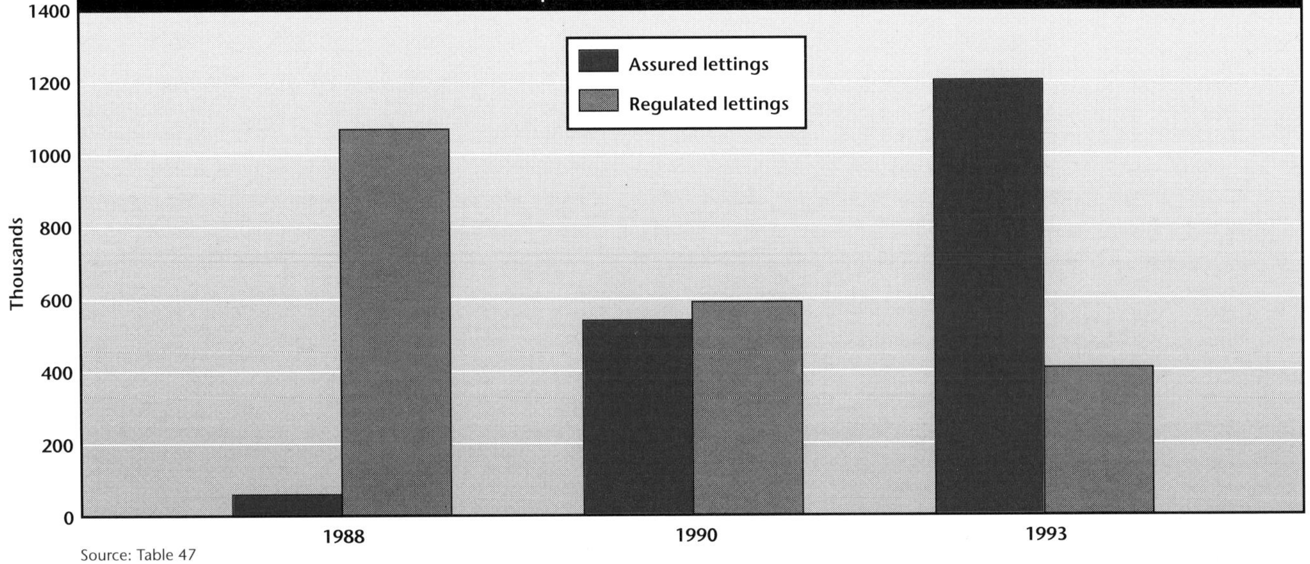

The Rowntree survey also found a small balance of landlords being more likely to decrease their lettings over the next two years, but with the net outcome being highly sensitive to the relative movements in rents and house prices.[6]

The most common form of tenancy in the private rented sector is now the assured shorthold tenancy (Table 47). Altogether there were by 1993 three times as many assured as regulated tenancies (Figure XIII). Something like one in eight of the assured tenancies with longer-term security of tenure, subject to the specified grounds for possession, are lettings arising from the Business Expansion Scheme tax breaks (Table 48).

Over the five years to 1993/94 the BES initiative has created almost 75,000 lettings. The average income tax relief cost works out at just over £16,000 per letting; in round terms this represents a 40% subsidy on the average capital cost per dwelling let under the scheme.

The ending of the BES tax breaks for rented housing will end the flow of new lettings from that source; some dwellings currently let under the scheme are expected to be sold at some point after they fulfil the minimum four-year period of renting required as a condition of the tax breaks.

Figure XIII Private lettings
Assured tenancies take over in the private rented sector

Source: Table 47

Rather more are likely to be retained for renting than was feared at the inception of the BES arrangements, however, as a result of the proportion of investment in companies linked to universities (28%) and housing associations (11%). Mortgage lender companies accounted for a further 25% of all investments; only 36% of the funding was raised by the 'entrepreneurial' landlord companies of the kind envisaged when the scheme was first launched.[7]

Nonetheless the changing tide of the BES lettings could be sufficient on its own to result in a decline in the private rented sector in the years ahead. The new restrictions on eligible rents for housing benefits, due to be introduced in 1996, are also likely to have some impact in limiting effective demand for private renting (see Chapter 6).

The proposal for 'housing investment trusts' to promote institutional investment in privately rented housing has now been taken up by the Government, and is featured in the June 1995 Housing White paper.[8] The trusts will have the benefit of exemption from capital gains tax and a reduced rate of corporation tax. It remains to be seen whether these tax breaks will be sufficient to overcome the long-term reluctance of institutional investors to enter the private rented market.

References

1 *Coping with Mortgage Default: Lessons from the Recession*, Steve Wilcox and Peter Williams, Council of Mortgage Lenders, 1995.
2 Page 51, *Mortgage Arrears and Possessions: Perspectives from borrowers, lenders and the courts*, Janet Ford, Elaine Kempson and Marilyn Wilson, Department of the Environment, HMSO 1995.
3 Pages 60 - 63, ibid.
4 Page 32, *The Supply of Privately Rented Homes*, ADH Crook, John Hughes and Peter Kemp, Joseph Rowntree Foundation 1995.
5 Table A1.3, *Private Renting in England 1993/94*, S Carey, OPCS, HMSO 1995.
6 Page 45, Crook *et al.*, *op. cit.*
7 Page 18, Crook *et al.*, *op. cit.*
8 Page 22, *Our Future Homes: The Government's housing policies for England and Wales*, Department of the Environment and Welsh Office, Cm 2901, HMSO 1995.

Key reading

Mortgage Arrears and Possessions: Perspectives from borrowers, lenders and the courts, Janet Ford, Elaine Kempson and Marilyn Wilson, Department of the Environment, HMSO 1995.

Housing Finance, Quarterly Journal of the Council of Mortgage Lenders.

The Compendium of Housing Finance Statistics, Council of Mortgage Lenders 1995.

The Supply of Privately Rented Homes, ADH Crook, John Hughes and Peter Kemp, Joseph Rowntree Foundation 1995.

chapter 4

UK housing expenditure plans

United Kingdom

Housing policies and expenditure plans for Scotland, Wales and Northern Ireland have their own dynamics, that only correspond to a limited degree with the policy agenda and financial choices made by the Department of the Environment (DoE) for England.

For example, housing still represents a larger share of the Welsh Office budget now compared to 1988/89 (Table 49), largely because of a substantial increase in provision for private sector improvement expenditure in 1992/93. Meanwhile in Scotland, Scottish Homes has maintained its budget for housing association investment (at least in cash terms) in 1995/96 rather than following the sharp reductions imposed in England and Wales (Table 52).

For all the differences between the 'territories' of England, Scotland, Wales and Northern Ireland, however, the common overall downward trend in public provision for housing investment is only too apparent, with gross investment in 1994/95 a third lower (in real terms) than in 1989/90 (Table 50b). A further reduction of the same order is now in store over the years to 1997/98, for local authorities (Table 51) and housing associations (Table 52) alike.

England

The 1994 Budget has further reduced financial provision for both local authority and housing association investment in 1995/96 compared to the previous year's plans. The financial impact on local authorities will be exacerbated by the run down of the usable capital receipts accumulated during the 1992/93 capital receipts 'holiday'. Altogether new capital resources for English social housing investment in 1995/96 will be nearly £800 million down on 1994/95.

Local authorities

In 1993/94 central government provision for local authority housing investment was reduced, on the basis that this would be more than offset by the temporary relaxation in the capital receipts rules announced in the 1992 Autumn Statement. However, for both 1994/95 and 1995/96 central government provision has been reduced again, notwithstanding the ending of the capital receipts 'holiday' as planned at the end of December 1993.

Central government provision for local authority investment has fallen by some 20% over the four-year period from 1992/93 to 1995/96. Overall capital provision for 1995/96 of £1,161 million is some £90 million lower than envisaged in the expenditure plans set out in the DoE 1994 Annual Report, and more than £600 million lower than the equivalent provision for 1991/92 (Table 55).

Basic credit approvals for English councils have fallen to only £779 million, with £90 million 'top-sliced' from the total credit approval provision to provide for special programmes favoured by the DoE. No further financial support is to be provided for the 'flats over shops' initiative, and the special programmes for 1995/96 are:

- £60 million for cash incentives grants, to assist council tenants to vacate their tenancy to buy in the open market for home-ownership.

- £30 million to extend the 'housing partnership' programme introduced in 1993/94 for schemes with matching private finance, and contributions from councils' own capital resources.

The 1995/96 annual capital guidelines (ACG) for housing investment total £994 million. In addition to the £779 million basic credit approvals, this includes £215 million of "receipts taken into account". The housing ACG, together with an £278 million provision for specified capital grant (for home improvements grants etc.), comprise councils' Housing Investment Programme (HIP) allocations, which total £1,272 million for all English councils.

Estate Action

Since 1994/95 funding for Estate Action schemes has been included within the new Single Regeneration Budget (SRB), which also includes provision for Urban Development Corporations, and the Derelict Land Grant, City Grants and other budgets now administered by the Urban Regeneration Agency. In previous years Estate Action schemes had been financed as a 'top-sliced' element of the provision for local authority credit approvals.

In 1995/96, some £314 million continuation funding has been provided for already established Estate Action schemes as part of the SRB budget. This compares with £372 million in 1994/95. No new Estate Action schemes are now planned, and the financial provision for the completion of existing schemes will clearly now decline rapidly in the years ahead. At the same time provision for estate improvement investment comprises only a very small part of the overall funding for the new style SRB comprehensive regeneration projects.

Capital receipts

Nationally new gross housing receipts are running at around £1.5 billion per annum. Of those, however, only some £900 million are receipts from new Right-to-Buy sales. The balance is derived from capital repayments on local authority mortgages, housing land sales and large-scale voluntary transfers. Total receipts have declined markedly since the £3.3 billion new gross receipts obtained in 1989/90 and are set to fall further in the years ahead, with the exception of receipts arising from stock transfers.

Despite the reduction in new usable receipts and new capital provision in 1994/95, local authority housing investment was a little higher than in 1993/94. This was because of the time lag between authorities obtaining and spending the additional useable capital receipts accumulated during the 1992/93 holiday. Latest estimates are that out-turn investment, including Estate Action spending, was some £3.16 billion in 1994/95, compared to £3.06 billion in 1993/94 (Table 54a).

The cushion of capital receipts from previous years has now, however, been largely exhausted, and it is estimated that English councils are likely to carry forward only some £0.5 billion useable housing receipts into 1995/96. Taking these into account, together with revenue contributions to capital outlay (RCCOs) now running at over £500 million per annum, new gross council investment of only £2.7 billion can be anticipated this coming year, with further reductions in the years ahead (see Figure XIV).

Detailed regional estimates of local authorities' future expenditure plans can be found in the increasingly authoritative annual housing finance survey undertaken jointly by the Association of District Councils (ADC) and the Association of Metropolitan Authorities (AMA).

The overall gross investment figures from the ADC/AMA survey, however, still come out somewhat lower than DoE figures, despite grossing up for non-response (by just over one in four authorities). The expenditure trends shown by the survey nonetheless correspond closely with those to be found in DoE figures.

Local authority policy and provision

Throughout the 1980s, the main impact of expenditure constraints was on local authority new-build activity. New starts of council housing in England fell from almost 28,000 in 1980 to just 400 in 1994. There was also a reduction in the level of local authority funding for housing association schemes over the same period, from £465 million in 1979/80 to £295 million in 1992/93 (at 1993/94 prices). Local authority support for housing association investment did, however, rise to £393 million in 1993/94, as authorities applied capital receipts from the 1992/93 holiday, before falling back to an estimated £346 million in 1993/94 (Table 54b).

In contrast, real investment levels in public and private sector renovation activity have been largely

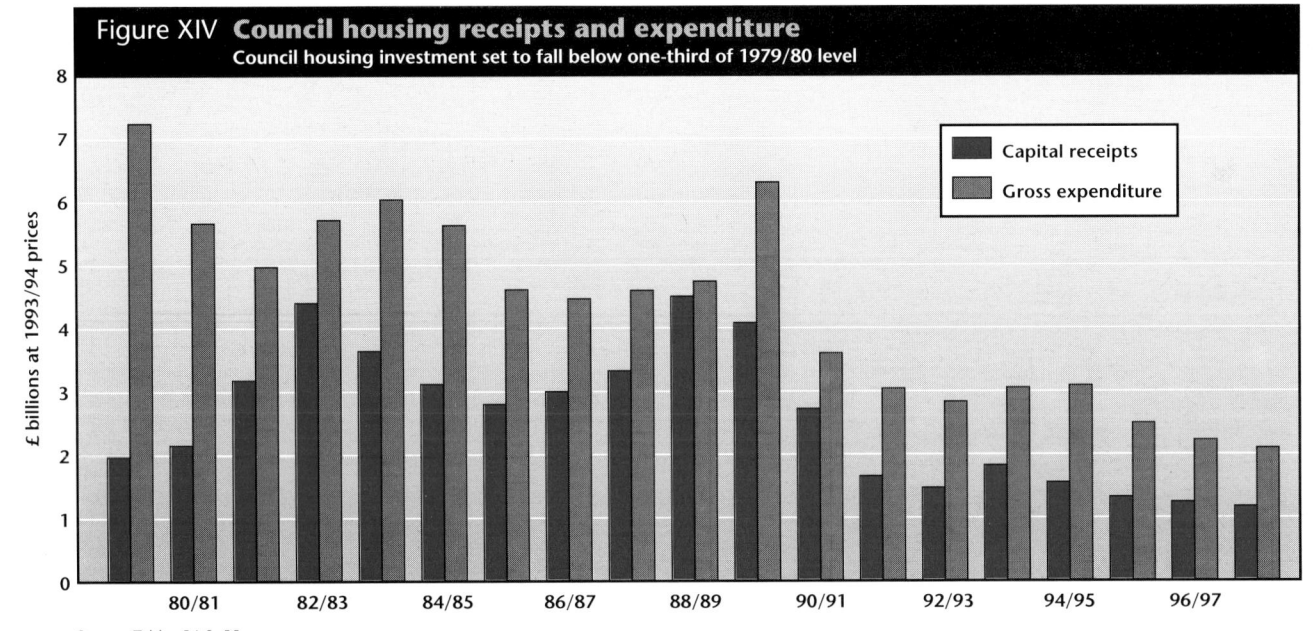

Figure XIV **Council housing receipts and expenditure**
Council housing investment set to fall below one-third of 1979/80 level

Source: Tables 54 & 55

maintained and account for an ever greater share of council investment resources. Investment in council stock renovation fell from £1.78 billion in 1979/80 to £1.68 billion in 1993/94, but rose to £1.89 billion in 1994/95. Over the same period investment in private sector renovation grants and related activities increased from £559 million to £578 million (all figures at 1993/94 prices).

Given the virtual end of new building by councils, the constraints on future investment resources must now inevitably begin to bear ever more heavily on investment in improvements and major repairs to the existing council stock. These financial pressures will in turn increase the need for councils to adopt alternative strategies if they are to secure the investment resources they require.

The proposals to abolish most mandatory private renovation grants, replacing them with discretionary grants, are described in the Government's 1995 White Paper as being necessary to enable local authorities to have strategic control over private renovation investment, and to focus investment within designated renewal areas. They will, of course, also make it easier for the Government to reduce financial support for renovation grants in the years ahead.

Housing associations

To a limited extent increased government provision for new housing association investment has offset the decline in provision for new local authority housing. The housing association programme was particularly boosted by the 'housing market package', launched by the 1992 Autumn Statement to clear 20,000 properties from the languishing home-ownership market before the end of the 1992/93 financial year. However, the Government has since made a series of reductions in the Housing Corporation budget for 1993/94 and subsequent years, reducing new housing association investment far more sharply than overall local authority housing investment.

The overall Housing Corporation budget for 1992/93 was boosted by the housing market package to £2,369 million; while the 1993/94 budget was reduced, from the previously planned £2 billion, to £1,843 million. Following successive reductions in the 1993 and 1994 Budgets, the 1995/96 Corporation capital budget has been cut back to just £1,197 million (Table 56). In real terms this is a reduction of nearly 40%, when compared to 1991/92, the year before the housing market package.

These financial constraints have not, however, had quite so great an impact on associations' investment output. This is partly because procurement costs have been competitive in a depressed construction industry, and financing costs have been relatively favourable with the prevailing low interest rates.

For the main part, however, output has been maintained by requiring associations to raise more private finance, supported by either higher rents or associations' reserves (Figure XV) in order to compensate for reduced levels of housing association grant new schemes. With average grant rates at 72% in 1992/93 a £100 million grant levered in £39 million private finance; with grant rates at just 58% for

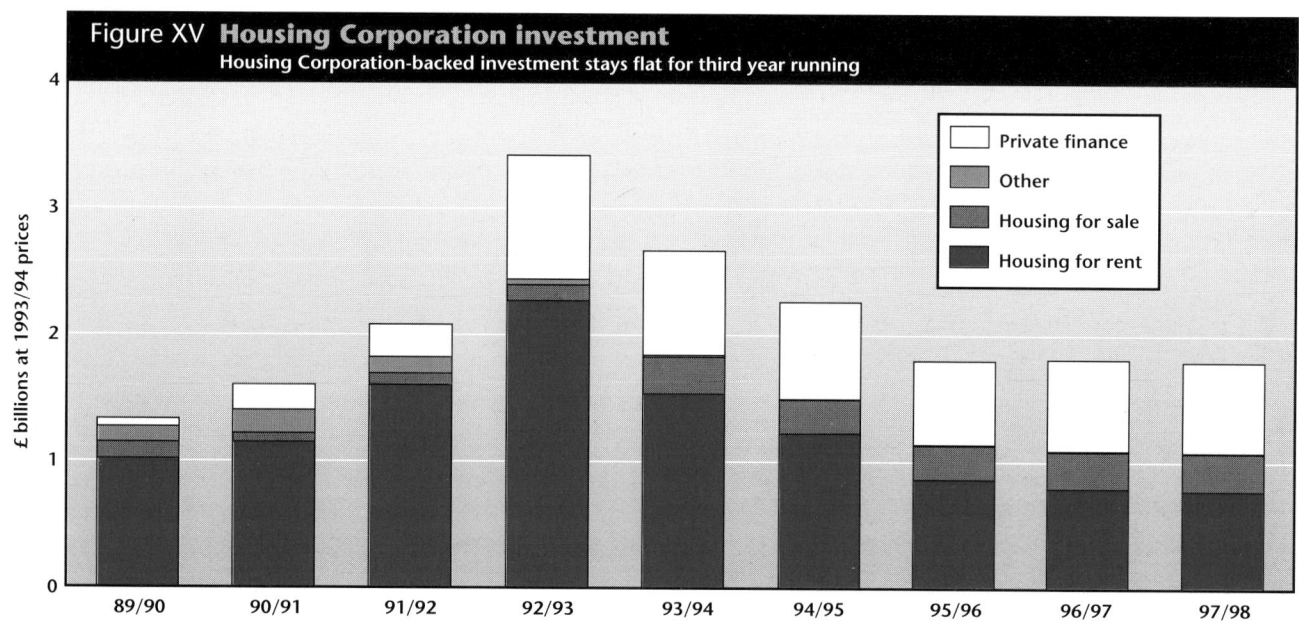

Figure XV **Housing Corporation investment**
Housing Corporation-backed investment stays flat for third year running
Source: Table 56

1995/96, a £100 million grant now levers in £72 million private finance.

The impact on the provision of new rented housing association dwellings has, however, been compounded by the Government's insistence that a greater proportion of the Corporation's 1995/96 Approved Development Programme be devoted to shared ownership and other low-cost home-ownership schemes. While this is in keeping with the Government's stated objective of promoting further growth in home-ownership, it is also entirely out of step with the Treasury and Department of Social Security policies to depress the home-ownership market and to restrict income support assistance with mortgage costs.

Approvals for new permanent housing association rented dwellings ran at almost 40,000 in 1991/92; with the housing market package this increased to just over 55,000 in 1992/93. However, in 1993/94 the figure fell to 37,000, and in 1995/96 it is now expected to fall below 20,000, before returning to around 25,000 in each of the next two years.

Grant rates

The average Housing Association Grant (HAG) rate in England for 1994/95 was 62%, compared to 65% in 1993/94. That rate has been further reduced to 58% in 1995/96, notwithstanding a critical report from the all-party House of Commons Environment Committee in 1994. Out-turn average grant aid rates are, however, somewhat lower as the result of competitive bidding by associations seeking to maintain or increase their share of the development programme, and the provision of free local authority land to complement grants.

In England the Housing Corporation has, until now, openly allocated resources by prioritising schemes that minimise the need for grant aid. Other factors are also taken into account, including the views of the local authority, but no account has been taken of the widely ranging rent levels charged by different associations.

By contrast, the Welsh counterpart to the Housing Corporation, Tai Cymru, has explicitly taken into account associations' rent levels, as well as the call on grant aid, in determining priorities in its allocations. It is now clear, however, that the Housing Corporation will also follow this approach in future years, under pressure from Department of Social Security concerns about the housing benefit costs arising from higher housing association rent levels.

Social housing rents

In both the council and housing association sectors, the DoE's policy over the last few years has been to increase rents in real terms, and to continue the switch from bricks-and-mortar subsidies to means-tested help with housing costs (see Table 63).

The Department does, however, now seem to accept that there are few or no financial gains to be derived from continuing to push council or housing association rents ever higher. This acknowledgement (expressed in both the Annual Report and the White Paper) is clearer with regard to council rents, despite the fact that it is housing association rents that are generally far higher. The detailed financial issues involved in the trade-off between housing association grant rates and housing benefit costs are discussed in Chapter 6.

In 1994/95, the rent guidelines on which subsidy to English councils is based increased by an average of 7.5%, taking the national subsidy guideline rent figure to £31.60 per week. Out-turn rent increases were higher, as existing rents were already on average more than £4.00 higher than the rent guidelines, in some cases because of management and maintenance expenditure exceeding subsidy allowances and in others because of the use of rental income for capital investment (the £500 million RCCOs in 1994/95 referred to above — see Table 61). In 1995/96 the rent guidelines have been increased by a further £2.28 per week, or 7.25%, taking the guideline rent figure to £33.88. The ADC/AMA survey estimates that out-turn average rents for 1995/96 have risen to £38.28 per week.[1]

One consequence of these rent increases is that English council housing has ceased to be a net recipient of basic housing subsidy. The DoE estimate for 1995/96 is that councils still in receipt of basic housing subsidy will get £804 million. However, 'negative entitlements', which are set against rent rebate subsidy, are estimated at £1,030 million. In other words, English council housing as a whole will be £226 million in surplus in 1995/96; there will be no net bricks-and-mortar subsidy. That net surplus will grow to almost £700 million by 1997/98 (Table 62).

While housing associations still receive subsidy, in the form of capital grants toward the cost of new schemes, because much more of their investment has been in recent years few associations have the benefits of substantial historic low debt assets. As a result of this, and of higher management and maintenance costs, average housing association assured rents in 1994 were some 28% higher than council rents (Table 63).

Rent levels for lettings of new housing association schemes are higher still, averaging £53.42 per week by mid-1994, reflecting the limited extent of rent pooling exercised by housing associations. Those rents represent almost 19% of average male manual earnings.

In some cases housing association rents are now very close to the average rents for similar size properties let by private landlords (Table 64). This is particularly the case for bedsit and one-bedroom dwellings, and for lettings in the northern regions. It must be noted, however, that the average rents shown in Table 64 take no account of any qualitative differences between the properties and services provided by housing associations and private landlords.

The majority of privately rented bedsits, for example, are not self-contained flats. Nor are the private rent figures wholly representative, because they are based on housing benefit cases only. Nonetheless, the proximity of some private and housing association rents is a genuine cause for concern in the context of the new limits on eligible rents for housing benefit due to be introduced in October (see Chapter 6). The housing association rents can also be seen to be far higher than the equivalent council rents shown in Table XXIX.

There should also be concern about the now far closer proximity of housing association rents and mortgage costs for first-time buyers (see Figure XVI). The gap between mortgage costs and rents for lettings of new dwellings are lower still, especially when it is remembered that the average dwelling purchased by first-time buyers is larger than the average dwelling rented from associations.

The convergence between the costs of renting and buying undermines the main rationale for conventional shared-ownership schemes, while the conversion to a low inflation economy also makes it a far more problematic proposition. That there is still a level of demand for shared ownership is testimony to the difficulties that confront aspiring home-buyers without savings or access to 100% mortgages.

There are, however, alternative policy instruments (such as local authority mortgage guarantees) that are more appropriate and cost-effective, where the issues are about access and security, rather than straight affordability. It is ironic that the Department of the Environment has insisted that the Housing Corporation budget for shared ownership and other housing for sale initiatives be increased at a time when the market rationale for most (but not all) such schemes is greatly diminished.

Table XXIX Average local authority rent by region, size and type of dwelling in 1993/94
£ per week

Region	Low/medium rise flats:			High rise flats:			Houses and bungalows:			
	1 bed-room	2 bed-room	3 bed-room or more	1 bed-room	2 bed-room	3 bed-room or more	1 bed-room	2 bed-room	3 bed-room	4 bed-room or more
North	24.08	25.44	24.67	25.05	26.03	21.21	24.44	26.19	28.18	28.22
Yorkshire & Humberside	23.17	24.05	23.39	20.75	22.66	23.91	23.53	23.95	25.13	26.51
North West	25.72	28.89	29.71	27.29	29.10	31.52	24.76	29.60	31.76	36.35
West Midlands	27.06	29.32	31.55	27.00	29.35	28.80	28.45	30.65	32.97	36.36
East Midlands	26.31	27.58	29.37	31.61	33.14	38.42	26.10	27.34	28.96	32.73
East Anglia	27.90	31.74	33.20	28.21	33.91	37.73	30.25	32.57	35.42	38.31
Greater London	35.97	39.95	44.42	35.44	40.41	43.03	38.66	42.42	48.33	53.13
Rest of South East	33.39	36.34	40.98	34.99	37.62	38.59	33.23	37.06	41.73	46.18
South West	29.97	31.19	33.19	27.58	31.08	32.92	31.42	33.52	35.61	40.31

Source: Department of the Environment

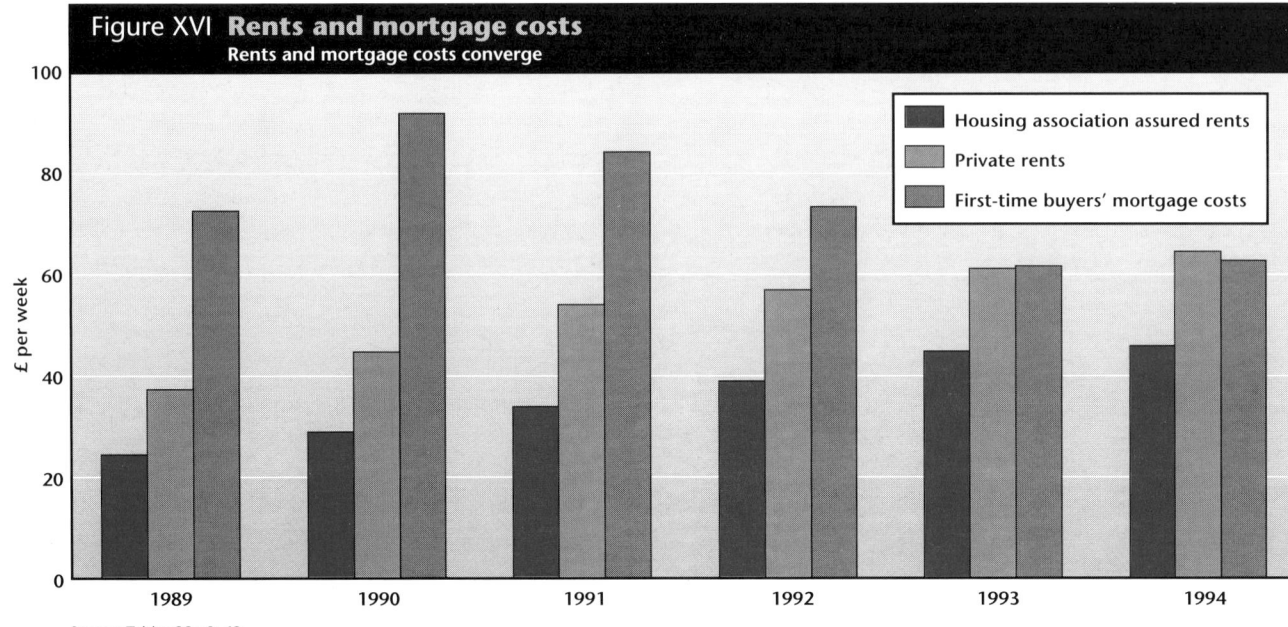

Figure XVI **Rents and mortgage costs**
Rents and mortgage costs converge
Source: Tables 39a & 63

Figure XVII **Gross social housing investment in Wales**
Welsh social housing investment falls back 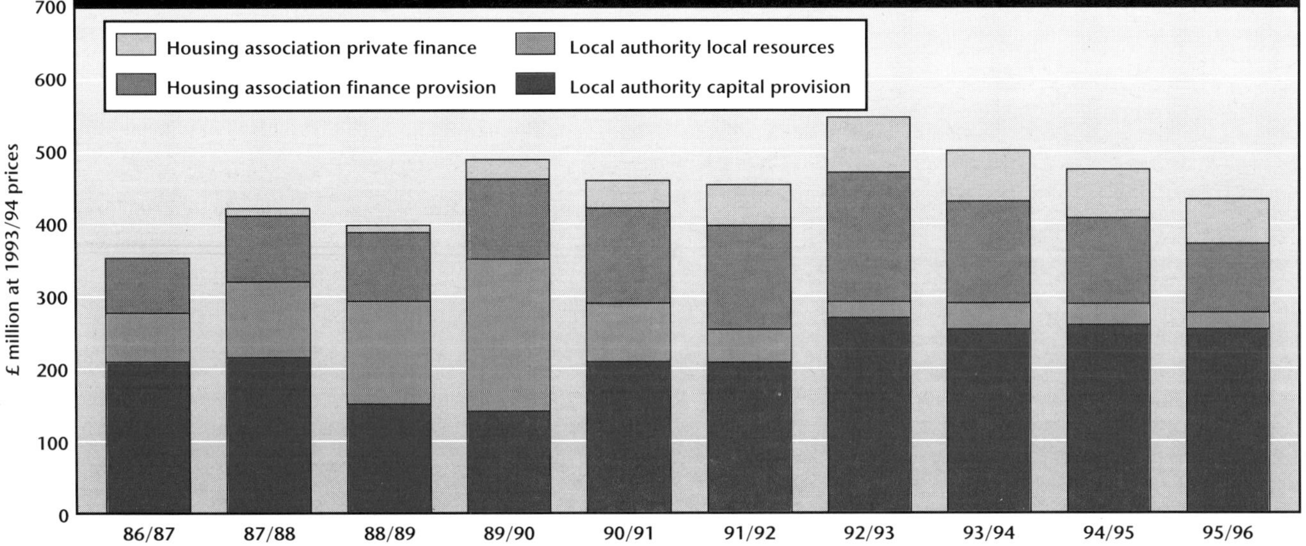
Source: Table 66

Large-scale voluntary transfers

One now familiar response by local councils to the financial constraints on housing investment imposed by successive expenditure plans and the new financial regimes introduced in England and Wales by the Local Government and Housing Act 1989 has been a wave of large-scale voluntary transfers (LSVT) of council stock to new landlord bodies. In all but one case to date, these have taken the form of housing associations newly created specifically for that purpose.

As at the end of March 1995, 40 councils had successfully transferred their housing stock, and this has resulted in over £400 million in net capital receipts becoming available for new investment by those councils, although not all of this has been used by councils for housing investment (Table 60). A further significant impact on housing investment has also been achieved by the new landlord bodies, which have been able to raise over £1 billion in private finance, primarily to undertake major repairs and improvements to the transferred stock.

Further details of the stock transfer programme and the development of proposals for local housing companies are discussed in the fourth *Contemporary Issues* article.

Wales

As noted above, the most distinctive feature of housing investment in Wales is the substantial hike in private sector improvement grants made in 1992/93 (Table 65). Since then, however, investment provision has been gradually reduced, and in 1995/96 total social housing investment will be lower in real terms than in 1991/92, as shown in Figure XVII.

Nonetheless, overall investment by local authorities still remains higher than in 1991/92 (Table 66), although other areas of investment have been squeezed by the focus on private sector investment grants. The Housing for Wales budget for housing association investment has also been cut back in 1995/96, as it has been in every year since 1992/93.

The Welsh Office cash plans for 1996/97 and 1997/98 show overall provision for housing capital and revenue spending rising from £610 million in 1995/96 to £626 and £633 million respectively. Over the two years this implies further reductions in real terms. The Welsh Office does not follow the general conventions for expenditure plans and provide any breakdown of housing expenditure plans beyond 1995/96.

It has, however, provided projections of local authority housing subsidy costs to 1997/98 (Table 68), and these show an increase from £228 million in 1995/96 to £243 million in 1997/98. This would account for more than two-thirds of the cash increase in the Welsh Office housing budget over that period. If the planned budget provision remains unchanged, this implies either that council rents will be increased even more rapidly in the next two years or that provision for capital investment will fall even further.

Even on current assumptions the levels of surpluses generated from council rents are projected to rise from £64 million in 1995/96 to £82 million in 1997/98, when they will offset more than a quarter of the gross rent rebate subsidy costs. Only a tiny minority of Welsh councils now receive positive basic housing subsidy entitlements, amounting to only some £2 million per annum (Table 68).

The Housing for Wales policy on rents has had a positive impact in restraining housing association rents, and Welsh associations' average assured rents increased by only 50 pence per week in 1994 (Table 69), and fell as a proportion of average earnings for the first time since assured rents were introduced in 1989.

The downward pressures on rents in Wales have been reinforced by the way Housing for Wales has taken rents into account when determining capital allocations for associations in 1995/96. Within any one local authority area, if an association's rent bid was more than 10% higher than the lowest bid for that area, then no allocation for new developments was given to that association. As a result five (out of 29) Welsh associations received no funding for new developments in 1995/96.[2]

Questions have been raised about the detailed rent-bidding methodology applied by Housing for Wales — and not just by those associations excluded from the new development programme in 1995/96. There are genuine difficulties in comparing and monitoring associations' bids and performance on rent levels. However, there can be no doubt that this pro-active policy by Housing for Wales is right in principle, and that it will succeed in limiting housing association rent rises in Wales, and improving the affordability of association rents.

Scotland

Provision for social sector housing investment in Scotland will be cut by one-sixth in real terms in the three years to 1997/98 (Table 70). This accelerates a decade-long decline in investment (Figure XVIII), that in overall terms will see provision reduced by 30% in real terms over the decade. Even if account is taken of the private finance now raised by housing associations (Table 73) the reduction over the decade will still exceed 20%.

Within that overall reduction, however, housing associations in Scotland have been spared the 1995/96 budget cuts visited on their counterparts south of the border. In cash terms the Scottish Homes capital budget for associations is unchanged from 1994/95, and the impact of inflation is more or less compensated for by a small increase in the proportion of private finance associations are expected to raise in 1995/96.

If housing associations in Scotland have been spared, this is because the Scottish Office has more severely cut back the provision for local authority investment. In real terms over the decade to 1997/98 there will have been a cut-back of over 40%, even assuming that Scottish councils increasingly apply rental income to supplement the reduced investment resources available for estate renovation (Table 72).

It is, however, rather easier for Scottish councils to make rental income available for investment as, unlike their counterparts south of the border, they still enjoy a subsidy regime that does not require them to

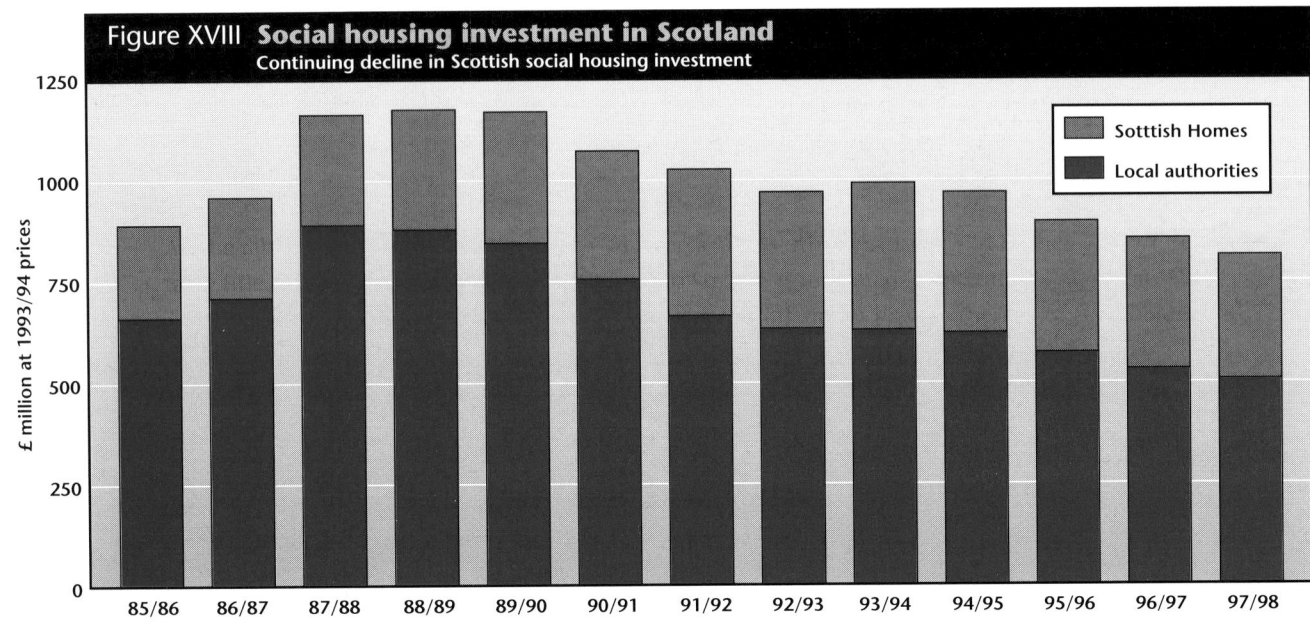

Figure XVIII Social housing investment in Scotland
Continuing decline in Scottish social housing investment

Source: Table 71
Note: Local authorities includes towns. Scottish Homes excludes NLF repayments, but includes predecessors.

contribute rental income towards the costs of housing benefits. In 1994/95 only a half of all Scottish councils received any housing support grant, and only in 8 cases did this amount to more than £5 per week per dwelling.[3] In overall terms, housing support grant makes up just 2% of the total housing revenue account income of Scottish councils, with rents contributing 98% (Table 75).

The relatively benign subsidy regime in Scotland continues to make it easier for councils not in receipt of subsidy to keep their rents below subsidy guidelines. Scottish council rents in 1994 were £27.79 per week, more than £7 per week lower than the subsidy guideline. Nonetheless, council rents in Scotland have risen in real terms, to represent just over 10% of average male manual earnings (Table 76).

The subsidy guidelines for council rents have been increased by 7.5% for 1995/96, but again these will have no impact on authorities no longer receiving subsidy. The cuts in capital resources for HRA investment represent a more significant upward pressure on rents.

While the Scottish Office Annual Report does give forward figures on the main housing budget heads to 1997/98 (unlike the Welsh Office) the section on housing is very thin on detail.

Northern Ireland

Public housing expenditure in Northern Ireland will be increased by some 6% in real terms over the three years to 1997/98 (Table 77). Those increases are shared by the Northern Ireland Housing Executive (NIHE) and provision for private sector renovation grants (Table 78).

In cash terms, provision for housing association investment has been restored in 1995/96 to the level provided in 1993/94. This boost is to allow associations to take over the development of some schemes originally planned to be undertaken by the NIHE and to inject an element of private finance into their funding. Already housing associations in Northern Ireland have raised some £9 million in private finance in 1994/95; the Northern Ireland Office clearly wishes to see this figure grow in future years.

Formally the expenditure plans show housing association investment falling back in 1996/97 and 1997/98. If they succeed in raising private finance for the schemes taken over from the NIHE in 1995/96, however, a future switch of capital resources in their favour is highly likely. Meanwhile provision for investment by the Northern Ireland Co-ownership Housing Association will continue to run at £5.2 million per annum, while the balance of the housing association programme is for rented housing.

NIHE rents have been raised ahead of inflation in line with the average increases in subsidy guidelines imposed by the Department of the Environment in England. In 1994 the average rent of £29.63 per week represented 12.3% of average earnings in Northern Ireland; higher than in Scotland, but lower than in England and Wales (Table 79).

The Northern Ireland Office Annual Report is more informative than the Scottish and Welsh Office reports, providing detailed forward financial and output plans to 1997/98 on all the main housing programmes. Among the useful data it sets out, for example, is an estimate of the balance of the capital assets of the NIHE, which totalled £1.8 billion at the end of March 1994.

References

1 Page 3, *Housing Finance Survey 1995-96*, ADC/AMA 1995. Figure is for responding authorities only.
2 See 'Rent bidding for housing associations', John Bader and Peter Lawler, in *Welsh Housing Quarterly Issue* 19, 1995, University of Cardiff.
3 See Table 17, *The Scottish Office Statistical Bulletin*, Housing Series HSG/1995/4, May 1995, HMSO.

Key reading

Annual Report 1995, The Government's Expenditure Plans 1995-96 to 1997-98 Department of the Environment, Cm 2807, HMSO 1995.

Our Future Homes, The Goverment's Housing Policies for England and Wales, Department of the Environment and the Welsh Office, HMSO 1995.

Departmental Report, The Government's Expenditure Plans 1995-96 to 1997-98, Welsh Office, Cm 2815, HMSO 1995.

Serving Scotland's Needs, The Government's Expenditure Plans 1995-96 to 1997-98, Scottish Office, Cm 2814, HMSO 1995.

Northern Ireland Expenditure Plans and Priorities, The Government's Expenditure Plans 1995-96 to 1997-98, Northern Ireland Office, Cm 2816, HMSO 1995.

Housing Finance Survey 1995-96, ADC/AMA 1995.

Meen, G & Wilcox, S (1995), *The cost of higher rents*, National Federation of Housing Associations, London.

Wilcox, S (1995), *Competitive Local Rents,* HACAS, London.

chapter 5

Housing needs and homelessness

Housing needs and homelessness

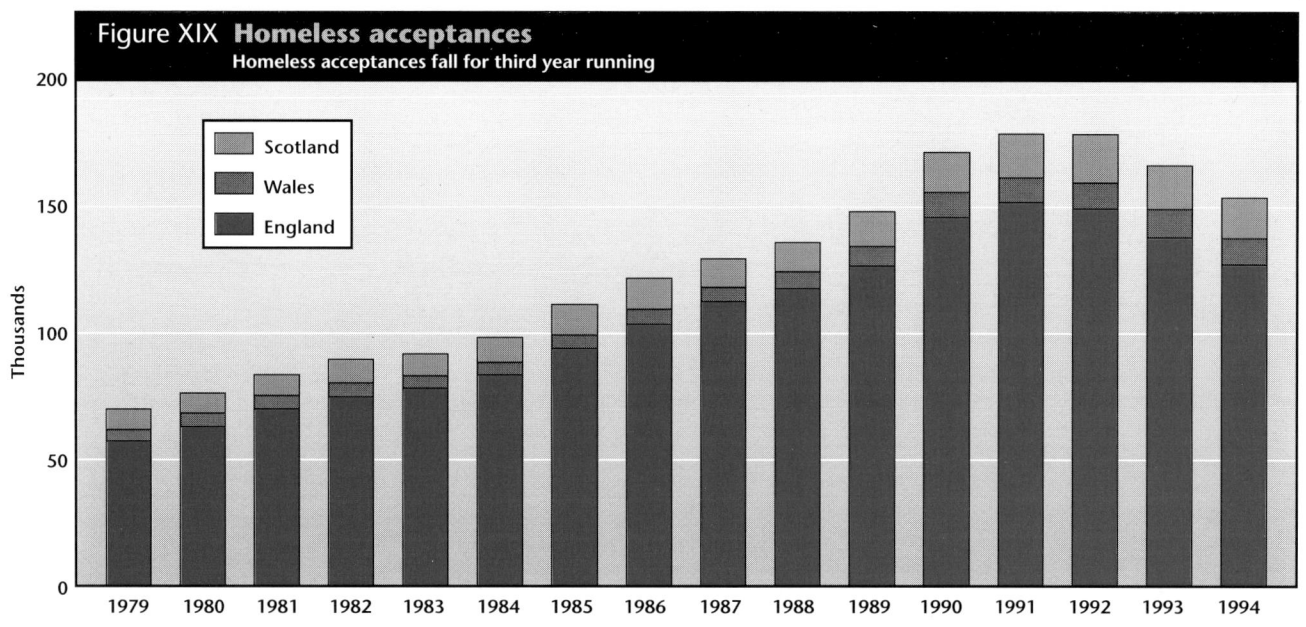

Figure XIX **Homeless acceptances**
Homeless acceptances fall for third year running
Source: Table 80
Note: Estimated 1994 figure for Scotland

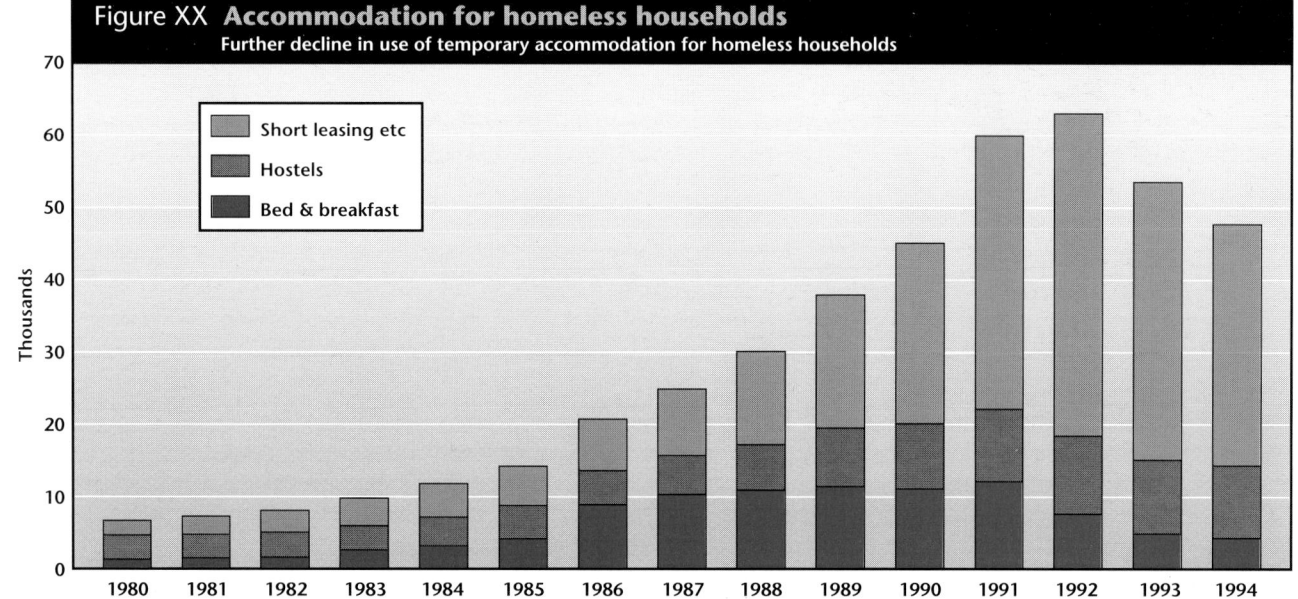

Figure XX **Accommodation for homeless households**
Further decline in use of temporary accommodation for homeless households
Source: Table 81

The housing policy White Paper has confirmed again the Government's determination to go ahead with amendments to substantially weaken the statutory duties of local authorities to provide long-term housing for homeless households.

The numbers of homeless households in England, Scotland and Wales are falling (Table 80 and Figure XIX). In England, homeless acceptances have now fallen in every year since 1991 and, although the acceptance figures do not tell the whole story,[1] there are genuine grounds for welcoming this trend. The numbers of homeless households in temporary accommodation in England also fell in 1994 (Table 81 and Figure XX), although there has subsequently been a slight upturn at the end of the first quarter of 1995.

The main reduction has been in the use of private sector leasing (Table 81), which in some cases has been linked to councils reducing the levels of voids. The numbers of households in bed-and-breakfast accommodation at the end of 1994 was also down — to 4,330, lower than at any time since 1985. The fall in the numbers of households in temporary accommodation has been particularly marked in London, which has seen a 30% reduction in just two years (Table 83).

Lettings increase ... for now

The main reason for the decline in homeless acceptances (in England) and households in temporary accommodation has undoubtedly been the increase in lettings made available to new tenants by housing associations (Table 89). These increased from just 69,000 in 1991/92 to 90,000 in 1992/93 and 112,000 in 1993/94.

These increases reflect both the gradual impact of local authority stock transfers to housing associations and the one-off housing market package at the end of 1992/93. Many of the lettings of dwellings purchased under that package fell into 1993/94. The impact of the subsequent cuts in the Housing Corporation budget are only now beginning to be reflected in completions (Table 90b), but by 1996/97 they will be 20,000 lower than in 1994/95.

Lettings to new tenants by local authorities have also been remarkably stable over the last few years (Table 86), despite the impact of stock transfers. The long-term impact of the Right-to-Buy on lettings must inevitably, however, begin to show through more in the years ahead. An anomaly in the way that lettings to new local authority and housing association tenants are counted is also particularly significant when the two figures are added together (Table 91). Local authority tenants moving to housing association lettings are counted as lettings to new tenants, rather than as transfer cases.

This definition of a 'new letting' is applied consistently to the figures for new lettings over all the years since 1979/80, but has a greater impact now that housing associations are virtually the sole providers of new dwellings, and nationally provide roughly one-third of all lettings. Back in 1979/80 existing council tenants would transfer to new council developments, and their move would not have counted as a letting to a new tenants.

CORE figures show that some one in four new housing association lettings are to households who last occupied a council dwelling. If these are netted off, there is still a fair increase in total social sector lettings to new tenants over the last few years, but it is far less pronounced than the published figures suggest at first sight.

The number of council tenants transferring to housing association lettings is also an important factor in the resilience of local authority relet figures, and these will also decline as the numbers of housing association completions fall. There is, however, a delay before local authority lettings figures become available, and it will be 1997 before the now predictable decline in new lettings is reflected in the published figures.

Lettings and homelessness

As the numbers of lettings decline this will, once again, accentuate the pressures on local authorities responding to the needs of homeless households. It is notable, for example, that the downturn in homeless acceptances and the numbers of homeless households in temporary accommodation over the last two years has been as the proportion of new lettings going to waiting list and other applicants increased from 65% to 68% in 1993/94 (Table 87b).

At the same time, the proportion of homeless households previously living with parents, relatives or friends fell sharply from over 40% to just 34% in 1994 (Table 82). These households are at the centre of the concerns about the overlap of the homeless and waiting list routes to council rehousing; the figures demonstrate the simple point that if waiting times can be limited (by an improved supply of lettings) then there will be fewer crises with parents and relatives providing temporary accommodation that result in homeless applications.

The regional local authority lettings figures, and those for Wales (Table 92) and Scotland (Table 93) show that outside of London only a fifth to a third of local authority lettings are now made to homeless households. Focusing more specifically on secure lettings of family size dwellings, only in London and the South East are more than a half provided for homeless households. Housing associations now let the same proportion of secure lettings of family size dwellings to homeless households as local authorities (Table 88).

Housing needs

The fact that the DoE has broken with a decade of silence and has now published formal estimates of the need for new social housing in England should be warmly welcomed (Table XXX). The DoE estimates broadly confirm the assessments made by a range of commentators in recent years,[2] suggesting that something like 100,000 new social rented dwellings a year are required to meet the needs that cannot be met through owner-occupation or relets of existing social sector housing.

The DoE has, however, chosen to emphasise its lower range estimate of a requirement for 60,000 dwellings per annum, rather than its higher range estimate of 100,000. The lower range estimate relies on an assumption that owner-occupation will grow over time, not just for older households as a lagged result of increased home-buying by younger households in previous decades, but also for younger households.

Table XXX Official estimate of housing needs in England
Thousands

	Range of estimates	
	Lower	Upper
Number of additional households	1,831	1,831
- Additional owner-occupiers	1,947	1,437
+ Estimated Right-to-Buy sales	600	500
- Additional private renters	0	0
= Number of additional households potentially needing social housing	484	894
+ Dwelling losses to demolition etc	95	95
+ Other adjustments	14	14
= Potential additional demand for social housing 1991-2001	593	1,003
Annual requirement for additional social housing to prevent increase in outstanding housing needs	59	100

Source: Department of the Environment, 1995
Notes: The lower estimates make optimistic assumptions about the potential for future growth in owner-occupation. Both the lower and upper estimates exclude any provision to reduce outstanding housing needs. For a fuller critique see text.

The assumption that an increased proportion of younger households will be home-buyers in the year 2001, relative to the base year of 1991, is simply not credible. There is clear evidence that, as a result of the recession, the proportion of younger households becoming home-buyers has fallen since 1991. Only 26% of heads of household aged under 25 were home-owners in 1993, for example, compared to 36% in 1991.

If the unrealistic assumption of growth in the proportions of younger home-owners is removed, the housing needs shown by the DoE assessment can be corrected to a more credible range of 80,000 to 100,000 new social rented dwellings per annum. It should also be emphasised that the DoE assessment only deals with future housing needs and includes no target for removing — or even reducing — the level of unmet housing needs outstanding in 1991, the base year for the assessment.

The emphasis given by the DoE to the lower figure of 60,000 is understandable, given that this figure is close to its total measure of new lettings created. This is arrived at by adding together the numbers of local authority completions, local-authority-funded housing association schemes, council relets created through the Cash Incentive Scheme and the output of the Housing Corporation programme (Tables 90a and b).

These figures are, however, not wholly comparable with the estimate of the need for new social rented dwellings. They count the one-off lettings generated through incentive schemes, for example, in the same total as the provision of new dwellings that will sustain a number of lettings over their lifetime. They also include the provision of low-cost home-ownership dwellings, when the provision of such dwellings through programmes over the last 15 years are already reflected in their estimates of the potential growth in home-ownership by the year 2001.

Forward projections of housing needs do have inherent limitations. They do inevitably involve a range of judgements and assumptions that are open to reasonable debate. There are also clearly a range of possible policy responses to assessments of housing needs, other than simply the provision of additional social sector rented dwellings.

However, the formal DoE assessment of housing needs can only be taken as confirmation that on current policies the housing shortage in England will worsen in the coming years. The proposed changes to the homeless legislation will do no more than reshape the way in which that housing shortage is allocated. In that context, the additional discretion to be provided by the proposed changes to those councils with avowedly 'mean and nasty' policies for homeless households must inevitably be a considerable cause for concern.

References

1. See 'Homelessness - the problem that won't go away', Angela Evans, Jackie Dix and Chris Allen, in *Housing Finance Review 1994/95*, Joseph Rowntree Foundation 1994.
2. See *A Review of Housing Needs Assessment*, Christine Whitehead and Mark Kleinman, The Housing Corporation 1992.

Key reading

Homelessness Statistics, Department of the Environment.

Provision for Social Housing - Background Analysis, submission by the Department of the Environment to the Environment Committee of the House of Commons, 1995.

chapter 6

Help with housing costs

Help with housing costs

The decline of MIRAS ...

The Government is now two-fifths of the way towards the abolition of MIRAS, having reduced the rate of mortgage interest tax relief from 25% in 1993/94 in two steps to just 15% in 1995/96. The savings in the costs of MIRAS have been even greater as a result of lower interest rates and average gross mortgage repayments. Altogether the costs of MIRAS have fallen from a peak of £7.7 billion in 1990/91 to £2.8 billion in 1995/96 (Table 95).

For individual home-buyers the average annual value of MIRAS over that period fell from £820 to £270. However, because of falling interest rates this has not resulted in a general increase in net mortgage costs. For a household with a standard £40,000 mortgage, net repayments fell from £431 per month in 1990/91 to £331 per month in 1992/93, and to £289 per month in 1995/96.

Since the abolition of higher rate mortgage interest tax relief at the end of 1990/91, the value of MIRAS has been far more evenly distributed across income bands (Table 96), and the share of MIRAS taken by London and the South East has also fallen (Table 97). It is still the case that MIRAS is mildly regressive but not that home-owners in London and the South East take a disproportionate share of MIRAS compared to those in other regions.

The case for the phased complete abolition of MIRAS remains but, given the current state of the housing market, and the proximity of the next general election, it will be some time before the next step is either desirable or feasible.

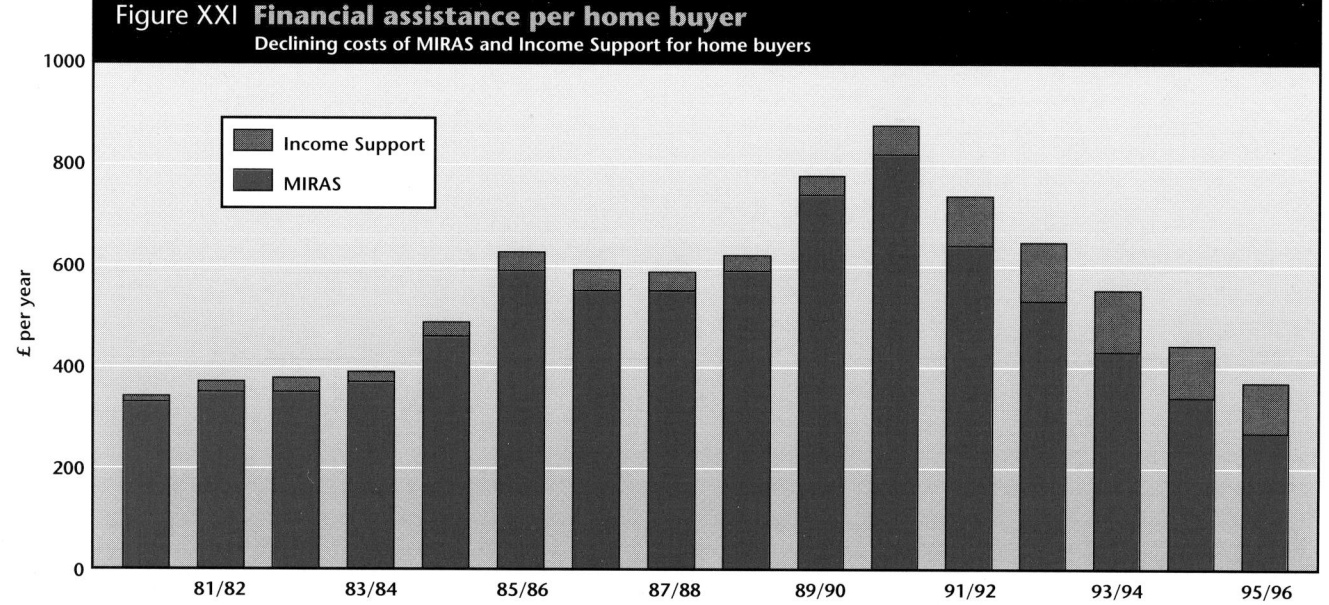

Figure XXI **Financial assistance per home buyer**
Declining costs of MIRAS and Income Support for home buyers

Source: Tables 95 & 99

... the fall of housing subsidies

While the abolition of MIRAS has been partially achieved, bricks-and-mortar subsidies for council housing have been virtually eliminated. While a minority of councils continue to receive some general subsidy, we have already seen that most councils in England and Wales not only receive no general subsidy, but are required to generate surpluses to contribute towards the costs of housing benefits (Tables 62 and 68).

In net terms, 'Council Housing UK' has now generated financial surpluses over the last two years (Table 98a), and these are set to rise from £300 million in 1995/96 to some £750 million in 1997/98. These surpluses have arisen only partially because of rent increases, which have offsetting costs in higher housing benefit payments and other ways (see below).

The rent surpluses also reflect the decline in new investment and the income generated by the requirement that 75% of the receipts from council house sales are set aside against outstanding housing debt. (Another reminder that the release of capital receipts imposes subsidy costs in much the same way as increased investment backed by borrowing.)

Erosion of income support for home-owners

Without doubt the most radical housing policy change this year is the restrictions on income support help for home-owners. These are discussed in detail in the fourth *Contemporary Issues* article, while the wider impact on the fortunes of the housing market and the economy are discussed in Chapter 1.

Table XXXI Average mortgage interest taken into account for income support by region

Region	Number of cases (000s):					Average mortgage interest (£ per week):				
	1990	1991	1992	1993	1994	1990	1991	1992	1993	1994
North Western	50	58	68	73	70	25.33	28.38	27.34	27.27	26.05
North East	45	52	60	69	68	23.25	29.91	29.93	26.34	25.30
Midlands	52	69	80	89	83	25.47	35.30	33.31	32.93	29.87
London North	51	80	100	112	105	48.12	59.43	60.72	57.82	51.65
London South	47	67	87	103	97	52.98	63.51	61.34	59.70	54.09
South Western	25	40	52	53	48	39.05	51.30	48.30	45.64	40.69
Wales	26	27	34	34	33	23.58	34.80	33.67	29.63	27.45
Scotland	14	18	19	22	24	32.64	35.33	32.59	27.99	26.26
Great Britain	310	411	499	555	529	34.33	44.41	44.02	42.18	38.18

Source: Hansard, Answer to parliamentary question by Ms Armstrong, 9/5/95

Figure XXII Housing assistance to households on income support
Cost of housing assistance to private tenants on income support now higher than for home-buyers

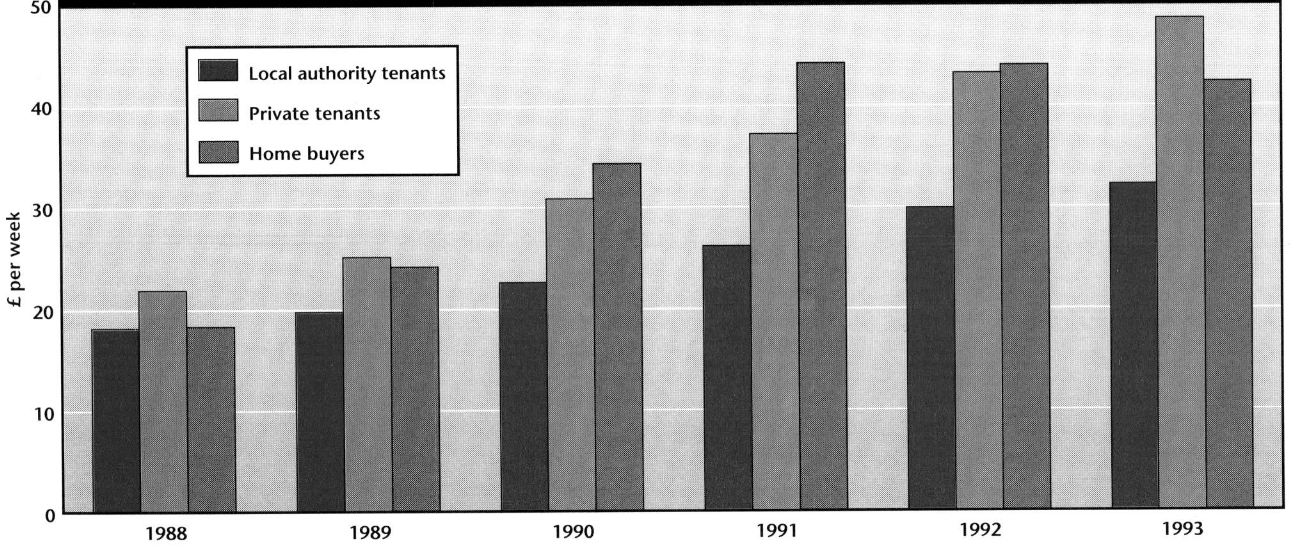

Source: Tables 99 & 104

It is worth noting, however, that while the costs of income support help with mortgage interest payments (ISMI) more than doubled over the years of the housing market recession, those costs are now falling (Table 99). The falls in the average amount of mortgage interest eligible for assistance are also shown in the regional figures in Table XXXI.

The average cost of ISMI is also below the average cost of housing benefits paid to private tenants in receipt of income support (Figure XXII), or indeed the average housing benefit paid to all private tenants, including those in low-paid work who only receive partial benefit, as can be seen from the regional figures in Table XXXII.

There is also some evidence that the failure to prevent the scale of repossessions over the last five years has contributed towards the rapid growth in the costs of housing benefits. Some four out of five repossessed households move into rented accommodation, and of those nearly a half move into the private rented sector.[1] An analysis based on the 1993 *Survey of English Housing* also suggests that the rapid increases in unemployment levels in the private rented sector in the early 1990s may also reflect the forced movements of ex-home-owners into renting.[2]

The numbers of such movements would have been significantly lower if the Government had responded positively to the proposal for a mortgage benefit scheme, to help home-owners with low incomes but ineligible for Income Support. Moreover, in many cases the Government is now clearly paying more in housing benefit to help the same households than it

Table XXXII Housing benefit caseload and payments by tenure and region

Region	Number of recipients:			Average weekly housing benefit:		
	Local authority tenants 000's	Housing association tenants 000's	Private tenants 000's	Local authority tenants £	Housing association tenants £	Private tenants £
North	233	35	52	26.60	34.30	40.90
Yorkshire & Humberside	302	37	91	24.50	39.80	39.90
North West	370	76	139	28.90	34.40	45.40
West Midlands	305	47	73	29.20	38.90	39.50
East Midlands	192	23	68	27.40	39.50	41.30
East Anglia	76	24	38	31.00	33.80	47.50
Greater London	427	105	235	43.00	48.00	68.20
Rest of South East	339	101	204	36.40	41.90	56.20
South West	165	35	115	33.00	42.60	48.30
England	2,409	483	1,014	31.90	40.10	52.00
Wales	152	26	58	30.50	39.30	42.30
Scotland	445	35	69	24.80	31.30	44.00
Great Britain	3,006	544	1,141	30.70	39.50	51.10

Source: *Housing Benefit and Council Tax Benefit Summary Statistics*, Department of Social Security
Note: Caseload figures are averages for 1994/95; payment figures are for May 1994.

would have paid out in mortgage benefits to enable them to retain their homes.

New rent limits for housing benefit

The inevitable consequence of declining subsidies and higher rents for social housing has been increased costs in housing benefits, despite the succession of restrictions imposed on the housing benefit scheme during the 1980s (Table 103).

Concern about those rising costs were announced by Peter Lilley, Secretary of State for Social Security, in a DSS report *The Growth of Social Security* published in 1993. Following extensive inter-departmental debates proposals were announced in the 1994 Budget for new cut-backs in the housing benefit scheme, in the form of further limits on the private rent levels eligible for 100% housing benefit.

This proposed that any rents in excess of "local reference rents" will only be 50% eligible for housing benefit. These rents are to be based on the averages prevailing in the private rented sector for accommodation of the same size and in the same locality. Following consultations, the proposals have been modified to exclude hostels and the lettings of housing associations or voluntary agencies where care and support is provided for residents. The local reference rents for one-room dwellings will also take account of whether or not the dwelling is self-contained.

The new scheme will come into operation in January 1996, and only then will we see how it will work in practice, as much will rest on the judgements of rent officers. The new scheme will apply to housing association lettings not covered by the care and support exemption, where local authorities make a rent officer referral because they consider that the rents may be excessive.

Some 3,000 housing association cases in England and Wales were referred in 1993/94, and just over one in eight resulted in a lower determination. A concern for associations must be that an unintended by-product of the new arrangements could be an increased level of referrals, and that the rents for their lettings may well exceed local reference rents levels even when the rents are not themselves judged excessive given the quality of the accommodation being provided.

Work incentives

The increases in rent levels in all sectors have also extended the range of the housing benefit poverty trap, making it far more difficult for households to secure jobs that lead to any significant improvement in their net household incomes.[3] The earnings levels required for different households to escape the housing benefit poverty trap are set out in Table 108. For a family with two children a rent of £65 means that they need earnings in excess of average male manual earnings to escape housing benefit dependency. A lone parent with one child and a rent of just £40 needs earnings in excess of the female manual average, even before taking account of childcare costs.

Since 1988 the real value of the earnings disregards for low-income working tenants have been eroded by the failure to uprate them for inflation. Some positive changes have been made to the earnings disregards for lone parents, and in October 1994 a further earnings disregard for up to £40 of weekly child care costs was introduced.

In May 1995 the level of family credit entitlement was also increased by £10 per week for households where at least one person is working more than 30 hours per week, and this will be disregarded when calculating housing benefit entitlement.

While these changes are welcome, they are no substitute for a general increase in the levels of earnings disregards.

Costs of higher rents

There is also new evidence that the policy of increasing social sector rents is no longer resulting in any net public expenditure savings. This is because higher rents not only lead directly to increased housing benefit costs, but also impose other costs on the DSS and the Treasury. Higher rents increase inflation, and this adds to the costs for the DSS in uprating the non-means-tested benefits that are directly linked to the Retail Prices Index (RPI). There is also a wider deflationary impact on the economy, leading to increased unemployment. Higher rents also extend the housing benefit poverty trap higher up the income scale, further eroding the limited incentives for tenants to undertake low or modestly paid work.

When all these additional costs are taken into account, Figure XXIII shows that they can outweigh the savings in council housing subsidy and impose a net cost on the Treasury. The position for housing associations is more complicated, as the Government makes up-front capital savings through grant rate reductions, while the costs of higher rents only have an impact as revenue costs over a run of years. It can take some 12 to 20 years before those revenue costs cancel out the grant rate savings, depending on the assumptions made about inflation, interest and discount rates etc.

The logic of these costings has now been accepted by the Government, and both the Annual Report and this year's White Paper suggest that it does not envisage further significant rises in council and housing association rents.

This nonetheless leaves in place a differential between housing association and council rents for which there is no coherent policy rationale, and rent levels that

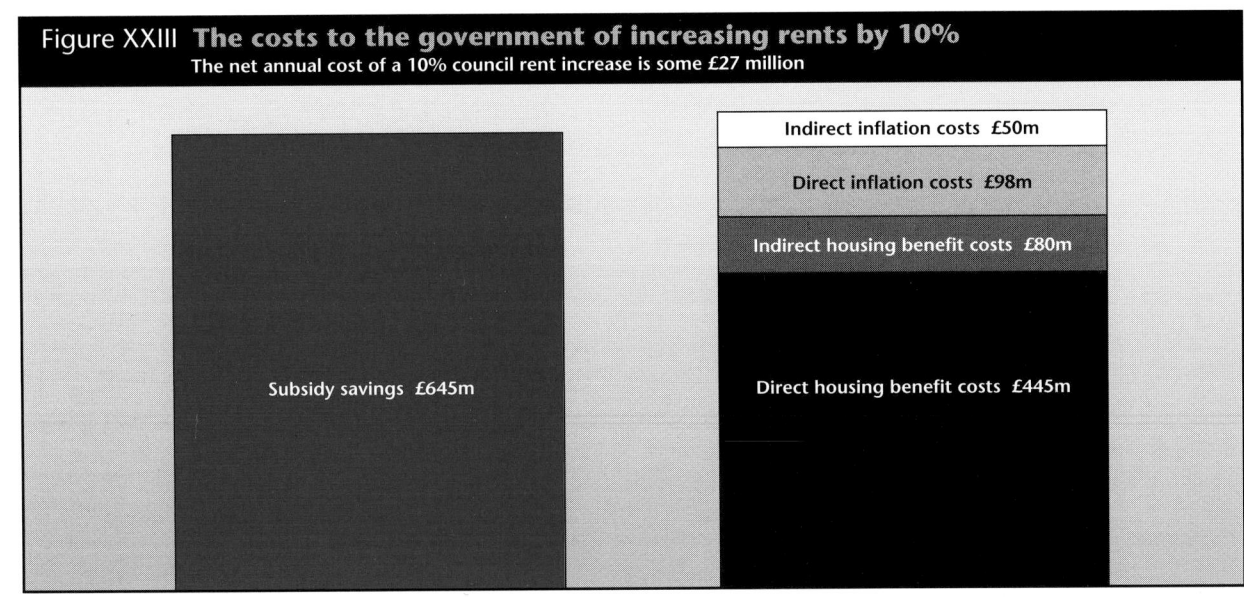

Figure XXIII **The costs to the government of increasing rents by 10%**
The net annual cost of a 10% council rent increase is some £27 million

- Subsidy savings £645m
- Indirect inflation costs £50m
- Direct inflation costs £98m
- Indirect housing benefit costs £80m
- Direct housing benefit costs £445m

Source: *The Cost of Higher Rents*, Geoff Meen and Steve Wilcox, NFHA 1995.
Notes: (1) A 10% rise in council rents adds almost 0.3% to the Retail Prices Index. This has a direct cost for the DSS in up-rating non-means-tested benefits and an indirect cost due to the impact of higher inflation on the wider economy.
(2) A rise in council rents has a direct impact on the housing benefit bill, but there is also an indirect cost as the housing benefit poverty trap is expanded and disincentives to work are increased.

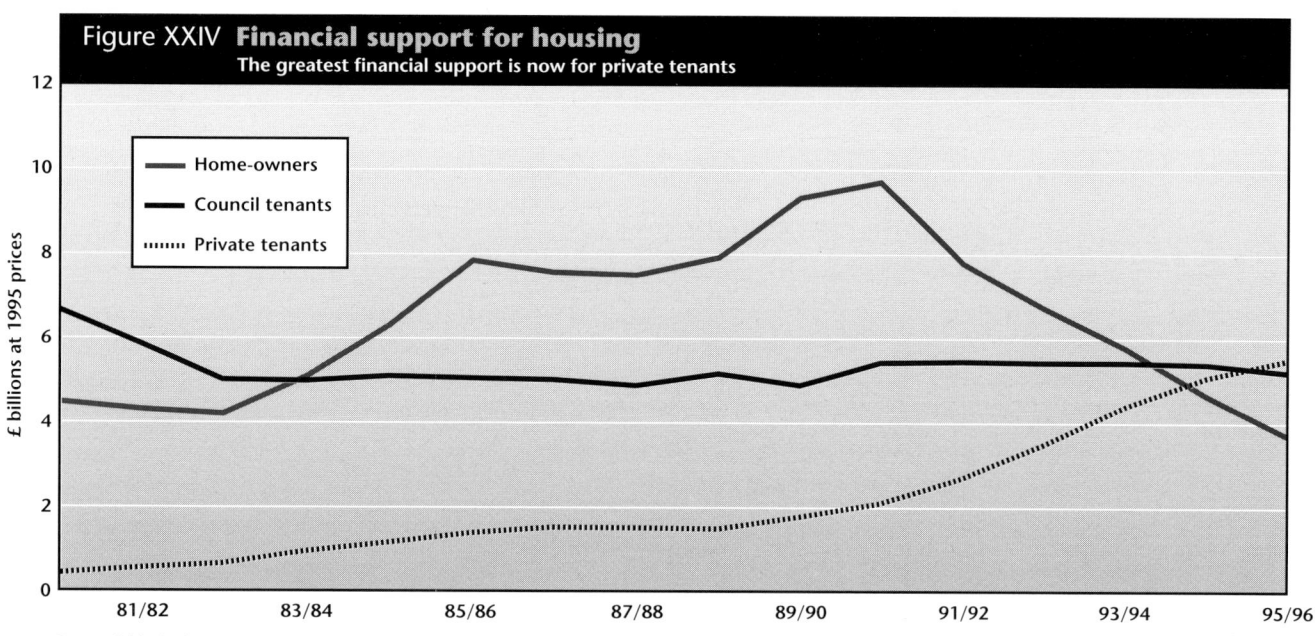

Figure XXIV **Financial support for housing**
The greatest financial support is now for private tenants

Source: Table 110b

ensnare far too many households in an inescapable housing benefit poverty trap.

Changing balance of housing help

As a result of the various housing, rent and benefit policy changes over the last fifteen years there has been a substantial shift in the balance of assistance with housing costs. The most obvious change is in terms of the shift from 'bricks and mortar' to 'personal' subsidies. Only within the owner-occupied sector does the general subsidy in the form of MIRAS continue to exceed the means-tested help given through the income support scheme (Table 110a).

Looking at all forms of assistance it can also be seen that, while the overall financial support for council housing has remained fairly constant, the least financial support is now given to home ownership,[4] while the greatest support is now provided in the form of rent allowances to private and housing association tenants, as shown in Figure XXIV.

This once again highlights the tenure bias in the current structure of assistance with housing costs that uniquely excludes low-income working home-buyers from any means-tested help with their housing costs. The inequity of that anomaly will become ever more pronounced when the phased abolition of MIRAS recommences.

References

1. Table 6.1, *Mortgage Arrears and Possessions: Perspectives from borrowers, lenders and the courts*, Janet Ford, Elaine Kempson and Marilyn Wilson, Department of the Environment, HMSO 1995.
2. Page 117, Chapter 9, Alan Holmans, in *Housing in England 1993/94*, Hazel Green and Jacqui Hansbro, OPCS, HMSO 1995.
3. See *Contemporary Issue* 6 in the 1994/95 edition of the Review for an extended discussion of housing costs and work disincentive issues.
4. The figures are not comprehensive, as they do not include the value of capital gains tax relief for owner-occupiers, or the value of renovation grants or capital grants to housing associations.

Key reading

Social Security Departmental Report, *The Government's Expenditure Plans 1995/96 to 1997/98*, Cm 2813, HMSO 1993.

Social Security Statistics 1994, Department of Social Security, HMSO 1994.

Income Support Statistics, Quarterly Enquiry, May 1994, Department of Social Security 1995.

Housing Benefit and Council Tax Benefit, Summary Statistics 1995

Inland Revenue Statistics 1994, Inland Revenue, HMSO, 1994.

The cost high rents, Geoff Meen & Steve Wilcox, NFHA 1995.

Economic prospects and public expenditure

Macro-economy

Table 1 Key economic trends

Year	1980	1981	1982	1983	1984	1985	1986	1987	1988	1989	1990	1991	1992	1993	1994
Gross Domestic Product															
£ bn (cash)	231.8	254.9	279.0	304.5	325.9	357.3	384.8	423.4	471.4	516.0	551.1	575.3	597.1	630.2	667.8
£ bn (1990 prices)	423.5	418.0	425.3	440.9	451.1	468.1	488.1	511.6	537.2	548.9	551.1	540.3	537.6	548.7	569.4
% real growth	-2.1	-1.3	1.7	3.7	2.3	3.8	4.3	4.8	5.0	2.2	0.4	-2.0	-0.5	2.1	3.8
Unemployment															
000s	1,364	2,172	2,545	2,788	2,916	3,028	3,098	2,805	2,273	1,782	1,661	2,286	2,765	2,901	2,637
%	5.1	8.1	9.5	10.5	10.7	10.9	11.1	10.0	8.0	6.2	5.8	8.0	9.7	10.3	9.4
Inflation %	18.0	11.9	8.6	4.5	5.0	6.1	3.4	4.2	4.9	7.8	9.5	5.9	3.7	1.6	2.4
Interest rates %	14.0	14.5	10.1	9.0	9.6	11.5	11.0	8.5	13.0	15.0	14.0	10.5	7.0	5.5	6.3

Sources: UK National Accounts, Economic Trends, Financial Statistics.
Notes: Gross Domestic Product is shown at current market prices ('money GDP') - (CAOB) and 1990 market prices (CAOO).
Unemployment figures are seasonally adjusted (BCJD & BCJE). Inflation is the General Index of Retail Prices (CZBH).
Interest rates are the base rates of selected retail banks at the year end (Table 7.1J Financial Statistics).

Table 2 Average male and female earnings in Great Britain

Year	1980	1981	1982	1983	1984	1985	1986	1987	1988	1989	1990	1991	1992	1993	1994
£ per week															
All full-time men	124.5	140.5	154.5	167.5	178.8	192.4	207.5	224.0	245.8	269.5	295.6	318.9	340.1	353.5	362.1
All full-time women	78.8	91.4	99.0	108.8	117.2	126.4	137.2	148.1	164.2	182.3	201.5	222.4	241.1	252.6	261.5
All full-time manual men	111.7	121.9	133.8	143.6	152.7	163.6	174.4	185.5	200.6	217.8	237.2	253.1	268.3	274.3	280.7
All full-time manual women	68.0	74.5	80.1	87.9	93.5	101.3	107.5	115.3	123.6	134.9	148.0	159.2	170.1	177.1	181.9
Percentages															
All women's earnings as a % of all men's earnings	63.3	65.1	64.1	65.0	65.5	65.7	66.1	66.1	66.8	67.6	68.2	69.7	70.9	71.5	72.2
All manual women's earnings as a % of all manual men's earning	60.9	61.1	59.9	61.2	61.2	61.9	61.6	62.2	61.6	61.9	62.4	62.9	63.4	64.6	64.8

Sources: Regional Trends, New Earnings Surveys.
Note: Earnings figures are inclusive of overtime.

Table 3 Personal disposable income, consumer spending and savings

Year	1980	1981	1982	1983	1984	1985	1986	1987	1988	1989	1990	1991	1992	1993	1994
£ billion															
Personal disposable income	161.0	177.7	191.0	205.5	223.6	243.5	264.5	285.5	317.7	352.9	379.3	407.8	438.5	460.2	477.3
− Consumer spending	139.6	155.4	169.4	185.6	198.8	217.5	241.6	265.3	299.4	327.4	347.5	365.0	382.4	405.8	427.0
= Savings	21.4	22.3	21.6	19.9	24.8	26.0	23.0	20.2	18.2	25.5	31.8	42.8	56.1	54.4	50.3
Savings ratio (%)	13.3	12.5	11.3	9.7	11.1	10.7	8.7	7.1	5.7	7.2	8.4	10.5	12.8	11.8	10.5
Increases over previous years:															
Personal disposable income															
% (cash)	18.1	10.4	7.5	7.6	8.8	8.9	8.6	7.9	11.3	11.1	7.5	7.5	7.5	4.9	3.7
% (constant prices)	1.5	−0.8	−1.1	2.6	3.7	3.4	4.5	3.5	5.9	4.9	1.9	0.1	2.7	1.5	1.0
Consumer spending															
% (cash)	16.4	11.3	9.8	9.6	7.1	9.3	11.0	10.1	12.9	9.4	6.0	4.9	5.2	5.2	5.2
% (constant prices)	0.0	0.1	1.1	4.5	2.1	3.8	6.8	5.6	7.5	3.3	0.5	−2.3	0.5	1.8	2.5

Sources: UK National Accounts; Economic Trends & Financial Statistics for 1994 data.
Notes: 'Real' disposable income and consumer expenditure increases are calculated with reference to the Consumer Expenditure Deflator (GIEF).
The 'Savings Ratio' is the ratio of savings to personal disposable income.

Macro-economy

Table 4 **Regional unemployment rates**

Region	1980	1981	1982	1983	1984	1985	1986	1987	1988	1989	1990	1991	1992	1993	1994	1995
North	6.6	10.5	12.7	14.3	14.7	15.3	15.5	15.0	12.8	10.9	8.7	9.3	10.7	11.8	11.8	10.8
Yorkshire & Humberside	4.0	7.6	9.8	11.2	11.3	11.8	12.4	12.2	10.1	8.1	6.6	7.4	9.4	10.6	10.0	8.9
North West	5.2	8.8	11.5	13.0	13.5	13.6	13.7	13.4	11.3	9.3	7.6	8.2	10.3	11.0	10.3	8.7
West Midlands	4.0	8.3	11.5	12.7	12.6	12.8	12.8	12.5	10.0	7.4	5.7	6.6	9.7	11.2	10.3	8.5
East Midlands	3.3	6.4	8.2	9.2	9.5	9.8	9.9	9.8	7.9	6.0	4.9	5.8	8.4	9.7	9.2	8.0
East Anglia	2.9	5.4	6.9	7.9	7.8	7.9	8.4	8.2	6.1	3.9	3.3	4.6	7.1	8.3	7.8	6.5
South East	2.4	4.5	6.3	7.2	7.5	8.0	8.2	8.0	6.1	4.3	3.6	5.1	8.4	10.4	9.8	8.2
South West	3.7	5.8	7.5	8.5	8.7	9.1	9.4	9.0	7.1	4.9	3.8	5.3	8.4	9.8	9.0	7.5
Wales	5.3	9.3	11.6	12.8	12.7	13.5	13.7	13.0	10.6	8.3	6.6	7.6	9.6	10.5	10.1	8.5
Scotland	5.9	8.7	10.9	12.0	12.4	12.6	13.0	13.7	12.0	10.3	8.4	8.1	9.1	9.9	9.5	8.4
Great Britain	3.9	6.8	9.0	10.1	10.3	10.7	10.9	10.7	8.7	6.7	5.4	6.4	9.0	10.4	9.8	8.4
Northern Ireland	7.9	11.8	13.5	15.0	15.8	15.7	16.5	17.4	16.1	14.9	13.3	12.8	13.6	14.2	13.3	12.2
United Kingdom	4.0	7.0	9.1	10.2	10.5	10.8	11.1	10.9	8.9	6.9	5.6	6.6	9.1	10.5	9.9	8.5

Source: Economic Trends.
Note: Seasonally adjusted figures, 1st quarter of each year

Table 5 **Personal housing wealth, borrowing and net equity**
£ billion

	1980	1981	1982	1983	1984	1985	1986	1987	1988	1989	1990	1991	1992	1993	1994
Net equity	262.5	269.2	288.3	339.0	378.9	430.3	498.2	612.8	860.9	914.5	863.7	837.0	753.8	761.6	755.6
+ House loans	52.5	62.0	76.4	91.5	108.6	127.4	154.3	183.6	223.7	258.0	295.0	320.5	337.9	354.3	372.4
= Gross assets	315.0	331.2	364.7	430.5	487.5	557.7	652.5	796.4	1,084.6	1,172.5	1,158.7	1,157.5	1,091.7	1,115.9	1,128.0
Index of growth of gross assets	100.0	105.1	115.8	136.7	154.8	177.0	207.1	252.8	344.3	372.2	367.8	367.5	346.6	354.3	1,128.0
÷ Deflator for gross domestic capital formation	100.0	110.0	113.1	116.9	121.8	128.5	134.2	140.4	150.3	163.4	172.7	173.2	168.4	168.7	171.5
= Index of real growth of gross assets	100.0	95.6	102.3	116.9	127.1	137.8	154.4	180.1	229.1	227.8	213.0	212.1	205.8	209.9	208.8

Sources: UK National Accounts 1994 Tables 1.7 & 12.2; Financial Statistics Table 3.2C; author's estimate of 1994 gross assets.

Table 6 Equity withdrawal
£ million

Year	1979	1980	1981	1982	1983	1984	1985	1986	1987	1988	1989	1990	1991	1992	1993	1994
Net mortgage lending	6,461	7,282	9,308	14,142	14,319	17,108	19,184	27,372	29,573	40,111	34,054	33,243	25,956	18,358	15,663	19,492
+ Private housing grants	122	159	187	351	826	1,079	697	550	534	550	514	515	461	578	594	572
− Domestic capital formation	5,312	6,115	6,174	6,850	7,757	9,186	9,683	11,526	13,439	18,013	19,142	17,212	15,681	16,108	16,725	18,259
− Council house sales	485	786	1,039	2,035	1,572	1,310	1,240	1,339	1,648	2,665	3,153	2,215	1,447	1,229	1,226	1,088
= Equity withdrawal	786	540	2,282	5,608	5,816	7,691	8,958	15,057	15,020	19,983	12,273	14,331	9,289	1,599	(1,694)	717
Consumer spending £bn	120.0	139.6	155.4	169.4	185.6	198.8	217.5	241.6	263.5	299.4	327.4	347.5	365.0	382.4	405.8	427.0
Equity withdrawal as % of consumer spending	0.7	0.4	1.5	3.3	3.1	3.9	4.1	6.2	5.7	6.7	3.7	4.1	2.5	0.4	-0.4	0.2

Sources: Mortgage Lending - Financial Statistics (AAPR), Private Housing Grants - Housing and Construction Statistics, Domestic Capital Formation - UK National Accounts (DFDF), Council House Sales - UK National Accounts (CTCS), Consumer Spending - UK National Accounts (AIIK).

Table 7 Gross fixed investment in dwellings
Percentage of Gross Domestic Product

	1980	1981	1982	1983	1984	1985	1986	1987	1988	1989	1990	1991	1992	Average 1980-92
Canada	5.6	5.8	4.7	5.3	5.1	5.3	6.1	7.2	7.3	7.6	6.7	6.1	6.5	6.1
Italy	6.7	6.9	6.6	6.8	6.4	6.1	5.6	5.2	5.1	5.0	5.2	5.3	5.3	5.9
France	7.4	7.1	6.6	6.3	5.8	5.5	5.3	5.3	5.4	5.4	5.2	5.1	5.0	5.8
Germany [1]	6.8	6.5	6.2	6.3	6.3	5.5	5.3	5.2	5.1	5.0	5.2	5.3	5.3	5.7
Japan	6.7	6.1	5.9	5.3	5.0	4.8	5.0	5.8	6.2	6.0	6.2	5.5	5.2	5.7
Netherlands	6.4	5.9	5.5	5.3	5.3	5.0	5.1	5.3	5.8	5.6	5.2	4.7	4.8	5.4
Australia	6.1	5.9	4.8	4.9	5.2	5.1	4.5	4.5	5.4	5.4	4.8	4.6	5.0	5.1
Sweden	5.0	4.8	4.5	4.4	4.6	4.4	4.1	4.4	5.0	5.4	5.9	6.5	5.9	5.0
New Zealand	3.8	4.2	4.2	4.4	4.5	4.5	4.4	4.5	4.3	4.7	4.6	4.0	4.1	4.3
Norway	4.7	4.6	4.8	4.6	4.2	4.1	4.8	5.1	5.0	3.8	3.0	2.1	n/a	4.2
USA	4.5	4.0	3.3	4.4	4.7	4.6	5.1	5.0	4.7	4.4	3.5	3.1	3.0	4.2
Belgium	5.9	3.4	3.0	2.8	2.7	2.8	2.8	2.9	3.5	4.0	4.3	4.2	4.7	3.6
UK	3.8	3.2	3.2	3.4	3.7	3.4	3.7	3.9	4.4	4.3	3.8	3.0	3.0	3.6

Source: National Accounts Vol II 1980 - 1992, OECD 1994, Table 1
Notes: Gross fixed investment in dwellings and GDP are at market prices. 1. The Federal Republic as constituted before reunification.

Public expenditure

Table 8 **Growth of real Gross Domestic Product**
Percentage changes from previous period

	1980	1981	1982	1983	1984	1985	1986	1987	1988	1989	1990	1991	1992	1993	Estimates and projections 1994	1995	1996	Average 1980-96
Japan	3.6	3.6	3.2	2.7	4.3	5.0	2.6	4.1	6.2	4.7	4.8	4.3	1.1	0.1	1.0	2.5	3.4	3.6
Spain	1.3	-0.2	1.6	2.2	1.5	2.6	3.2	5.6	5.2	4.7	3.6	2.2	0.8	-1.0	1.7	2.9	3.3	2.6
USA	-0.5	1.8	-2.2	3.9	6.2	3.2	2.9	3.1	3.9	2.5	1.2	-0.6	2.3	3.1	3.9	3.1	2.0	2.5
Germany	1.0	0.1	-0.9	1.8	2.8	2.0	2.3	1.5	3.7	3.6	5.7	5.0	2.2	-1.1	2.8	2.8	3.5	2.4
Italy	4.1	0.6	0.2	1.0	2.7	2.6	2.9	3.1	4.1	2.9	2.1	1.2	0.7	-0.7	2.2	2.7	2.9	2.2
France	1.6	1.2	2.5	0.7	1.3	1.9	2.5	2.3	4.5	4.3	2.5	0.8	1.2	-1.0	2.2	3.1	3.2	2.2
Belgium	4.3	-0.9	1.5	-1.7	4.5	0.8	1.4	2.0	4.9	3.5	3.2	2.3	1.9	-1.7	2.3	3.0	3.1	2.2
UK	-2.2	-1.3	1.7	3.7	2.3	3.8	4.3	4.8	5.0	2.2	0.4	-2.0	-0.5	2.0	3.5	3.4	3.0	2.1
Netherlands	0.9	-0.7	-1.5	1.4	3.1	2.6	2.7	1.2	2.6	4.7	4.1	2.1	1.4	0.4	2.5	2.9	3.2	2.1
Greece	1.8	0.1	0.4	0.4	2.8	3.1	1.6	-0.5	4.4	4.0	-1.0	3.2	0.8	-0.5	1.0	1.5	2.3	1.6
Sweden	1.7	0.0	1.0	1.8	4.0	1.9	2.3	3.1	2.3	2.4	1.4	-1.1	-1.9	-2.1	2.3	2.3	2.5	1.5

Source: Table A1, OECD Economic Outlook, December 1994

Table 9 **General Government Financial Balances as a percentage of Gross National Product**
Surpluses (+) or deficits (-)

	1980	1981	1982	1983	1984	1985	1986	1987	1988	1989	1990	1991	1992	1993	Estimates and projections 1994	1995	1996
Greece	-2.9	-9.0	-6.9	-7.8	-9.3	-12.5	-11.6	-10.9	-12.4	-14.5	-13.9	-13.0	-11.8	-13.5	-13.1	-11.6	-10.1
Sweden	-4.0	-5.3	-7.0	-5.0	-2.9	-3.8	-1.2	4.2	3.5	5.4	4.2	-1.1	-7.4	-13.5	-11.2	-10.2	-9.7
Italy	-8.6	-11.6	-11.3	-10.7	-11.6	-12.6	-11.6	-11.0	-10.7	-9.9	-10.9	-10.2	-9.5	-9.6	-9.7	-9.1	-7.8
Spain	-2.2	-3.7	-5.4	-4.6	-5.2	-6.9	-6.0	-3.1	-3.3	-2.8	-4.1	-4.9	-4.2	-7.5	-6.8	-6.1	-5.2
Belgium	-9.3	-13.0	-11.0	-11.5	-9.2	-8.7	-9.2	-7.4	-6.6	-6.3	-5.4	-6.5	-6.7	-6.6	-5.3	-4.6	-4.1
France	0.0	-1.9	-2.8	-3.2	-2.8	-2.9	-2.7	-1.9	-1.7	-1.2	-1.6	-2.2	-3.9	-5.8	-5.7	-5.0	-4.0
UK	-3.4	-2.6	-2.5	-3.3	-3.9	-2.8	-2.4	-1.4	1.0	0.9	-1.2	-2.7	-6.2	-7.7	-6.8	-4.7	-3.2
Netherlands	-3.9	-5.1	-6.6	-5.9	-5.9	-3.9	-3.5	-5.1	-4.2	-4.7	-5.1	-2.8	-3.8	-3.3	-3.8	-3.6	-2.9
Japan	-4.4	-3.8	-3.6	-3.6	-2.1	-0.8	-0.9	0.5	1.5	2.5	2.9	3.0	1.8	-0.2	-2.0	-1.8	-1.8
USA	-1.3	-1.0	-3.4	-4.1	-2.9	-3.1	-3.4	-2.5	-2.0	-1.5	-2.5	-3.2	-4.3	-3.4	-2.0	-1.8	-1.8
Germany	-2.9	-3.7	-3.3	-2.6	-1.9	-1.2	-1.3	-1.9	-2.2	0.1	-2.0	-3.3	-2.9	-3.3	-2.7	-2.4	-1.8

Source: Annex Table 29, OECD Economic Outlook, December 1994.   Note: OECD forecasts for future years.

Economic prospects and public expenditure

Table 10 **The Budget Economic Forecast** [1]
Percentage changes on a year earlier unless otherwise stated

	1993	Forecast 1994	1995	Average errors from past forecasts[2]
GDP and domestic demand at constant prices				
Domestic demand of which:	2¼	3	2¾	1½
Consumer expenditure	2½	2½	2½	1¾
General government consumption	1	1¼	¼	1
Fixed investment	¼	3¾	5¾	4
Change in stockbuilding[3]	¼	½	0	½
Exports of goods and services	3	8¼	7	2¼
Imports of goods and services	2¾	4¾	5¼	3¼
Gross domestic product	2	4	3¼	1½
Non-oil GDP	1¾	3½	3¼	1¼
Manufacturing output	1¼	4¼	4¼	1¾
Balance of payments current account				
£ billion	-10½	-4	-3½	7
per cent of GDP	-1¾	-½	-½	1
Inflation				
RPI excluding mortgage interest payments (fourth quarter)	2¾	2	2½	1
Producer output prices (fourth quarter)[4]	3	2½	2¾	1
GDP deflator at market prices (financial year)	3	2	3¼	1¼
Money GDP at market prices (financial year)				
£ billion	639	678	720	
percentage change	5¾	6	6¼	2
PSBR (financial year)				
£ billion	45½	34½	21½	10½
per cent GDP	7	5	3	1½

Source: Table 3.8, Financial Statement and Budget Report 1995-6, HM Treasury, November 1994
Notes: 1. This forecast is consistent with output, income and expenditure estimates and other series for the period to the third quarter of 1993 released by the Central Statistical Office (CSO) on 18 November 1994. All figures are rounded to the nearest quarter.
2. Average absolute error in autumn forecasts over past ten years.
3. Per cent of GDP.
4. Excluding food, beverages, tobacco and petroleum industries.

Table 11a General government expenditure
£ billion

	Outturn	Forecast		Projections			
	1993-94	1994-95	1995-96	1996-97	1997-98	1998-99	1999-2000
Control total	241.4	249.6	255.7	263	272	280	289
+ Cyclical social security	14.3	14.1	14.1	14	14	15	15
+ Central government debt interest	19.2	22.1	24.5	26	26	26	26
+ Accounting adjustments	8.0	9.5	10.7	13	13	13	12
= General Government Expenditure	282.9	295.2	305.0	316	325	333	341

Table 11b General government receipts
£ billion

	Outturn	Forecast		Projections			
	1993-94	1994-95	1995-96	1996-97	1997-98	1998-99	1999-2000
Income Tax	58.4	64.2	70.1	75	79	85	90
+ Other taxes, duties and royalties	116.6	129.4	146.4	160	171	177	186
+ Social security contributions	38.7	42.5	44.5	47	49	52	54
+ Other receipts	17.1	16.3	17.8	17	18	18	19
+ Privatazation receipts	5.4	6.3	3.0	3	2	1	1
= General government receipts	236.2	258.8	281.9	301	318	333	350

Table 11c **Public Sector Borrowing Requirement**
£ billion

	Outturn	Forecast			Projections		
	1993-94	1994-95	1995-96	1996-97	1997-98	1998-99	1999-2000
General Government Expenditure	282.9	295.2	305.0	316	325	333	341
- General government receipts	236.2	258.8	281.9	301	318	333	350
= General government borrowing requirement	46.7	36.5	23.1	15	7	0	-8
+ Public corporations' market and overseas borrowing	-1.3	-2.0	-1.6	-2	-2	-1	-1
= Public Sector Borrowing Requirement	45.4	34.5	21.5	13	5	-1	-9

Table 11d **General Government Expenditure receipts and borrowing as a percentage of Gross Domestic Product**

	Outturn	Forecast			Projections		
	1993-94	1994-95	1995-96	1996-97	1997-98	1998-99	1999-2000
Money Gross Domestic Product (GDP) - £ billion	639	678	720	758	796	834	873
Percentages of money GDP							
General Government Expenditure	44.3	43.5	42.4	41.7	40.8	39.9	39.1
General government receipts	37.0	38.2	39.2	39.7	39.9	39.9	40.1
General government borrowing requirement	7.3	5.4	3.2	2.0	0.9	0.0	-0.9
Public Sector Borrowing Requirement	7.1	5.1	3.0	1.7	0.6	-0.1	-1.0

Source: Tables 4.1., 4.4. & 4.5., Financial Statement and Budget Report 1995-96, HM Treasury, HMSO 1994.
Notes: Projections are rounded to the nearest billion from 1996-97 onwards, and constituent items may not sum to total because of rounding.
Privatisation receipts are included along with other government receipts; General Government Expenditure (GGE) is shown excluding those receipts.
Generally the government prefers to use a measure of GGE that is net of those receipts, in effect treating them as 'negative expenditure'.

Table 12 General Government Expenditure, Gross Domestic Product and the Public Sector Borrowing Requirement
£ billion

Year	1980/81	1981/82	1982/83	1983/84	1984/85	1985/86	1986/87	1987/88	1988/89	1989/90	1990/91	1991/92	1992/93	1993/94	1994/95	1995/96	1996/97	1997/98
General Government Expenditure (GGE)																		
Net	108.6	120.5	132.7	140.5	150.8	158.5	164.8	173.2	179.8	200.8	218.1	236.3	260.2	277.6	288.9	301.8	312.4	322.8
Receipts	0.2	0.5	0.5	1.1	2.0	2.7	4.5	5.1	7.1	4.2	5.3	7.9	8.2	5.5	6.3	3.0	3.0	2.0
Gross	108.8	121.0	133.1	141.6	152.8	161.2	169.3	178.4	186.9	205.0	223.5	244.2	268.4	283.0	295.2	304.8	315.4	324.8
1993/94 prices	225.7	228.7	235.2	239.2	245.7	245.7	250.4	250.6	245.9	252.2	254.6	261.7	276.7	283.0	289.4	289.5	292.3	294.2
Public Sector Borrowing																		
Requirement (PSBR)	12.5	8.6	8.9	9.7	10.1	5.6	3.6	-3.4	-14.5	-7.9	-0.5	13.8	36.7	45.4	34.4	21.5	13.0	5.0
Gross Domestic Product (GDP)																		
Cash	237.7	261.0	285.8	310.0	332.1	364.9	392.7	434.8	484.1	525.8	556.8	580.8	604.8	639.0	678.0	719.0	757.0	795.0
1993/94 prices	493.2	493.4	504.9	523.6	533.9	556.3	580.9	610.7	637.0	646.7	634.2	622.5	623.5	639.0	664.7	682.8	701.6	720.1
GDP deflator index	48.2	52.9	56.6	59.2	62.2	65.6	67.6	71.2	76.0	81.3	87.8	93.3	97.0	100.0	102.0	105.3	107.9	110.4
Public spending ratios																		
GGE as a % of GDP	46.6	47.2	47.4	46.5	46.9	45.0	43.9	41.8	39.3	39.7	40.1	42.0	44.4	44.3	43.5	42.4	41.7	40.9
PSBR as a % of GDP	5.3	3.3	3.1	3.1	3.0	1.5	0.9	-0.8	-3.0	-1.5	-0.1	2.4	6.1	7.1	5.1	3.0	1.7	0.6

Source: Public Expenditure Cm 2821, HM Treasury February 1995, Tables 1.1 & 1.4.
Notes: Government receipts are from privatisations, such as BP etc, but do not include local authority capital receipts which are already 'netted off' from the gross General Government Expenditure figures. Percentages for the GGE to GDP ratio are for Gross GGE, and for the years up to 1989-90 are adjusted to remove the distortion caused by the abolition of domestic rates. Outturn figures for years to 1993/94; estimated outturn figures for 1994/95; plans for 1995/96 onwards.

Table 13 **Public sector capital expenditure**
£ billion

		1979/80	1980/81	1981/82	1982/83	1983/84	1984/85	1985/86	1986/87	1987/88	1988/89	1989/90	1990/91	1991/92	1992/93	1993/94	1994/95	1995/96	1996/97	1997/98
	Central government	3.0	3.4	3.6	4.6	4.8	5.4	5.5	4.9	5.1	6.0	7.7	9.6	10.3	10.9	9.9	9.2	8.3	9.0	9.0
+	Local government	4.0	4.1	2.7	3.3	4.7	4.9	4.8	4.7	4.8	3.6	6.9	5.9	7.0	6.9	6.5	7.9	6.9	6.7	6.5
=	General government	6.9	7.5	6.3	7.9	9.4	10.2	10.2	9.7	9.9	9.7	14.7	15.5	17.3	17.8	16.5	17.1	15.2	15.7	15.5
+	Public corporations	6.9	7.3	7.5	8.1	8.2	7.0	5.7	5.2	4.8	4.9	5.6	5.2	4.3	5.3	5.3	6.1	6.2	5.4	5.0
+	Reserve allocation																	0.3	0.6	0.9
=	Total public sector capital expenditure	13.8	14.8	13.8	16.0	17.6	17.2	15.9	14.9	14.7	14.6	20.3	20.7	21.6	23.1	21.7	23.2	21.7	21.7	21.4
-	Depreciation	7.9	9.5	10.4	10.7	11.1	11.1	10.6	10.7	10.5	11.3	11.7	10.9	9.9	10.1	10.1	10.3	10.3	10.4	10.7
=	Net public sector capital expenditure	5.9	5.3	3.4	5.3	6.5	6.2	5.4	4.2	4.2	3.3	8.6	9.8	11.7	13.0	11.7	12.9	11.4	11.3	1.7
	Total public sector capital expenditure at 1993/94 prices	33.9	30.7	26.1	28.3	29.7	27.7	24.2	22.0	20.6	19.2	25.0	23.6	23.2	23.8	21.7	22.7	20.6	20.1	19.4

Source: HM Treasury, Public Expenditure Cm 2821.
Note: Capital expenditure is shown net of receipts from the sale of physical assets. For further definitions see Chapter 5, Annex A, Financial Statement and Budget Report 1994-95, HM Treasury, 1993.

Table 14a General Government Expenditure by function
£ billion

	1980-81 outturn	1981-82 outturn	1982-83 outturn	1983-84 outturn	1984-85 outturn	1985-86 outturn	1986-87 outturn	1987-88 outturn	1988-89 outturn	1989-90 outturn	1990-91 outturn	1991-92 outturn	1992-93 outturn	1993-94 outturn	1994-95 estimated outturn	1994-95 % of total expenditure
Social security	24.3	29.6	33.6	36.9	40.0	43.5	46.8	48.9	50.2	53.2	59.5	70.6	80.0	87.6	90.6	34.5
Health & personal social services	14.1	15.8	17.2	18.3	19.6	20.7	22.3	24.5	27.0	29.5	33.1	37.4	41.0	43.2	46.4	17.7
Education	12.8	13.9	15.0	15.8	16.4	17.0	18.7	20.4	22.0	24.6	26.5	29.4	31.8	33.6	35.1	13.4
Defence	11.5	12.8	14.6	15.7	17.4	18.2	18.4	18.9	19.2	20.8	21.7	22.9	22.9	22.8	22.2	8.5
Law, order & protective services	4.0	4.6	5.2	5.7	6.4	6.6	7.2	8.0	9.0	10.2	11.5	13.0	14.2	14.8	15.4	5.9
Transport	4.3	4.8	5.3	5.5	5.7	5.8	5.7	5.7	5.9	6.8	8.3	9.2	10.7	10.2	10.3	3.9
Other environmental services	3.8	3.9	4.5	4.6	4.4	4.5	5.3	5.5	5.6	6.7	7.4	8.2	8.7	8.8	9.6	3.7
Trade, industry, energy & employment	4.7	6.2	8.0	7.0	8.0	8.1	8.1	6.6	8.0	7.6	8.8	8.2	8.6	9.0	8.6	3.3
Housing	**5.6**	**4.2**	**3.8**	**4.4**	**4.4**	**4.1**	**4.0**	**4.1**	**3.2**	**5.1**	**4.8**	**5.7**	**6.2**	**5.4**	**5.5**	**2.1**
Agriculture, fisheries, food & forestry	1.6	1.7	2.2	2.4	2.4	2.9	2.2	2.4	2.2	2.2	2.9	3.1	3.2	4.1	3.9	1.5
Overseas services & aid	1.3	1.5	1.6	1.7	1.7	1.9	2.0	2.0	2.3	2.6	2.7	3.1	3.4	3.5	3.7	1.4
National Heritage	1.0	1.2	1.3	1.3	1.4	1.5	1.6	1.8	2.0	2.3	2.5	2.6	2.6	2.6	2.7	1.0
Miscellaneous expenditure [1]	3.0	3.3	3.9	3.4	3.9	3.8	4.4	5.3	5.0	6.9	7.0	5.9	7.8	8.1	8.3	3.2
Total expenditure on services	92.2	103.5	116.2	122.8	131.7	138.6	146.5	154.3	161.7	178.4	196.8	219.3	241.3	253.6	262.5	100.0%
+ General government debt interest	11.4	13.3	13.9	14.3	16.2	17.9	17.6	17.9	18.4	18.7	18.4	16.9	17.9	19.7	22.6	
+ Other accounting adjustments [2]	5.3	4.2	3.0	4.4	5.0	4.7	5.1	6.1	6.8	7.9	8.3	8.1	9.2	9.6	10.0	
- Privatisation proceeds	0.2	0.5	0.5	1.1	2.0	2.7	4.5	5.1	7.1	4.2	5.3	7.9	8.2	5.5	6.3	
= General Government Expenditure	108.6	120.5	132.7	140.4	150.8	158.5	164.8	173.2	179.8	200.8	218.1	236.3	260.2	277.6	288.9	

Source: Public Expenditure, Cm 2821, HM Treasury 1995, Table 1.2
Notes: 1. Includes contributions to the European Communities and activities required for the general maintenance of government such as tax collection and the registration of population.
2. These adjustments differ from those shown in tables linking the planning total with general government expenditure because of debt interest and the exclusion of market and overseas borrowing of public corporations from expenditure on services.

Table 14b: General Government Expenditure by function in real terms[1]

£ billion 1993-94 prices

	1980-81 outturn	1981-82 outturn	1982-83 outturn	1983-84 outturn	1984-85 outturn	1985-86 outturn	1986-87 outturn	1987-88 outturn	1988-89 outturn	1989-90 outturn	1990-91 outturn	1991-92 outturn	1992-93 outturn	1993-94 outturn	1994-95 estimated outturn	Real growth 1980-81 to 1994-95 %
Law, order & protective services	8.3	8.8	9.1	9.7	10.2	10.0	10.6	11.3	11.8	12.6	13.1	13.9	14.7	14.8	15.1	81.9
Social security	50.4	56.0	59.4	62.3	64.3	66.3	69.2	68.7	66.0	65.5	67.8	75.6	82.5	87.6	88.8	76.2
Health & personal social services	29.3	29.9	30.4	30.9	31.5	31.5	32.9	34.4	35.6	36.3	37.7	40.1	42.3	43.2	45.5	55.5
Overseas services & aid	2.8	2.8	2.8	2.9	2.7	2.9	2.9	2.8	3.0	3.2	3.1	3.3	3.5	3.5	3.7	32.1
National Heritage	2.1	2.2	2.2	2.2	2.3	2.3	2.4	2.5	2.6	2.8	2.8	2.8	2.7	2.6	2.7	30.1
Education	26.6	26.4	26.5	26.7	26.4	25.9	27.6	28.7	29.0	30.2	30.2	31.5	32.8	33.6	34.4	29.6
Other environmental services	7.9	7.4	7.9	7.7	7.0	6.8	7.8	7.7	7.4	8.3	8.5	8.8	9.0	8.8	9.4	19.4
Agriculture, fisheries, food & forestry	3.4	3.2	3.8	4.1	3.9	4.4	3.3	3.4	2.9	2.7	3.4	3.3	3.3	4.1	3.9	14.7
Transport	8.9	9.1	9.4	9.2	9.1	8.9	8.5	8.0	7.7	8.4	9.5	9.8	11.0	10.2	10.1	13.2
Defence	23.8	24.2	25.9	26.6	27.9	27.8	27.2	26.6	25.3	25.6	24.7	24.6	23.6	22.8	21.7	-8.8
Trade, industry, energy & employment	9.8	11.6	14.1	11.9	12.8	12.4	12.0	9.3	10.6	9.3	10.0	8.8	8.9	9.0	8.4	-13.5
Housing	**11.7**	**7.9**	**6.8**	**7.4**	**7.2**	**6.2**	**5.9**	**5.8**	**4.2**	**6.2**	**5.5**	**6.1**	**6.4**	**5.4**	**5.4**	**-53.9**
Miscellaneous expenditure	6.2	6.2	7.0	5.8	6.3	5.8	6.5	7.5	6.6	8.5	7.9	6.3	8.1	8.1	8.2	31.7
Total expenditure on services	191.2	195.8	205.2	207.3	211.6	211.2	216.7	216.7	212.8	219.5	224.2	235.0	248.7	253.6	257.3	34.6
+ General government debt interest	23.7	25.1	24.5	24.2	26.0	27.2	26.1	25.1	24.3	23.0	20.9	18.1	18.4	19.7	22.2	
+ Other accounting adjustments	11.0	8.0	5.4	7.5	8.0	7.1	7.6	8.6	8.9	9.7	9.5	8.6	9.5	9.6	9.6	
- Privatisation proceeds	0.4	0.9	0.8	1.9	3.3	4.1	6.6	7.2	9.3	5.2	6.1	8.5	8.4	5.5	6.2	
= General Government Expenditure	225.4	228.0	234.3	237.0	242.3	241.5	243.8	243.3	236.6	247.1	248.5	253.2	268.2	277.6	283.2	25.7

Source: Public Expenditure, Cm 2821, HM Treasury 1995, Table 1.3.
Note: 1. Cash figures adjusted to 1993-94 price levels by excluding the effect of general inflation.

Table 15a **Control total by department**
£ million

Department	1989-90 outturn	1990-91 outturn	1991-92 outturn	1992-93 outturn	1993-94 outturn	1994-95 estimated outturn	1995-96 plans	1996-97 plans	1997-98 plans
Defence [1]	20,777	21,709	22,913	22,910	22,757	22,173	21,723	21,924	22,317
Foreign & Commonwealth	898	968	1,132	1,278	1,276	1,386	1,158	1,160	1,183
Overseas Development	1,688	1,738	1,993	2,143	2,231	2,366	2,363	2,419	2,478
Agriculture, Fisheries & Food	1,487	2,137	2,159	2,198	2,880	2,646	3,026	3,003	2,959
Trade & Industry	1,615	3,506	3,144	2,668	2,667	1,989	1,379	795	748
ECGD	358	372	215	117	(60)	(11)	(16)	11	6
Employment	3,579	3,643	3,467	3,482	3,509	3,708	3,468	3,503	3,469
Transport	3,570	4,692	5,390	6,605	6,010	5,956	4,387	4,445	5,075
DoE - Housing [2]	2,938	6,743	7,493	8,232	7,735	7,439	6,895	6,907	6,925
DoE - Local government [3,4]	19,756	20,522	28,356	31,175	29,376	29,930	30,307	30,904	30,865
DoE - Other environment	1,191	1,538	1,617	2,011	2,145	2,158	1,983	1,918	1,907
DoE - PSA, PH etc	(56)	(31)	(86)	(198)	(93)	(131)	(206)	(221)	(241)
Home Office	4,077	4,839	5,517	5,821	5,962	6,261	6,415	6,416	6,565
Lord Chancellors	1,376	1,638	2,000	2,331	2,422	2,600	2,796	2,875	2,878
Education [4]	4,866	5,656	6,336	7,124	9,807	10,483	10,949	11,204	11,212
National Heritage	706	775	868	989	961	957	1,001	961	924
Health & OPCS [4]	20,000	22,521	25,653	28,264	29,816	31,765	32,957	33,271	34,114
Social Security [2,4,5]	45,999	48,926	55,069	61,774	67,889	70,840	72,798	75,950	79,200
Scotland [3]	8,948	9,717	11,697	12,713	13,559	14,235	14,412	14,577	14,688
Wales [3]	3,801	4,442	5,309	5,992	6,305	6,585	6,778	6,871	6,927
Northern Ireland	5,395	5,525	6,018	6,580	7,086	7,492	7,711	7,868	8,014
Exchequer	3,152	3,344	3,392	3,429	3,351	3,338	3,223	3,185	3,144
Cabinet & Parliament	1,166	1,290	1,407	2,231	2,474	2,497	2,462	2,491	2,544
European Communities	2,316	2,027	707	1,898	1,873	2,043	2,821	2,765	2,639
Local authority self financed expenditure	15,533	15,285	11,221	9,714	9,931	11,800	11,700	12,000	12,200
Reserve							3,000	5,700	8,700
Allowance for shortfall						(1,000)			
Control total	175,134	193,521	212,987	231,481	241,867	249,500	255,500	262,800	271,500
Cyclical social security	6,711	7,833	10,923	13,300	14,339	14,200	14,000	14,000	14,400

Source: Public Expenditure, Cm 2821, HM Treasury 1995, Tables 2.1, 2.2 & B.1.
Notes: 1. The outturns for the Ministry of Defence in 1990/91 & 1991/92 are net of other governments' contributions to the cost of the Gulf conflict.
2. Central government support to local authorities for rent rebates is included against DoE-Housing from 1990/91 and against Department of Social Security in earlier years.
3. Includes revenue/rate support grant and non-domestic rates and certain transitional grants associated with the change from rates to the commumity charge.
4. The years after 1992-93 are affected by transfers between departments and spending sectors. The main changes relate to further education and the transfer of responsibility for community care from central government to local authorities.
5. Excludes cyclical social security ie unemployment benefit and non-pensioner Income Support.

Table 15b Control total by department in real terms
£ million 1993/94 prices

Department	1989-90 outturn	1990-91 outturn	1991-92 outturn	1992-93 outturn	1993-94 outturn	1994-95 estimated outturn	1995-96 plans	1996-97 plans	1997-98 plans
Defence [1]	25,561	24,726	24,554	23,611	22,757	21,738	20,626	20,309	20,219
Foreign & Commonwealth	1,104	1,103	1,213	1,317	1,276	1,359	1,100	1,074	1,071
Overseas Development	2,076	1,979	2,136	2,208	2,231	2,320	2,244	2,242	2,245
Agriculture, Fisheries & Food	1,829	2,434	2,314	2,265	2,880	2,594	2,873	2,781	2,681
Trade & Industry	1,986	3,993	3,369	2,749	2,667	1,950	1,309	736	678
ECGD	440	423	230	120	(60)	(10)	(15)	10	6
Employment	4,403	4,150	3,715	3,588	3,509	3,636	3,293	3,245	3,143
Transport	4,392	5,344	5,776	6,807	6,010	5,839	4,166	4,118	4,598
DoE - Housing [2]	3,615	7,680	8,030	8,484	7,735	7,293	6,547	6,399	6,274
DoE - Local Government [3,4]	24,305	23,375	30,387	32,129	29,376	29,343	28,778	28,629	27,963
DoE - Other Environment	1,465	1,752	1,733	2,073	2,145	2,116	1,883	1,777	1,728
DoE - PSA, PH etc	(69)	(36)	(92)	(205)	(93)	(129)	(196)	(204)	(218)
Home Office	5,016	5,512	5,912	5,999	5,962	6,138	6,091	5,944	5,948
Lord Chancellors	1,693	1,866	2,143	2,403	2,422	2,549	2,655	2,664	2,607
Education [4]	5,987	6,442	6,790	7,342	9,807	10,278	10,396	10,379	10,158
National Heritage	869	883	930	1,019	961	939	951	890	837
Health & OPCS [4]	24,605	25,651	27,491	29,129	29,816	31,143	31,294	30,821	30,907
Social Security [2,4,5]	56,590	55,725	59,014	63,664	67,889	69,451	69,124	70,350	71,750
Scotland [3]	11,008	11,067	12,535	13,102	13,559	13,956	13,684	13,504	13,307
Wales [3]	4,676	5,059	5,690	6,175	6,305	6,456	6,436	6,365	6,276
Northern Ireland	6,638	6,293	6,449	6,781	7,086	7,345	7,322	7,288	7,261
Exchequer	3,878	3,809	3,635	3,534	3,351	3,273	3,060	2,951	2,849
Cabinet & Parliament	1,435	1,469	1,508	2,299	2,474	2,448	2,338	2,308	2,305
European Communities	2,849	2,309	757	1,956	1,873	2,003	2,679	2,561	2,391
Local authority self financed expenditure	19,109	17,410	12,024	10,012	9,931	11,600	11,100	11,100	11,000
Reserve							2,800	5,300	7,900
Allowance for shortfall						(1,000)			
New control total	215,457	220,417	228,245	238,564	241,867	244,600	242,600	243,500	246,000
Cyclical social security	8,255	8,921	11,707	13,711	14,339	13,922	13,295	12,975	13,043

Source: Public Expenditure, Cm 2821, HM Treasury 1995, Tables 2.1, 2.3 & B.1.
Notes: See Table 15a.

Dwellings and households

Dwellings and households

Table 16a **Dwellings by tenure in England, Wales and Scotland**
Thousands

	1981	1982	1983	1984	1985	1986	1987	1988	1989	1990	1991	1992	1993	1994
England														
Owner-occupiers	10,499	10,819	11,104	11,364	11,626	11,929	12,264	12,648	12,971	13,171	13,288	13,386	13,517	13,664
+ Privately rented	2,044	2,035	2,032	2,028	2,005	1,953	1,899	1,848	1,849	1,906	1,969	2,023	2,045	2,056
+ Housing association	422	432	447	464	483	495	512	534	567	613	647	707	767	834
+ Local authority	5,061	4,886	4,763	4,670	4,584	4,504	4,403	4,254	4,081	3,944	3,880	3,810	3,740	3,661
= All dwellings	18,025	18,172	18,346	18,525	18,697	18,882	19,078	19,284	19,468	19,634	19,787	19,927	20,070	20,215
Wales														
Owner-occupiers	682	704	719	733	747	761	777	798	822	836	846	857	867	878
+ Privately rented	103	100	98	95	93	90	88	85	83	80	96	95	94	93
+ Housing association	12	14	15	16	18	19	20	21	23	27	30	32	35	38
+ Local authority	293	278	271	267	262	258	253	244	232	226	219	217	214	211
= All dwellings	1,089	1,096	1,103	1,112	1,120	1,128	1,137	1,148	1,159	1,169	1,191	1,201	1,210	1,220
Scotland														
Owner-occupiers	718	747	781	816	850	884	922	972	1,033	1,088	1,133	1,178	1,220	1,259
+ Privately rented	191	182	174	167	161	154	147	139	133	126	153	152	150	149
+ Housing association	36	38	41	45	47	50	54	59	62	65	57	62	67	72
+ Local authority	1,027	1,016	1,001	987	974	962	943	914	877	845	816	784	756	731
= All dwellings	1,970	1,983	1,998	2,015	2,032	2,050	2,067	2,084	2,104	2,124	2,160	2,175	2,193	2,210

Table 16b **Dwellings by tenure in England, Wales and Scotland**
Percentages

		1981	1982	1983	1984	1985	1986	1987	1988	1989	1990	1991	1992	1993	1994
	England														
	Owner-occupiers	58.2	59.5	60.5	61.3	62.2	63.2	64.3	65.6	66.6	67.1	67.2	67.2	67.4	67.6
+	Privately rented	11.3	11.2	11.1	10.9	10.7	10.3	10.0	9.6	9.5	9.7	10.0	10.2	10.2	10.2
+	Housing association	2.3	2.4	2.4	2.5	2.6	2.6	2.7	2.8	2.9	3.1	3.3	3.5	3.8	4.1
+	Local authority	28.1	26.9	26.0	25.2	24.5	23.9	23.1	22.1	21.0	20.1	19.6	19.1	18.6	18.1
=	All dwellings	100.0	100.0	100.0	100.0	100.0	100.0	100.0	100.0	100.0	100.0	100.0	100.0	100.0	100.0
	Wales														
	Owner-occupiers	62.6	64.2	65.2	66.0	66.7	67.5	68.3	69.5	70.9	71.5	71.0	71.4	71.6	71.6
+	Privately rented	9.4	9.1	8.9	8.6	8.3	8.0	7.7	7.4	7.1	6.8	8.0	7.9	7.8	7.6
+	Housing association	1.1	1.2	1.4	1.5	1.6	1.7	1.7	1.8	1.9	2.3	2.5	2.7	2.9	3.1
+	Local authority	26.9	25.4	24.5	24.0	23.4	22.8	22.3	21.3	20.0	19.4	18.4	18.1	17.7	17.3
=	All dwellings	100.0	100.0	100.0	100.0	100.0	100.0	100.0	100.0	100.0	100.0	100.0	100.0	100.0	100.0
	Scotland														
	Owner-occupiers	36.4	37.7	39.1	40.5	41.8	43.1	44.6	46.7	49.1	51.2	52.5	54.2	55.6	57.0
+	Privately rented	9.7	9.2	8.7	8.3	7.9	7.5	7.1	6.7	6.3	6.0	7.1	7.0	6.8	6.7
+	Housing association	1.8	1.9	2.1	2.2	2.3	2.5	2.6	2.8	2.9	3.1	2.6	2.9	3.3	3.3
+	Local authority	52.1	51.2	50.1	49.0	47.9	46.9	45.6	43.9	41.7	39.8	37.8	36.0	35.1	35.1
=	All dwellings	100.0	100.0	100.0	100.0	100.0	100.0	100.0	100.0	100.0	100.0	100.0	100.0	100.0	100.0

Table 16c **Dwellings by tenure in Great Britain, Northern Ireland and the United Kingdom**
Thousands

	1981	1982	1983	1984	1985	1986	1987	1988	1989	1990	1991	1992	1993	1994
Great Britain														
Owner-occupiers	11,898	12,270	12,604	12,913	13,225	13,575	13,962	14,418	14,826	15,094	15,267	15,421	15,604	15,801
+ Privately rented	2,337	2,318	2,304	2,290	2,258	2,198	2,134	2,072	2,064	2,112	2,218	2,270	2,289	2,298
+ Housing association	469	483	504	525	548	565	586	614	652	706	734	801	869	944
+ Local authority	6,380	6,180	6,035	5,924	5,820	5,723	5,600	5,412	5,190	5,015	4,915	4,811	4,710	4,603
All dwellings	21,085	21,251	21,447	21,653	21,844	22,060	22,282	22,516	22,732	22,927	23,138	23,303	23,473	23,645
Northern Ireland														
Owner-occupiers	271	282	289	296	317	327	339	348	360	373	379	388	400	
+ Privately rented	38	35	32	29	25	26	24	23	23	23	22	22	21	
+ Housing association	3	4	4	5	6	6	7	8	9	9	10	11	12	
+ Local authority	190	190	185	183	182	180	176	175	172	167	163	160	158	
All dwellings	502	510	509	512	530	540	545	553	563	571	573	580	590	
United Kingdom														
Owner-occupiers	12,169	12,552	12,893	13,209	13,540	13,902	14,301	14,765	15,186	15,466	15,646	15,809	16,004	
+ Privately rented	2,375	2,353	2,336	2,318	2,283	2,224	2,157	2,095	2,087	2,135	2,240	2,292	2,310	
+ Housing association	472	487	508	530	553	570	593	622	661	715	744	812	881	
+ Local authority	6,570	6,370	6,219	6,107	6,002	5,903	5,776	5,587	5,361	5,182	5,078	4,971	4,868	
All dwellings	21,586	21,761	21,956	22,165	22,378	22,600	22,827	23,069	23,297	23,497	23,711	23,883	24,063	

Table 16d Dwellings by tenure in Great Britain, Northern Ireland and the United Kingdom
Percentages

	1981	1982	1983	1984	1985	1986	1987	1988	1989	1990	1991	1992	1993	1994
Great Britain														
Owner-occupiers	56.4	57.7	58.8	59.6	60.5	61.5	62.7	64.0	65.2	65.8	66.0	66.2	66.5	66.8
+ Privately rented	11.1	10.9	10.7	10.6	10.3	10.0	9.6	9.2	9.1	9.2	9.6	9.7	9.8	9.7
+ Housing association	2.2	2.3	2.3	2.4	2.5	2.6	2.6	2.7	2.9	3.1	3.2	3.4	3.7	4.0
+ Local authority	30.3	29.1	28.1	27.4	26.6	25.9	25.1	24.0	22.8	21.9	21.2	20.6	20.1	19.5
All dwellings	100.0	100.0	100.0	100.0	100.0	100.0	100.0	100.0	100.0	100.0	100.0	100.0	100.0	100.0
Northern Ireland														
Owner-occupiers	54.0	55.3	56.8	57.8	59.9	60.7	62.1	62.8	64.0	65.3	66.1	66.8	67.8	
+ Privately rented	7.6	6.9	6.2	5.6	4.7	4.8	4.3	4.1	4.0	3.9	3.8	3.8	3.5	
+ Housing association	0.5	0.7	0.8	0.9	1.0	1.1	1.3	1.4	1.5	1.6	1.7	1.8	2.0	
+ Local authority	37.9	37.2	36.2	35.7	34.4	33.4	32.3	31.6	30.5	29.2	28.4	27.6	26.7	
All dwellings	100.0	100.0	100.0	100.0	100.0	100.0	100.0	100.0	100.0	100.0	100.0	100.0	100.0	
United Kingdom														
Owner-occupiers	56.4	57.7	58.7	59.6	60.5	61.5	62.6	64.0	65.2	65.8	66.0	66.2	66.5	
+ Privately rented	11.0	10.8	10.6	10.5	10.2	9.8	9.5	9.1	9.0	9.1	9.4	9.6	9.6	
+ Housing association	2.2	2.2	2.3	2.4	2.5	2.5	2.6	2.7	2.8	3.0	3.1	3.4	3.7	
+ Local authority	30.4	29.3	28.3	27.6	26.8	26.1	25.3	24.2	23.0	22.1	21.4	20.8	20.2	
All dwellings	100.0	100.0	100.0	100.0	100.0	100.0	100.0	100.0	100.0	100.0	100.0	100.0	100.0	

Source: Housing and Construction Statistics (various editions), Scottish Office, Welsh Office.
Notes: All figures are for the December of the year shown. Owner-occupiers includes shared owners and long leaseholders.
Private renting includes renting with a job or business. Local authority tenants includes new town tenants.
1994 figures for Northern Ireland were not available at time of publication.

Table 17 **Gross fixed capital formation in dwellings**
£ million

	1980	1981	1982	1983	1984	1985	1986	1987	1988	1989	1990	1991	1992	1993	1994
Private sector:															
New dwellings	3,129	2,924	3,358	4,087	4,697	4,417	5,691	6,910	9,000	8,565	7,143	6,100	6,697	7,440	8,139
+ Improvements to existing dwellings	2,986	3,250	3,492	3,670	4,489	5,266	5,835	6,529	9,013	10,577	10,069	9,581	9,411	9,285	10,120
= Total private sector	6,115	6,174	6,850	7,757	9,186	9,683	11,526	13,439	18,013	19,142	17,212	15,681	16,108	16,725	18,259
+ Public sector	2,559	1,964	2,070	2,690	2,746	2,536	2,614	2,916	2,914	3,846	4,227	2,820	2,584	2,742	2,678
= Whole economy	8,674	8,138	8,920	10,447	11,932	12,219	14,140	16,355	20,927	22,988	21,439	18,501	18,692	19,467	20,937
Gross Domestic Product (£ bn)	231.8	254.9	279.0	304.5	325.9	357.3	384.8	423.4	471.4	516.0	551.1	575.3	597.1	630.2	667.8
Gross fixed capital formation in dwellings as a percentage of Gross Domestic Product	3.7	3.2	3.2	3.4	3.7	3.4	3.7	3.9	4.4	4.5	3.9	3.2	3.1	3.1	3.1

Sources: UK National Accounts, and Central Statistical Office
Notes: All figures at current market prices.

Provision of dwellings

Table 18a **Housing starts in England**

	1980	1981	1982	1983	1984	1985	1986	1987	1988	1989	1990	1991	1992	1993	1994
Local authorities	27,869	20,405	27,605	27,983	23,046	18,020	16,195	15,400	12,980	12,576	6,383	2,719	1,470	1,158	404
+ New towns	5,541	1,160	1,076	1,735	885	567	472	137	0	0	0	0	0	0	0
+ Government departments	224	297	93	169	122	176	307	517	443	369	108	260	131	100	87
= Total public sector	33,634	21,862	28,774	29,887	24,053	18,763	16,974	16,054	13,423	12,945	6,491	2,979	1,601	1,258	491
+ Housing associations	13,154	10,007	15,155	12,541	11,070	10,393	11,078	9,515	10,403	11,018	14,361	16,406	28,111	33,638	32,969
+ Private sector	84,123	101,633	123,227	150,971	138,027	144,365	158,764	172,613	193,965	141,881	110,711	112,309	99,586	116,702	131,488
= All dwellings	130,911	133,502	167,156	193,399	173,150	173,521	186,816	198,182	217,791	165,844	131,563	131,694	129,298	151,598	164,948

Table 18b **Housing completions in England**

	1980	1981	1982	1983	1984	1985	1986	1987	1988	1989	1990	1991	1992	1993	1994
Local authorities	67,337	45,969	28,442	28,443	27,196	22,523	18,728	15,565	15,712	13,920	13,956	8,065	3,274	1,413	1,086
+ New towns	6,973	8,648	3,069	1,182	1,742	703	660	435	163	0	0	0	0	0	0
+ Government departments	525	287	109	242	211	98	235	597	233	690	142	75	235	24	16
= Total public sector	74,835	54,904	31,620	29,867	29,149	23,324	19,623	16,597	16,108	14,610	14,098	8,140	3,509	1,437	1,102
+ Housing associations	19,299	16,838	11,157	14,292	13,973	11,318	10,464	10,411	9,958	9,646	13,695	15,343	20,789	29,635	30,462
+ Private sector	110,232	98,797	108,826	129,234	138,699	135,376	147,942	157,580	169,786	151,537	132,118	128,738	119,533	115,445	118,979
= All dwellings	204,366	170,539	151,603	173,393	181,821	170,018	178,029	184,588	195,834	175,793	159,911	152,221	143,831	145,661	150,543

Dwellings and households

Table 18c Housing starts in Wales

	1980	1981	1982	1983	1984	1985	1986	1987	1988	1989	1990	1991	1992	1993	1994
Local authorities	2,343	1,130	1,933	1,898	777	770	742	909	658	501	338	174	261	75	124
+ New towns	96	41	188	110	131	121	0	0	58	0	0	0	0	0	0
+ Government departments	7	5	0	0	0	2	1	2	6	0	0	1	0	0	0
= Total public sector	2,446	1,176	2,121	2,008	908	893	743	911	722	501	338	175	261	75	124
+ Housing associations	384	460	695	640	326	579	507	1,014	1,522	1,568	2,199	2,496	2,657	3,198	2,602
+ Private sector	5,033	4,494	5,437	6,224	5,608	7,217	7,111	8,741	10,794	9,970	7,643	6,722	5,997	7,310	7,236
= All dwellings	7,863	6,130	8,253	8,872	6,842	8,689	8,361	10,666	13,038	12,039	10,180	9,393	8,915	10,583	9,962

Table 18d Housing completions in Wales

	1980	1981	1982	1983	1984	1985	1986	1987	1988	1989	1990	1991	1992	1993	1994
Local authorities	3,493	3,370	1,771	1,543	1,997	992	744	810	793	566	608	418	133	172	255
+ New towns	209	160	104	195	155	81	126	0	0	58	0	0	0	0	0
+ Government departments	2	6	5	0	0	2	0	2	1	6	0	0	1	0	0
= Total public sector	3,704	3,536	1,880	1,738	2,152	1,075	870	812	794	630	608	418	134	172	255
+ Housing associations	917	540	794	529	593	607	534	467	708	1,642	1,652	2,446	2,460	2,853	2,684
+ Private sector	5,932	5,105	5,082	5,395	6,276	6,540	7,026	7,975	9,535	9,121	7,719	7,251	7,050	6,262	6,993
= All dwellings	10,553	9,181	7,756	7,662	9,021	8,222	8,430	9,254	11,037	11,393	9,979	10,115	9,644	9,287	9,909

Table 18e Housing starts in Scotland

		1980	1981	1982	1983	1984	1985	1986	1987	1988	1989	1990	1991	1992	1993	1994
	Local authorities	4,281	2,152	3,198	2,609	2,248	2,017	2,251	2,598	1,922	1,029	946	860	441	482	749
+	New towns	1,155	733	765	194	126	190	141	374	484	557	720	134	395	428	309
+	Government departments	5	14	11	14	1	59	259	40	0	64	5	0	0	0	0
=	Total public sector	5,441	2,899	3,974	2,817	2,375	2,266	2,651	3,012	2,406	1,650	1,671	994	836	910	1,058
+	Housing associations	1,261	1,051	2,446	1,068	1,239	1,487	1,356	1,863	1,912	2,639	2,111	3,448	3,051	5,062	4,243
+	Private sector	9,681	11,027	12,135	15,196	14,642	14,123	14,685	13,115	15,072	18,427	16,873	15,941	14,668	17,183	21,295
=	All dwellings	16,383	14,977	18,555	19,081	18,256	17,876	18,692	17,990	19,390	22,716	20,655	20,383	18,555	23,156	26,596

Table 18f Housing completions in Scotland

		1980	1981	1982	1983	1984	1985	1986	1987	1988	1989	1990	1991	1992	1993	1994
	Local authorities	6,167	5,549	2,987	2,819	2,400	2,610	2,030	2,388	2,473	1,874	1,173	1,162	740	470	282
+	New towns	1,288	1,516	729	667	233	201	157	107	257	409	720	550	276	456	207
+	Government departments	33	1	17	6	14	17	114	139	85	0	69	0	0	0	0
=	Total public sector	7,488	7,066	3,733	3,492	2,647	2,828	2,301	2,634	2,815	2,283	1,962	1,712	1,016	926	489
+	Housing associations	881	1,928	1,167	1,271	2,076	1,148	1,466	1,169	1,278	1,620	1,430	1,920	1,974	1,677	1,203
+	Private sector	12,242	11,021	11,523	13,166	14,115	14,435	14,870	13,904	14,179	16,287	16,543	15,705	14,592	17,823	16,942
=	All dwellings	20,611	20,015	16,423	17,929	18,838	18,411	18,637	17,707	18,272	20,190	19,935	19,337	17,583	20,426	18,634

Dwellings and households

Table 18g Housing starts in Great Britain

	1980	1981	1982	1983	1984	1985	1986	1987	1988	1989	1990	1991	1992	1993	1994
Local authorities	34,493	23,687	32,736	32,490	26,071	20,807	19,188	18,907	15,560	14,106	7,667	3,753	2,172	1,715	1,277
+ New towns	6,792	1,934	2,029	2,039	1,142	878	613	511	542	557	720	134	395	428	309
+ Government departments	236	316	104	183	123	237	567	559	449	433	113	261	131	100	87
= Total public sector	41,521	25,937	34,869	34,712	27,336	21,922	20,368	19,977	16,551	15,096	8,500	4,148	2,698	2,243	1,673
+ Housing associations	14,799	11,518	18,296	14,249	12,635	12,459	12,941	12,392	13,837	15,225	18,671	22,350	33,819	41,898	39,814
+ Private sector	98,837	117,154	140,799	172,391	158,277	165,705	180,560	194,469	219,831	170,278	135,227	134,972	120,251	141,195	160,019
= All dwellings	155,157	154,609	193,964	221,352	198,248	200,086	213,869	226,838	250,219	200,599	162,398	161,470	156,768	185,337	201,506

Table 18h Housing completions in Great Britain

	1980	1981	1982	1983	1984	1985	1986	1987	1988	1989	1990	1991	1992	1993	1994
Local authorities	76,997	54,888	33,200	32,805	31,593	26,125	21,502	18,763	18,978	16,324	15,780	9,645	4,147	2,055	1,623
+ New towns	8,470	10,324	3,902	2,044	2,130	985	943	542	420	445	720	550	276	456	207
+ Government departments	560	294	131	248	225	117	349	738	319	696	211	75	236	24	16
= Total public sector	86,027	65,506	37,233	35,097	33,948	27,227	22,794	20,043	19,717	17,465	16,711	10,270	4,659	2,535	1,846
+ Housing associations	21,097	19,306	13,118	16,092	16,642	13,073	12,464	12,047	11,944	12,908	16,777	19,709	25,223	34,165	34,349
+ Private sector	128,406	114,923	125,431	147,797	159,090	156,351	169,838	179,379	193,465	176,987	156,380	151,694	141,175	139,530	142,914
= All dwellings	235,530	199,735	175,782	198,986	209,680	196,651	205,096	211,469	225,126	207,360	189,868	181,673	171,058	175,374	179,086

Provision of dwellings

Table 18i Housing starts in Northern Ireland

	1980	1981	1982	1983	1984	1985	1986	1987	1988	1989	1990	1991	1992	1993
Northern Ireland Housing Executive	2,901	2,509	3,247	4,357	3,074	2,352	1,920	1,595	2,061	927	1,059	999	718	1,132
+ Government departments	11	97	190	1	7	1	0	9	0	13	0	137	69	0
= Total public sector	2,912	2,606	3,437	4,358	3,081	2,353	1,920	1,605	2,061	940	1,059	1,136	787	1,132
+ Housing associations	112	670	541	547	641	395	626	725	572	498	764	791	718	489
+ Private sector	3,338	2,776	4,487	6,892	7,314	7,199	7,114	7,418	7,228	6,763	5,704	5,531	6,199	7,070
= All dwellings	6,362	6,052	8,465	11,797	11,036	9,947	9,660	9,748	9,861	8,201	7,527	7,458	7,704	8,691

Table 18j Housing completions in Northern Ireland

	1980	1981	1982	1983	1984	1985	1986	1987	1988	1989	1990	1991	1992	1993
Northern Ireland Housing Executive	2,507	2,859	2,814	4,044	3,588	3,233	2,580	1,764	1,712	1,708	1,299	953	1,049	810
+ Government departments	56	223	218	49	6	2	0	0	3	0	15	2	51	18
= Total public sector	2,563	3,082	3,032	4,093	3,594	3,235	2,580	1,764	1,715	1,708	1,314	955	1,100	828
+ Housing associations	325	129	395	641	695	611	537	546	715	685	442	791	675	671
+ Private sector	3,568	3,557	3,606	4,971	6,177	6,940	7,082	7,451	7,511	7,911	6,163	5,164	5,913	5,707
= All dwellings	6,456	6,768	7,033	9,705	10,466	10,786	10,199	9,761	9,941	10,304	7,919	6,910	7,688	7,206

Dwellings and households

Table 18k Housing starts in the United Kingdom

	1980	1981	1982	1983	1984	1985	1986	1987	1988	1989	1990	1991	1992	1993
Local authorities	37,394	26,196	36,016	36,733	29,233	23,191	21,096	20,429	17,428	14,963	8,695	4,752	2,890	2,847
+ New towns	6,792	1,934	2,029	2,039	1,142	878	613	511	533	680	720	134	395	428
+ Government departments	247	413	294	184	130	237	565	568	449	469	113	398	200	100
= Total public sector	44,433	28,543	38,339	38,956	30,505	24,306	22,274	21,508	18,430	16,112	9,528	5,284	3,485	3,375
+ Housing associations	14,911	12,188	18,813	14,802	13,292	12,848	13,729	13,634	15,043	16,447	19,384	23,141	34,537	42,387
+ Private sector	102,175	119,930	145,276	179,285	165,629	172,878	187,241	204,175	228,624	176,714	141,172	140,524	126,450	148,265
= All dwellings	161,519	160,661	202,428	233,043	209,426	210,032	223,242	239,317	262,097	209,273	170,084	168,949	164,472	194,028

Table 18l Housing completions in the United Kingdom

	1980	1981	1982	1983	1984	1985	1986	1987	1988	1989	1990	1991	1992	1993
Local authorities	79,504	57,747	36,058	36,877	35,287	29,348	24,128	20,573	20,714	18,160	16,908	10,598	5,196	2,865
+ New towns	8,470	10,324	3,902	2,044	2,130	985	943	542	420	467	720	550	276	456
+ Government departments	616	517	349	297	230	119	346	738	322	696	226	77	287	42
= Total public sector	88,590	68,588	40,309	39,218	37,647	30,452	25,417	21,853	21,456	19,323	17,854	11,225	5,759	3,363
+ Housing associations	21,422	19,435	13,532	16,777	17,308	13,734	13,068	13,117	13,479	14,598	17,221	20,500	25,898	34,836
+ Private sector	131,974	118,480	129,022	153,038	165,606	163,470	177,647	191,187	206,996	187,504	165,197	156,859	147,088	145,237
= All dwellings	241,986	206,503	182,863	209,033	220,561	207,656	216,132	226,157	241,931	221,425	200,272	188,584	178,746	183,436

Source: Housing and Construction Statistics

Table 19a Right to Buy in England

	1980	1981	1982	1983	1984	1985	1986	1987	1988	1989	1990	1991	1992	1993	1994	Cumulative Total
Local authorities	55	64,908	170,944	117,210	83,440	76,319	73,767	84,007	128,566	139,722	92,995	51,414	41,445	41,248	43,116	1,209,156
+ New towns	0	866	1,765	1,349	971	663	556	792	1,091	1,332	365	177	166	180	45	10,318
+ Housing associations	0	547	1,988	2,100	1,904	1,451	2,791	2,046	3,323	3,700	3,369	1,871	669	686	831	27,276
= Total	55	66,321	174,697	120,659	86,315	78,433	77,114	86,845	132,980	144,754	96,729	53,462	42,380	42,094	43,992	1,246,830

Table 19b Right to Buy in Wales

	1980	1981	1982	1983	1984	1985	1986	1987	1988	1989	1990	1991	1992	1993	1994	Cumulative Total
Local authorities	0	7,588	14,943	8,674	5,266	5,265	5,233	5,506	9,386	12,468	6,278	3,382	2,716	2,715	3,006	92,426
+ New towns	0	328	1,130	514	323	286	102	35	47	58	52	20	32	35	25	2,987
+ Housing associations	0	0	15	40	61	71	85	68	172	227	156	101	75	64	99	1,234
= Total	0	7,916	16,088	9,228	5,650	5,622	5,420	5,609	9,605	12,753	6,486	3,503	2,823	2,813	3,130	96,646

Table 19c Right to Buy in Scotland

	1980	1981	1982	1983	1984	1985	1986	1987	1988	1989	1990	1991	1992	1993	1994	Cumulative Total
Local authorities	513	6,934	10,543	12,627	11,443	10,646	10,251	13,796	22,617	29,180	26,941	18,569	19,825	16,372	17,119	227,376
+ New towns	227	1,233	1,068	1,775	1,361	1,164	998	1,450	2,137	3,218	2,105	1,304	984	977	1,238	21,239
+ Housing associations	1,417	1,929	1,933	2,919	2,444	2,463	2,073	3,348	6,726	6,315	3,232	2,287	2,455	2,191	2,271	44,003
= Total	2,157	10,096	13,544	17,321	15,248	14,273	13,322	18,594	31,480	38,713	32,278	22,160	23,264	19,540	20,628	292,618

Dwellings and households

Table 19d Right to Buy in Great Britain

	1980	1981	1982	1983	1984	1985	1986	1987	1988	1989	1990	1991	1992	1993	1994	Cumulative Total
Local authorities	568	79,430	196,430	138,511	100,149	92,230	89,251	103,309	160,569	181,370	126,214	73,365	63,986	60,335	63,241	1,528,958
+ New towns	227	2,427	3,963	3,638	2,655	2,113	1,656	2,277	3,275	4,608	2,522	1,501	1,182	1,192	1,308	34,544
+ Housing associations	1,417	2,476	3,936	5,059	4,409	3,985	4,949	5,462	10,221	10,242	6,757	4,259	3,199	2,941	3,201	72,513
= Total	2,212	84,333	204,329	147,208	107,213	98,328	95,856	111,048	174,065	196,220	135,493	79,125	68,467	64,447	67,750	1,636,094

Source: Housing and Construction Statistics
Notes: Figures include shared ownership sales. Scottish housing association figures include Right to Buy and some voluntary sales by Scottish Homes.

Table 20 Changes in regional provision of social housing

| | Stock of dwellings (000s) | | | | | | Percentage change in provision 1981 - 1993 | | |
| | April 1981 | | | December 1993 | | | | | |
Region	Public sector	Housing association	All social housing	Public sector	Housing association	All social housing	Public sector	Housing association	All social housing
North	478	37	515	347	51	398	-27.4	37.8	-22.7
Yorkshire & Humberside	601	27	628	461	60	521	-23.3	122.2	-17.0
North West	720	53	773	537	107	644	-25.4	101.9	-16.7
West Midlands	615	40	655	469	65	534	-23.7	62.5	-18.5
East Midlands	413	19	432	305	38	343	-26.2	100.0	-20.6
East Anglia	190	13	203	124	42	166	-34.7	223.1	-18.2
Greater London	851	134	985	656	188	844	-22.9	40.3	-14.3
Rest of South East	885	60	945	576	161	737	-34.9	168.3	-22.0
South West	366	27	393	259	51	310	-29.2	88.9	-21.1
England	5,118	410	5,528	3,740	767	4,507	-26.9	87.1	-18.5
+ Wales	298	11	309	214	34	248	-28.2	209.1	-19.7
+ Scotland	1,031	33	1,064	770	71	841	-25.3	115.2	-21.0
= Great Britain	6,447	453	6,900	4,724	874	5,598	-26.7	92.9	-18.9
+ Northern Ireland	192	2	194	158	12	170	-17.7	500.0	-12.4
= United Kingdom	6,639	455	7,094	4,882	886	5,768	-26.5	94.7	-18.7

Source: Housing and Construction Statistics 1983 - 1993, Table 9.4.
Note: Public sector housing comprises local authority, new town and Northern Ireland Housing Executive dwellings.

Table 21a Households lacking amenities by tenure in Great Britain
Numbers

Tenure	England				Wales				Scotland				Great Britain			
	No bath or shower	No inside W.C.	Shared bath or shower	Shared inside W.C.	No bath or shower	No inside W.C.	Shared bath or shower	Shared inside W.C.	No bath or shower	No inside W.C.	Shared bath or shower	Shared inside W.C.	No bath or shower	No inside W.C.	Shared bath or shower	Shared inside W.C.
Outright home-owner	25,251	36,807	3,791	3,103	4,939	7,021	232	199	2,693	1,467	209	223	32,883	45,295	4,232	3,525
Home buyer	4,916	9,085	3,662	3,701	746	1,125	192	182	423	327	219	216	6,085	10,537	4,073	4,099
Furnished private renting	3,883	4,173	74,601	75,691	455	493	3,445	3,405	718	382	2,848	2,787	5,056	5,048	80,894	81,883
Unfurnished private renting	19,438	23,038	10,593	10,486	1,792	1,972	387	389	1,566	520	197	279	22,796	25,530	11,177	11,154
Rented with work	1,563	2,228	3,173	3,232	206	237	335	331	195	155	193	189	1,964	2,620	3,701	3,752
Housing association	1,168	1,777	9,085	6,291	93	160	166	164	72	48	170	159	1,333	1,985	9,421	6,614
Local authority	4,006	10,885	23,137	10,124	255	385	682	332	496	334	647	436	4,757	11,604	24,466	10,892
Total households	60,225	87,993	128,042	112,628	8,486	11,393	5,439	5,002	6,163	3,233	4,483	4,289	74,874	102,619	137,964	121,919

Source: 1991 Census Housing and the Availability of Cars, Table 8.

Table 21b Households lacking amenities by tenure in Great Britain
Percentages within each tenure and territory

Tenure	England				Wales				Scotland				Great Britain			
	No bath or shower	No inside W.C.	Shared bath or shower	Shared inside W.C.	No bath or shower	No inside W.C.	Shared bath or shower	Shared inside W.C.	No bath or shower	No inside W.C.	Shared bath or shower	Shared inside W.C.	No bath or shower	No inside W.C.	Shared bath or shower	Shared inside W.C.
Outright home-owner	0.6	0.8	0.1	0.1	1.4	2.0	0.1	0.1	0.8	0.4	0.1	0.1	0.6	0.9	0.1	0.1
Home buyer	0.1	0.1	0.0	0.0	0.2	0.3	0.0	0.0	0.1	0.0	0.0	0.0	0.1	0.1	0.0	0.0
Furnished private renting	0.6	0.6	10.8	11.0	1.4	1.5	10.3	10.2	1.5	0.8	5.8	5.7	0.7	0.7	10.5	10.6
Unfurnished private renting	2.7	3.2	1.5	1.5	5.0	5.5	1.1	1.1	3.2	1.1	0.4	0.6	2.9	3.2	1.4	1.4
Rented with work	0.4	0.6	0.9	0.9	1.1	1.3	1.8	1.8	0.5	0.4	0.5	0.5	0.5	0.6	0.9	0.9
Housing association	0.2	0.3	1.5	1.1	0.4	0.6	0.6	0.6	0.1	0.1	0.3	0.3	0.2	0.3	1.4	1.0
Local authority	0.1	0.3	0.6	0.3	0.1	0.2	0.3	0.2	0.1	0.0	0.1	0.1	0.1	0.2	0.5	0.2
Total households	0.3	0.5	0.7	0.6	0.8	1.0	0.5	0.4	0.3	0.2	0.2	0.2	0.3	0.5	0.6	0.6

Source: 1991 Census Housing and the Availability of Cars, Table 8.

Table 22a English housing conditions: repair costs and unfitness 1991
£s

Tenure	Estimated average cost of remedial repairs			Costs of remedying unfitness	
	Urgent repairs	General repairs	Comprehensive repairs	Average cost	Number of unfit dwellings (000s)
Owner-occupied	630	1,100	2,040	2,693	715
Private rented	1,320	1,960	3,540	4,012	333
Local authority	620	930	1,790	1,597	265
Housing association	470	720	1,350	2,871	41
Vacant	-	-	-	7,915	145
Total stock	680	1,130	2,100	3,301	1,498

Source: English House Condition Survey 1991
Notes: For repair costs vacant dwellings are allocated to tenures. All cost figures are mean averages at 1991 prices.

Table 22b English housing conditions: unfitness

Tenure	1986		1991		Change in unfitness
	(000s)	%	(000s)	%	%
Owner-occupied	769	6.6	715	5.5	-7.0
Private rented	361	25.4	333	20.5	-7.8
Local Authority	281	6.8	265	6.9	-5.7
Housing Association	23	4.9	41	6.7	78.3
Vacant	228	28.1	145	22.7	-36.4
Total stock	1,662	8.8	1,498	7.6	-9.9

Source: English House Condition Survey 1991.

Table 22c English housing conditions: repair costs
£s

Percentage of dwellings with costs exceeding given level	1986		1991		% Change 1986 - 1991	
	Urgent repairs	General repairs	Urgent repairs	General repairs	Urgent repairs	General repairs
2 %	5,930	8,760	4,850	7,190	18	18
5 %	3,600	5,760	2,880	4,480	20	22
10 %	2,330	3,830	1,750	2,930	25	23
25 %	1,010	1,820	650	1,290	36	29
50 % (median)	260	580	130	380	50	34
75 %	0	40	0	0	-	-
Average cost	880	1,480	680	1,130		

Source. English House Condition Survey 1991.

Table 23a Welsh housing conditions 1993

Tenure	Numbers of unfit dwellings				Total	Percentage of stock unfit	Fit dwellings	Average repair costs (£)	
	Pre-1919	1919-1944	1945-1964	Post-1964				Unfit dwellings	All dwellings
Owner-occupied	56,800	13,800	12,100	10,600	93,200	11.9	730	3,830	1,100
Private rented	14,700	1,900	600	700	17,900	25.6	1,370	4,570	2,190
Local authority	2,400	10,100	15,500	9,900	37,900	15.8	610	3,210	1,020
Housing association	900	800	0	300	2,100	6.0	200	2,850	360
Total unfit	74,800	26,600	28,200	21,500	151,200	13.4	-	-	-
Total stock	368,900	157,400	244,000	361,300	1,131,700	100.0	720	3,740	1,130

Source: 1993 Welsh House Condition Survey
Notes: Housing association figures should be treated with caution as they are based on a sample of just 80 dwellings.
Local authority includes the Development Board for Rural Wales (DBRW).

Table 23b Welsh housing conditions: unfitness rates - 1986 and 1993 compared

Tenure and age of dwelling	Unfitness rates Modelled 1986 %	1993 %	Actual 1993 %
Private sector	18.6	12.9	13.0
Social housing	22.1	14.8	14.4
Pre-1919	32.0	21.7	21.0
Post-1919	12.5	9.3	9.7
Total stock	19.5	13.3	13.3

Source: 1993 Welsh House Condition Survey.
Notes: Private housing is owner-occupied and private renting; social housing is local authority and housing association. Modelling is needed to compare results because of changes in definition between the 1986 and 1993 surveys.

Table 23c Welsh housing conditions: repair costs - 1986 and 1993 compared

Tenure	Mean repair costs per dwelling Comparable 1986 £	1993 £	Full 1993 £
Owner-occupied	1,378	1,045	1,098
Private rented	2,896	2,061	2,190
Social housing	780	919	934
Total	1,314	1,077	1,125

Source: 1993 Welsh House Condition Survey.
Note: Modelling is needed to compare results because of changes in definition between the 1986 and 1993 surveys.

Table 24 Scottish housing conditions 1991

Property character	Dwellings below tolerable standard Number (000s)	% Incidence	Dwellings with condensation Number (000s)	% Incidence	Dwellings with mould Number (000s)	% Incidence	Total occupied stock Number (000s)	%
Age :								
Pre-1919	50	11.8	77	18.1	59	13.8	426	20.9
1919-1944	16	4.5	82	22.5	51	13.9	365	18.0
1945-1964	18	3.6	116	23.7	73	14.9	491	24.1
Post-1964	9	1.2	118	15.7	70	9.3	753	37.0
Total	94	4.6	394	19.4	252	12.4	2,035	100.0
Tenure :								
Private	60	4.9	176	14.3	108	8.8	1,229	60.4
Public	34	4.3	218	27.1	145	18.0	806	39.6
Dwelling type :								
Houses	48	3.9	234	18.9	146	11.8	1,243	61.6
Flats	46	5.8	160	20.2	106	13.4	792	38.9

Source: Scottish House Condition Survey 1991: Preliminary Findings, Scottish Homes 1993.

Table 25a **Regional renovation grants paid to private owners under the Housing Act 1985 and earlier Acts in Great Britain**

	1980	1981	1982	1983	1984	1985	1986	1987	1988	1989	1990	1991	1992	1993	1994
North	5,923	4,907	8,049	16,842	14,613	7,778	7,048	6,897	7,393	7,354	7,157	1,445	225	122	4
Yorkshire & Humberside	9,478	7,667	12,249	25,275	20,763	12,420	10,120	11,801	11,662	13,046	13,872	3,354	217	41	12
North West	12,800	12,063	17,725	32,380	35,911	22,311	20,243	19,732	17,195	14,746	13,253	4,297	900	129	125
East Midlands	7,930	7,273	11,354	23,864	22,770	11,766	11,178	10,254	11,391	10,625	9,558	2,683	324	52	5
West Midlands	6,873	7,122	7,919	17,893	18,889	11,409	10,389	11,755	10,330	11,190	10,720	5,091	735	50	8
East Anglia	3,607	3,278	4,796	10,276	10,786	6,712	5,738	6,095	6,234	5,292	4,280	854	86	14	3
Greater London	10,460	9,450	12,978	27,269	42,995	30,559	20,759	14,483	13,639	10,437	10,384	3,343	672	124	27
Rest of South East	10,751	11,155	18,251	41,310	39,342	22,038	18,234	18,213	18,611	17,317	13,102	3,440	543	92	14
South West	6,643	6,026	10,707	24,717	23,038	11,419	9,619	9,678	8,848	8,210	6,754	1,706	177	36	7
England	74,465	68,941	104,028	219,826	229,107	136,412	113,328	108,908	105,303	98,217	89,080	26,213	3,879	660	205
Wales	7,342	7,100	10,989	27,323	29,978	17,152	18,571	19,097	20,187	20,174	25,112	10,084	1,219	109	155
Scotland	13,420	18,036	23,957	45,498	60,661	46,286	31,453	30,668	31,512	26,693	23,557	23,478	24,898	21,194	21,177
Great Britain	95,227	94,077	138,974	292,647	319,746	199,850	163,352	158,673	157,002	145,084	137,749	59,775	29,996	21,963	21,537

Source: Housing and Construction Statistics, Scottish Office
Notes: No new grants were made under the 1985 Act in England and Wales after June 1990; although payments continued for grants made before that date.

Table 25b **Regional renovation grants paid to private owners under the Local Government and Housing Act 1989**

	Mandatory Grants					Discretionary Grants					Minor Works Assistance					Total all grants and assistance				
	1990	1991	1992	1993	1994	1990	1991	1992	1993	1994	1990	1991	1992	1993	1994	1990	1991	1992	1993	1994
North	47	2,271	3,404	3,148	3,469	2	275	392	308	246	497	2,107	1,991	1,702	1,986	546	4,653	5,787	5,158	5,701
Yorkshire & Humberside	119	4,454	6,243	6,599	6,949	4	254	717	1,019	982	478	2,249	2,635	2,472	2,208	601	6,957	9,595	10,090	10,139
North West	78	4,160	8,125	7,787	8,763	3	379	796	610	419	1,551	5,146	3,641	3,239	4,599	1,632	9,685	12,562	11,636	13,781
East Midlands	38	2,464	4,854	4,858	5,743	8	273	490	522	981	814	3,094	2,735	2,498	3,017	860	5,831	8,079	7,878	9,741
West Midlands	54	2,891	5,463	5,467	5,900	197	430	335	322	397	736	3,918	3,511	2,205	3,785	987	7,239	9,309	7,994	10,082
East Anglia	48	1,165	1,909	2,131	2,593	12	221	328	252	318	238	916	1,106	1,230	1,645	298	2,302	3,343	3,613	4,556
Greater London	53	2,012	4,072	4,763	5,907	61	311	553	712	548	418	1,746	2,145	2,425	2,860	532	4,069	6,770	7,900	9,315
South East	91	4,087	7,303	9,166	10,078	20	817	1,376	1,286	1,152	1,283	6,471	6,720	5,906	5,893	1,394	11,375	15,399	16,358	17,123
South West	109	2,772	4,156	4,866	5,806	19	476	512	435	445	716	3,678	3,669	4,169	4,821	844	6,926	8,337	9,470	11,072
England	637	26,276	45,529	48,785	55,208	326	3,426	5,499	5,466	5,488	6,743	29,325	28,153	25,846	30,814	7,706	59,027	79,181	80,097	91,510
Wales	54	3,851	9,841	10,595	9,192	4	453	647	627	676	1,375	6,751	4,960	4,709	4,332	1,433	11,055	15,448	15,931	14,200
England and Wales	691	30,127	55,370	59,380	64,400	330	3,879	6,146	6,093	6,164	8,118	36,076	33,113	30,555	35,146	9,139	70,082	94,629	96,028	105,710

Source: Housing and Construction Statistics
Note: The 1989 Act grants system for England and Wales started in July 1990, apart from Minor Works Assistance, which started in April 1990. The Act does not apply in Scotland.

Table 26a **Number of local authorities and new town dwellings receiving renovation grants by region in Great Britain**

	1980	1981	1982	1983	1984	1985	1986	1987	1988	1989	1990	1991	1992	1993	1994
North	7,331	4,119	4,533	11,007	9,632	15,698	17,482	18,856	26,333	22,222	21,525	23,397	17,630	18,199	24,650
Yorkshire & Humberside	8,523	4,999	6,289	8,398	8,990	8,087	4,885	10,317	10,863	14,664	11,284	9,370	15,643	21,809	18,251
North West	16,436	8,480	12,542	13,360	10,487	13,291	15,226	13,914	13,921	17,921	31,119	23,534	32,588	35,646	29,061
East Midlands	7,522	5,626	5,533	8,477	8,918	8,791	11,320	14,143	15,704	16,072	20,461	13,992	13,250	12,958	15,959
West Midlands	8,554	6,390	5,905	6,817	5,987	8,944	16,208	20,209	24,231	27,264	40,684	19,847	21,633	34,731	29,606
East Anglia	1,517	1,249	1,337	2,036	2,626	2,947	3,947	5,032	3,429	5,120	4,922	3,322	3,708	7,038	11,531
Greater London	12,024	13,476	8,796	10,500	18,657	13,423	30,421	28,127	35,069	44,029	38,406	38,107	37,297	60,726	91,529
Rest of South East	11,303	6,666	9,344	19,922	16,380	19,191	22,059	25,625	28,349	32,888	29,330	27,767	21,397	32,213	50,554
South West	4,065	1,926	3,443	4,944	4,935	6,110	12,113	12,139	11,102	14,748	28,786	25,426	14,087	25,402	26,589
England	77,275	52,931	57,722	85,461	86,612	96,482	133,661	148,362	169,001	194,928	226,517	184,762	177,233	248,722	297,729
Wales	-	-	-	-	2,390	1,728	2,788	5,886	8,333	8,444	10,987	10,513	9,491	23,264	20,216
Scotland	22,295	26,065	51,214	41,583	33,774	58,993	71,397	86,912	72,373	53,277	87,448	74,464	82,759	92,229	95,967
Great Britain	-	-	-	-	122,776	157,203	207,846	241,160	249,707	256,649	324,952	269,739	269,483	364,215	413,912

Source: Housing and Construction Statistics, Scottish Office.
Note: Figures for Scotland are of work approved and include Scottish Homes.

Table 26b **Number of housing association dwellings receiving renovation grants**

	1980	1981	1982	1983	1984	1985	1986	1987	1988	1989	1990	1991	1992	1993	1994
North	2,161	1,193	2,299	1,687	1,444	1,034	1,196	731	1,099	531	360	143	236	340	-
Yorkshire & Humberside	1,304	744	1,359	1,184	1,178	1,001	1,019	851	622	523	560	523	381	492	-
North West	2,543	3,218	5,101	3,573	3,384	2,553	2,799	1,857	1,876	2,355	1,381	753	658	780	-
East Midlands	1,119	710	978	943	1,178	682	813	981	681	1,062	447	289	449	263	-
West Midlands	2,170	1,209	1,933	2,041	1,831	1,248	1,746	1,368	1,102	936	525	365	655	481	-
East Anglia	54	163	238	185	155	56	306	155	398	619	265	271	241	140	-
Greater London	4,348	3,302	4,321	3,845	7,271	3,842	3,538	3,888	4,486	4,855	3,754	2,596	3,430	2,335	-
Rest of South East	406	266	603	548	1,233	573	636	524	709	1,578	2,272	1,213	1,154	958	-
South West	571	438	532	507	781	361	661	581	264	565	1,089	266	328	223	-
England	14,676	11,243	17,364	14,513	18,455	11,350	12,714	10,936	11,237	13,024	10,653	6,419	7,532	6,012	-
Wales	252	694	1,009	993	760	945	907	948	867	812	399	305	322	300	287
Scotland	2,787	1,833	3,422	2,530	1,424	1,124	1,414	1,262	1,225	1,122	816	1,680	1,785	1,524	1,029
Great Britain	17,715	13,770	21,795	18,036	20,639	13,419	15,035	13,146	13,329	14,958	11,868	8,404	9,639	7,836	-

Sources: Housing and Construction Statistics, Scottish Office Statistical Bulletin Hsg/1995/4.

Dwellings and households

Table 27 **Property characteristics by tenure in Great Britain**
Percentages

	Owner-occupiers:		Rented:					Total
	Owned outright	With mortgage	With job or business	Local authority	Housing association	Private: unfurnished	Private: furnished	
Property type								
Houses:								
Detached	31	25	30	1	2	12	8	19
Semi-detached	35	36	22	26	11	21	11	31
Terraced	25	30	12	33	26	34	29	29
Flats:								
Purpose-built	6	6	16	37	46	13	15	15
Converted	3	3	9	3	14	20	36	5
With business	0	0	12	0	0	1	2	1
Total	100	100	100	100	100	100	100	100
Property age								
Pre-1919	26	24	39	4	25	50	51	22
1919 - 1944	24	23	12	20	10	26	19	22
1945 - 1964	25	18	23	39	10	9	11	23
Post-1964	25	35	26	37	56	14	19	32
Total	100	100	100	100	100	100	100	100

Source: General Household Surveys 1993, CSO
Notes: Flats includes maisonettes. Accommodation with business premises includes 'other'.
Figures do not total precisely due to rounding.

Table 28a Tenure profile of heads of household by age in Great Britain
Percentages

Item	Owner-occupiers:		Rented:				With job or business	All tenures
	Owned outright	With mortgage	Local authority	Housing association	Private: unfurnished	Private: furnished		
1980								
Age:								
Under 25	0	4	4	7	4	40	7	4
25 - 29	1	13	7	11	5	24	11	8
30 - 44	8	48	22	15	13	20	32	26
45 - 64	40	33	36	20	27	10	43	34
65 - 74	32	2	21	25	26	4	6	17
75 or over	20	0	12	23	25	2	1	10
All ages	100	100	100	100	100	100	100	100
1993								
Age:								
Under 25	0	2	5	7	12	38	4	4
25 - 29	0	11	9	11	14	25	15	8
30 - 44	5	45	26	23	19	24	36	28
45 - 59	21	33	16	13	15	9	34	24
60 - 69	32	6	16	14	11	1	8	15
70 - 79	29	2	19	23	15	1	3	14
80 or over	14	0	10	10	14	2	1	7
All ages	100	100	100	100	100	100	100	100

Source: General Household Surveys 1980 & 1993.

Dwellings and households

Table 28b Tenure profile of heads of household by sex and marital status in Great Britain
Percentages

Item	Owner-occupiers:		Rented:				With job or business	All tenures
	Owned outright	With mortgage	Local authority	Housing association	Private: unfurnished	Private: furnished		
1980								
Sex & marital status								
Men:								
Married	20	40	31	1	4	1	3	100
Single	17	22	25	1	11	22	3	100
Widowed	35	5	45	2	9	1	2	100
Divorced/separated	9	34	36	1	9	8	3	100
All men	20	37	31	1	5	2	3	100
Women:								
Married	13	41	32	2	2	10	2	100
Single	30	9	30	3	12	13	3	100
Widowed	36	3	46	3	11	0	0	100
Divorced/separated	13	16	58	3	6	3	1	100
All women	30	8	44	3	10	4	1	100
Total	23	30	34	1	6	3	3	100
1993								
Sex & marital status								
Men:								
Married	24	54	15	2	3	1	2	100
Single	15	32	20	4	9	17	2	100
Widowed	46	8	39	3	3	1	0	100
Divorced/separated	11	38	28	3	10	9	2	100
All men	24	49	17	2	4	3	2	100
Women:								
Married	7	48	26	7	11	0	0	100
Single	18	22	34	10	8	8	1	100
Widowed	50	5	33	5	6	0	0	100
Divorced/separated	11	38	37	5	6	2	1	100
All women	32	18	34	6	6	3	0	100
Total	26	41	22	3	4	3	1	100

Source: General Household Surveys 1980 & 1993

Table 28c Tenure profile of heads of household by socio-economic group and economic activity status[1] in Great Britain
Percentages

Item	Owner-occupiers:		Rented:				With job or business	All tenures
	Owned outright	With mortgage	Local authority	Housing association	Private: unfurnished	Private: furnished		
1980								
Socio-economic group:								
Professional	3	8	0	4	0	9	8	4
Employers/managers	10	24	3	3	4	9	25	12
Intermediate non-manual	4	11	2	4	5	17	8	6
Junior non-manual	5	10	6	7	6	18	13	8
Skilled manual [2]	15	34	27	19	17	21	23	25
Semi-skilled manual [3]	6	8	14	8	9	10	21	10
Unskilled manual	2	1	5	3	3	5	0	3
Economically inactive	56	4	42	52	55	11	1	33
Total	100	100	100	100	100	100	100	100
1993								
Socio-economic group:								
Professional	2	9	0	1	2	7	12	5
Employers/managers	6	24	2	4	9	9	28	13
Intermediate non-manual	3	14	2	4	5	12	11	8
Junior non-manual	3	7	4	4	8	8	8	5
Skilled manual [2]	11	26	16	11	16	16	18	19
Semi-skilled manual [3]	3	8	10	9	8	10	18	7
Unskilled manual	1	2	4	4	3	5	1	2
Economically inactive	71	10	61	64	48	34	4	41
Total	100	100	100	100	100	100	100	100

Source: General Household Surveys 1980 & 1993
Notes: 1. Excludes members of the armed forces, economically active full-time students and those who were unemployed and had never worked.
2. Includes own account non-professional.
3. Includes personal service.

Dwellings and households

Table 29a Race by tenure in Great Britain (1991 - 1993 average)
Percentages

Tenure	White	Indian	Pakistani/Bangladeshi	Black Caribbean	Other	All ethnic minorities	Total
Outright owner	26	18	12	6	10	11	25
Owner with mortgage	41	63	51	35	38	46	41
Rented :							
With job or business	1	2	2	1	3	2	1
Local authority or housing association	25	9	24	50	35	31	25
Private unfurnished	4	2	5	2	4	3	4
Private furnished	2	5	6	5	9	7	3
Total	100	100	100	100	100	100	100

Source : General Household Survey 1993, CSO.

Table 29b Race by dwelling type in Great Britain (1988 - 1991 average)
Percentages

	White	Indian	Pakistani/Bangladeshi	West Indian & Guyanese	Other	All ethnic minorities	Total
House:							
Detached	20	12	9	4	5	7	20
Semi-detached	32	28	28	15	20	22	32
Terraced	28	37	43	41	32	37	29
Flats:							
Purpose-built	14	16	11	24	28	21	14
Converted	4	6	4	14	12	10	4
With business premises	1	2	5	1	4	3	1
Total	100	100	100	100	100	100	100

Source: General Household Survey 1991, CSO.

Table 29c Race by bedroom standards in Great Britain (1988 - 1991 average)
Percentages

Bedroom standard	White	Indian	Pakistani/Bangladeshi	West Indian & Guyanese	Other	All ethnic minorities	Total
2 or more below standard	0	2	9	2	2	3	0
1 below standard	2	9	18	13	10	12	3
Equals standard	28	39	30	44	41	39	29
1 above standard	39	27	28	27	33	29	39
2 or more above standard	30	23	14	15	14	16	29

Source : General Household Survey 1991, CSO

Table 30 Tenure and consumer durables in Great Britain 1991
Percentage of households with specified durables

Item	Rented:				Owner-occupiers:			All households
	Local authority	Housing association	Private unfurnished	Rented furnished	With job/business	In process of purchasing	Outright owner	
No car	68	70	50	49	25	11	32	33
One car	27	26	38	38	54	50	49	44
Two or more cars	4	4	12	13	22	38	18	23
Central heating	77	85	49	65	78	89	82	82
Telephone	70	76	74	70	93	97	96	88
Washing machine	78	66	70	55	83	97	88	87
Freezer or fridge/freezer	71	67	69	55	87	93	85	84
Dishwasher	1	1	4	5	24	25	12	14
Video recorder	53	53	48	54	81	88	56	69
Home computer	12	12	11	15	23	33	11	21

Sources: Family Spending 1991, CSO, 1991 Census Housing and Availability of Cars, HMSO 1993.

Dwellings and households

Table 31 **Employment status of household heads by tenure**
Percentages

Year	Tenure	Employment status of household head		Unemployed	Retired	Disabled or sick	Economic inactive	Total
		In employment: Full time	Part time					
1981	Outright owners	37	4	3	44	2	10	100
	Home-buyers	92	1	3	2	1	1	100
	Council renting	43	4	9	28	4	11	100
	Housing association	42	4	6	34	3	10	100
	Unfurnished private	51	4	4	30	2	9	100
	Furnished private	65	1	9	5	1	19	100
	All tenures	58	3	5	24	2	8	100
1988	Outright owners	31	5	3	53	4	4	100
	Home-buyers	88	2	3	3	1	2	100
	Council renting	26	5	12	38	8	10	100
	Housing association	25	8	10	40	5	12	100
	Unfurnished private	50	6	5	33	2	5	100
	Furnished private	55	6	13	4	1	21	100
	All tenures	54	4	5	27	4	5	100
1993	Outright owners	23	6	3	62	3	4	100
	Home-buyers	82	4	5	5	2	2	100
	Council renting	22	6	13	37	9	13	100
	Housing association	23	5	13	37	8	15	100
	Unfurnished private	47	6	12	26	3	7	100
	Furnished private	53	3	19	2	2	21	100
	All tenures	31	5	7	28	4	6	100

Sources: Housing trailers to the 1981 & 1988 Labour Force Surveys, Survey of English Housing 1993.
Notes: Unemployed includes households that believe no work is avalable. The fifth column includes disabled and permanently sick only.
For 1984 and 1991 data see Table L in the 1994/95 edition of the Review.

Tenure profiles and characteristics

Table 32 **Employment status of recently moving household heads by tenure**
Percentages

Year	Tenure	In employment: Full time	Part time	All employed	Unemployed	Retired	Other economic inactive	Total
1984	Outright owner:	31	5	36	9	31	19	100
	Buying with mortgage:	94	1	95	3	-	2	100
	Council:	29	5	33	24	17	26	100
	Housing association:	40	12	52	16	12	10	100
	Private, unfurnished:	74	4	77	11	3	11	100
	Private, furnished:	52	4	56	16	1	28	100
1991	Outright owner:	37	5	42	6	42	8	100
	Buying with mortgage:	93	2	94	3	1	2	100
	Council:	28	3	31	22	20	27	100
	Housing association:	30	6	35	13	28	24	100
	Private, unfurnished:	75	4	7	9	2	9	100
	Private, furnished:	55	4	59	11	1	28	100
1993	Outright owner:	22	8	29	4	53	14	100
	Buying with mortgage:	90	3	93	3	2	2	100
	Council:	24	4	28	24	15	34	100
	Housing association:	25	6	31	22	16	32	100
	Private, unfurnished:	57	5	62	19	3	15	100
	Private, furnished:	53	3	56	16	22	28	100

Source: Housing trailers to the 1984 and 1991 Labour Force Surveys, Survey of English Housing 1993

Dwellings and households

Table 33 Average incomes of household heads by tenure in Great Britain
£ per week

Tenure	1972	1976	1980	1984	1988	1992	1993
Owners:							
Outright owner	25	59	81	107	157	194	183
With mortgage	39	96	142	195	267	320	319
Tenants:							
Local authority	22	58	68	76	93	110	113
Housing association	-	54	66	88	94	120	110
Private - unfurnished	19	48	60	77	110	149	154
Private - furnished	21	57	87	89	161	170	152

Source: General Household Surveys 1972 to 1993.
Notes: Income figures are mean averages for usual gross income of household heads. Local authority tenants includes tenants of new towns.

Table 34 Tenure and sources of income

| Sources of income | Rented unfurnished: | | | Rented furnished | Rent free | Owner-occupiers: | | All owners |
	Local authority	Housing association	Other			In process of purchasing	Outright owner	
Gross household weekly income	£ 171.17	£ 176.34	£ 241.85	£ 304.46	£ 241.80	£ 508.51	£ 297.00	£ 430.29
Percentage from:	%	%	%	%	%	%	%	%
Wages & salaries	45.9	43.1	59.4	66.4	65.2	78.9	34.5	67.6
Self employment	3.4	5.6	9.7	10.3	4.2	9.5	7.0	8.9
Investments	1.5	2.9	4.3	1.7	6.9	2.6	14.8	5.7
Pensions & annuities	3.8	6.3	4.9	0.6	4.9	2.3	20.0	6.8
Social security	43.6	39.6	19.8	8.9	16.4	5.0	23.0	9.6
Other sources	1.8	2.5	1.9	12.2	2.3	1.7	0.7	1.5
Total	100.0	100.0	100.0	100.0	100.0	100.0	100.0	100.0

Source: Family Spending 1993, CSO.
Note: Pensions and annuities excludes social security benefits.

Table 35 Tenure and gross weekly household income in Great Britain, 1993

Percentages of households in each gross income decile group

Income decile group	Lower income boundary	Rented unfurnished: Local authority	Housing association	Other	Rented furnished	Rent free	Owner-occupiers: In process of buying	Outright owner	Total
	£	%	%	%	%	%	%	%	%
Lowest		49.6	8.0	6.7	6.7	3.2	4.9	20.9	100.0
Second	74	45.1	6.2	5.3	3.0	2.4	9.2	28.8	100.0
Third	110	36.4	5.9	3.4	4.3	1.9	14.0	34.1	100.0
Fourth	156	25.1	4.7	3.9	3.7	1.6	25.4	35.7	100.0
Fifth	214	18.5	3.4	3.9	3.7	1.7	35.5	33.2	100.0
Sixth	278	15.1	2.2	2.7	3.4	1.7	49.2	25.7	100.0
Seventh	350	9.2	1.4	3.3	2.7	1.0	61.0	21.3	100.0
Eigth	426	6.4	1.4	2.6	2.7	0.7	67.0	19.1	100.0
Ninth	529	3.0	1.0	1.7	3.7	0.6	76.8	13.2	100.0
Highest	718	2.1	0.1	0.9	2.6	0.6	78.4	15.3	100.0
All		21.0	3.4	3.4	3.7	1.5	42.1	24.7	100.0

Source: Family Spending 1993, CSO.

Private housing

Level of market activity

Table 36a Numbers of property transactions in England and Wales
Thousands

Year 1980	1981	1982	1983	1984	1985	1986	1987	1988	1989	1990	1991	1992	1993	1994	1994 Qtr 1	Qtr 2	Qtr 3	Qtr 4	1995 Qtr 1
1,267	1,351	1,542	1,669	1,760	1,743	1,801	1,937	2,148	1,580	1,398	1,306	1,136	1,196	1,274	329	321	313	314	312

Source: Economic Trends, Inland Revenue Statistics
Note: Quarterly figures are seasonally adjusted.

Table 36b Residential property transactions in England and Wales
Thousands

Year	1986	1987	1988	1989	1990	1991	1992	1993	1994
All properties	1,801	1,937	2,148	1,580	1,398	1,306	1,136	1,196	1,274
Residential properties	1,600	1,744	1,990	1,467	1,283	1,225	1,032	1,114	1,168
Residential properties as share of all (%)	88.8	90.0	92.6	92.8	91.8	93.8	90.8	93.1	91.7

Source: Economic Trends, Inland Revenue Statistics.

Table 37 Numbers of mortgage advances per year in Great Britain
Thousands

	1980	1981	1982	1983	1984	1985	1986	1987	1988	1989	1990	1991	1992	1993	1994
Building societies	675	736	861	950	1,086	1,073	1,231	1,048	1,232	867	780	697	589	566	618
+ Banks				179	115	176	246	286	357	300	333	315	325	391	362
+ Insurance Companies	18	15	16	18	18	19	31	40	41	27	26	13			
+ Local authorities	16	73	111	47	36	23	12	10	11	11	8	3	3	3	2
= Total	709	824	988	1,194	1,255	1,291	1,520	1,384	1,641	1,205	1,147	1,028	917	960	982
Building societies' share of total (%)	95	89	87	80	87	83	81	76	75	72	68	68	64	59	63

Sources: Housing and Construction Statistics (Annual Volumes); Department of the Environment
Notes: Figures include council house sales. Abbey National Plc figures are included in the Banks figures from July 1989. Figures for insurance company mortgages have not been collected since 1991.

Table 38a **Building society advances**

	1980	1981	1982	1983	1984	1985	1986	1987	1988	1989	1990	1991	1992	1993	1994
Advances (£ million)															
New dwellings	1,406	1,456	1,716	2,330	2,900	2,900	3,516	3,488	4,696	4,221	3,775	3,770	3,351	3,231	4,127
+ Other dwellings	8,183	9,406	11,831	14,867	18,637	20,375	28,163	26,986	37,745	29,090	29,260	28,752	24,119	23,481	26,178
= All dwellings	9,589	10,862	13,547	17,197	21,537	23,275	31,679	30,474	42,441	33,311	33,035	32,522	27,470	26,712	30,305
+ Other advances		1,129	1,792	2,066	2,497	3,216	5,257	4,810	6,935	10,732	10,296	9,502	6,015	4,799	5,072
= Total advances	9,614	11,991	15,339	19,263	24,034	26,491	36,936	35,284	49,376	44,043	43,331	42,024	33,485	31,511	35,377
Number of dwellings (000s)															
New dwellings	94	87	94	111	130	119	122	106	118	88	78	71	62	60	74
+ Other dwellings	584	649	766	839	955	955	1,110	943	1,115	778	703	626	526	506	544
= All dwellings	675	736	861	950	1,086	1,073	1,231	1,048	1,232	867	780	697	589	566	617
Average advance															
New dwellings	14,696	17,000	18,890	20,666	22,404	24,205	27,945	31,607	38,628	45,363	47,157	49,694	50,048	51,002	53,110
Other dwellings	13,118	14,917	16,402	18,023	20,052	21,778	25,361	28,233	34,373	37,181	42,362	44,272	44,141	45,399	47,984
All dwellings	13,340	15,165	16,685	18,350	20,345	22,058	25,629	28,593	34,811	38,105	42,885	44,854	44,805	46,029	46,645
Average advance as a % of average house price	56.7	61.9	67.9	67.5	68.6	69.2	69.5	67.2	66.1	66.4	68.3	69.0	70.4	69.6	70.8

Source: Housing Finance, Council of Mortgage Lenders
Notes: The figures for number of loans are in respect of the number of houses purchased by building society borrowers and further advances etc.
However, until 1980 figures for amounts include further loans to borrowers and the second and subsequent advances of instalment mortgages.
From 1981 further advances etc are included in the 'Other' row. Figures for amounts and numbers of advances exclude Abbey National from July 1989

Table 38b **Building society advances**

	1991				1992				1993				1994			
	Qtr 1	Qtr 2	Qtr 3	Qtr 4	Qtr 1	Qtr 2	Qtr 3	Qtr 4	Qtr 1	Qtr 2	Qtr 3	Qtr 4	Qtr 1	Qtr 2	Qtr 3	Qtr 4
Advances (£ million)																
New dwellings	726	981	970	1,093	732	923	886	813	658	848	832	896	772	1,032	1,107	1,216
+ Other dwellings	6,053	7,216	8,072	7,411	5,913	6,572	7,505	4,145	4,369	6,244	6,739	6,153	5,539	6,946	7,560	6,133
= All dwellings	6,779	8,197	9,042	8,504	6,645	7,495	8,391	4,958	5,027	7,092	7,571	7,049	6,311	7,978	8,667	7,349
+ Other advances	2,327	2,467	2,480	2,228	1,750	1,470	1,507	1,269	1,388	1,278	1,055	1,051	1,122	1,111	1,318	1,521
= Total advances	9,106	10,664	11,522	10,732	8,395	8,965	9,898	6,227	6,415	8,370	8,626	8,100	7,433	9,089	9,985	8,870
Number of dwellings (000s)																
New dwellings	14	18	18	20	14	16	17	16	12	16	16	17	15	19	20	20
+ Other dwellings	137	158	174	158	128	143	162	93	94	132	143	137	124	141	155	124
= All dwellings	151	176	192	178	141	161	179	107	105	147	159	154	138	160	174	145
Average advance																
New dwellings	48,627	50,525	51,040	51,367	50,442	50,567	49,562	50,316	51,051	51,473	50,443	50,952	51,126	52,815	53,381	54,517
Other dwellings	44,172	44,589	46,150	45,591	44,850	44,388	45,299	42,754	44,109	45,655	46,172	45,149	45,805	49,492	48,839	47,337
All dwellings	44,624	45,239	46,646	46,287	45,427	45,083	45,718	43,834	44,882	46,277	46,616	45,842	46,425	49,908	49,394	48,432
Average advance as a % of average house price	67.7	68.3	69.0	70.3	71.4	70.1	69.6	71.1	71.9	70.9	69.5	69.1	70.1	69.7	71.0	72.3

Source: Housing Finance, Council of Mortgage Lenders
Notes: As Table 38a.

Private housing

Table 39a Advances to first-time buyers

Year	1980	1981	1982	1983	1984	1985	1986	1987	1988	1989	1990	1991	1992	1993	1994
Number of loans (000s)	318	364	467	502	566	570	619	505	582	453	413	330	301	305	339
Average dwelling price (A) (£)	17,533	18,166	17,762	19,513	22,174	23,742	27,444	30,097	35,807	39,748	45,234	47,094	46,401	47,597	48,057
Average advance (B) (£)	12,946	14,361	15,109	16,611	18,786	20,260	23,640	25,485	30,374	32,950	37,332	38,963	38,642	38,801	39,748
Average annual income (C) (£)	7,749	8,248	8,602	8,899	9,754	10,466	11,669	12,444	14,103	15,238	17,016	17,607	17,896	17,981	18,166
Average advance as percentage of dwelling price (B/A)	73.8	79.1	85.1	85.1	84.7	85.3	86.1	84.7	84.8	82.9	82.5	82.7	83.3	81.5	82.7
Ratio average advance/ average income (B/C)	1.67	1.74	1.76	1.87	1.93	1.94	2.03	2.05	2.15	2.16	2.19	2.21	2.16	2.16	2.19
Interest rates (%)	14.9	14.0	13.3	11.0	11.8	13.2	11.8	11.5	11.0	13.6	15.0	12.7	10.7	8.1	7.7
Average monthly repayment (D) (£)	122.60	129.82	131.45	126.41	150.48	174.84	191.01	205.92	244.00	314.80	398.18	364.84	317.95	267.05	271.88
Average repayment as percentage of average income (D/C)	19.0	18.9	18.3	17.0	18.5	20.0	19.6	19.9	20.8	24.8	28.1	24.9	21.3	17.8	18.0

Source: Housing Finance, Council of Mortgage Lenders
Notes: All figures relate to the UK. Average income data subject to variation in recording by different societies. From 1989 Q3 Abbey National are excluded from data on number of loans, but retained for other columns. Average mortgage payments are calculated on the basis of a conventional 25 year repayment mortgage, on the basis of the average building society mortgage rate for the year, adjusted to net repayments allowing for changes in tax and MIRAS rates, and the impact of the £30,000 limit on relief against the average advance.

Table 39b Annual changes in house prices, mortgage advances and incomes for first-time buyers
Percentages

Year	1980	1981	1982	1983	1984	1985	1986	1987	1988	1989	1990	1991	1992	1993	1994
Average dwelling price	17.5	3.6	-2.2	9.9	13.6	7.1	15.6	9.7	19.0	11.0	13.8	4.1	-1.5	2.6	1.0
Average advance	14.7	10.9	5.2	9.9	13.1	7.8	16.7	7.8	19.2	8.5	13.3	4.4	-0.8	0.4	2.4
Average income	23.2	6.4	4.3	3.5	9.6	7.3	11.5	6.6	13.3	8.0	11.7	3.5	1.6	0.5	1.0

Source: As Table 39a

Table 39c Advances to former owner-occupiers

Year	1980	1981	1982	1983	1984	1985	1986	1987	1988	1989	1990	1991	1992	1993	1994
Number of loans (000s)	358	373	395	448	517	505	612	542	648	414	367	367	287	259	273
Average dwelling price (A) (£)	28,959	30,110	30,634	34,260	36,717	39,390	45,200	49,987	61,540	71,353	76,170	76,253	76,098	77,284	81,612
Average advance (B) (£)	13,359	15,384	17,316	19,672	21,483	23,300	27,146	29,487	36,013	41,029	45,180	47,669	48,494	50,124	53,583
Average annual income (C) (£)	8,688	9,419	10,178	10,969	11,703	12,702	14,165	15,044	17,108	19,341	22,479	23,191	23,917	24,492	25,623
Average advance as percentage of dwelling price (B/A)	46.1	51.1	56.5	57.4	58.5	59.2	60.1	59.0	58.5	57.5	59.3	62.5	63.7	64.9	65.7
Ratio average advance/ average income (B/C)	1.54	1.63	1.70	1.79	1.84	1.83	1.92	1.96	2.11	2.12	2.00	2.06	2.03	2.05	2.09
Interest rates (%)	14.9	14.0	13.3	11.0	11.8	13.2	11.8	11.5	11.0	13.6	15.0	12.7	10.7	8.1	7.7
Average monthly repayment (D) (£)	126.51	139.07	150.65	149.70	172.08	201.08	219.34	236.19	339.43	434.07	460.72	431.31	376.72	356.28	377.48
Average repayment as percentage of average income (D/C)	17.5	17.7	17.8	16.4	17.6	19.0	18.6	18.8	23.8	26.9	24.6	22.3	18.9	17.5	17.7

Source: Housing Finance, Council of Mortgage Lenders
Notes: As Table 39a.

Table 39d Annual changes in house prices, mortgage advances and incomes for former owner-occupiers

Year	1980	1981	1982	1983	1984	1985	1986	1987	1988	1989	1990	1991	1992	1993	1994
Average dwelling price	20.3	4.0	1.7	11.8	7.2	7.3	14.7	10.6	23.1	15.9	6.8	0.1	-0.2	1.6	5.6
Average advance	12.9	15.2	12.6	13.6	9.2	8.5	16.5	8.6	22.1	13.9	10.1	5.5	1.7	3.4	6.9
Average income	22.3	8.4	8.1	7.8	6.7	8.5	11.5	6.2	13.7	13.1	16.2	3.2	3.1	2.4	4.6

Source: As Table 39c

Private housing

Table 40 Housing wealth, borrowing and equity

	USA 1989	France 1984	Germany 1988	UK: 1988	1992	1994
Billions (of the national currency)						
Gross Domestic Product	5,132	4,362	2,111	471	597	668
Value of owner-occupied stock	6,500	4,189	2,850	985	981	1,009
- House purchase debt	1,900	701	427	222	336	371
= 'Free Equity'	4,600	3,488	2,420	763	645	638
Percentages						
Value of stock as % of GDP	127	96	135	209	164	151
Debt as a % of GDP	37	16	20	47	56	56
Free equity as a % of GDP	90	80	115	162	108	96

Sources: Table 7, House Prices, Land Prices, The Housing Market and House Purchase Debt in Britain and Other Countries, A Holmans, Department of the Environment.
Note: UK figures updated and revised; they do not exactly correspond with figures in Table 5, as they have been adjusted to exclude values for housing association and non-corporate private landlords included within the personal sector.

Table 41 Regional land prices
£ 000s per hectare

	1981	1982	1983	1984	1985	1986	1987	1988	1989	1990	1991	1992	1993
North	76.3	79.6	71.9	80.2	121.6	123.0	105.2	120.7	277.8	216.0	323.0	268.0	243.6
North West	84.9	75.3	97.5	81.6	100.8	124.7	146.1	197.3	393.7	320.9	343.4	315.7	269.7
Yorks & Humberside	61.4	78.1	85.5	96.2	115.5	107.2	122.3	174.8	252.8	349.5	327.7	280.2	239.3
West Midlands	124.1	91.5	130.9	130.9	125.0	150.4	220.4	393.7	458.4	493.8	388.4	345.2	434.0
East Midlands	63.7	72.4	75.5	101.1	94.3	115.7	178.4	313.7	396.5	376.6	334.2	302.9	314.3
East Anglia	71.0	75.8	83.1	94.7	149.1	153.7	273.5	452.5	547.1	406.4	248.2	264.7	302.2
Greater London	390.1	486.0	754.6	600.5	888.2	1,532.3	2,138.4	2,168.0	3,095.8	2,184.7	1,607.0	1,562.7	1,330.2
Rest of South East	168.1	180.5	218.4	286.6	378.9	406.9	604.6	822.1	761.2	583.2	597.5	521.5	477.9
South West	78.9	94.5	138.3	121.7	197.1	196.0	309.1	496.7	493.5	323.3	414.8	404.2	267.3
England	112.0	119.4	155.1	150.7	199.7	240.9	345.3	461.4	454.0	402.5	407.7	350.6	342.4
Wales	31.6	48.8	49.2	74.5	89.0	76.6	83.8	97.8	219.4	228.4	160.0	176.0	169.6
England & Wales	107.3	116.2	150.3	147.0	195.6	233.5	338.1	442.8	435.7	394.1	405.1	343.1	331.4

Sources: Housing and Construction Statistics, Department of the Environment
Note: 1993 figures are provisional.

Table 42a **Average regional house prices**
£

Year	1980	1981	1982	1983	1984	1985	1986	1987	1988	1989	1990	1991	1992	1993	1994
North	17,710	18,602	18,071	20,034	22,604	22,786	24,333	27,275	30,193	37,374	43,655	46,005	48,347	49,337	49,380
Yorks & Humberside	17,689	19,202	18,180	20,870	22,356	23,338	25,607	27,747	32,685	41,817	47,231	52,343	52,278	54,346	53,439
North West	20,092	20,554	20,744	22,827	24,410	25,126	27,503	29,527	34,074	42,126	50,005	53,178	56,377	54,890	56,350
East Midlands	18,928	19,465	19,487	22,034	24,377	25,539	28,483	31,808	40,521	49,421	52,620	55,740	54,599	53,370	54,618
West Midlands	21,663	21,755	20,992	23,133	24,989	25,855	28,437	32,657	41,700	49,815	54,694	58,659	57,827	58,315	59,128
East Anglia	22,808	23,060	23,358	25,814	28,296	31,661	36,061	42,681	57,295	64,610	61,427	61,141	56,770	58,039	56,458
Greater London	30,968	30,757	30,712	34,632	39,346	44,301	54,863	66,024	77,697	82,383	83,821	85,742	78,254	78,399	85,197
Rest of South East	29,832	29,975	29,676	33,753	37,334	40,487	48,544	57,387	72,561	81,635	80,525	79,042	74,347	74,605	77,717
South West	25,293	25,365	25,514	27,996	30,612	32,948	38,536	44,728	58,457	67,004	65,378	65,346	61,460	60,791	62,903
Wales	19,363	20,155	19,662	22,533	23,665	25,005	27,354	29,704	34,244	42,981	46,464	48,989	49,685	52,072	52,144
Scotland	21,754	23,014	22,522	23,822	25,865	26,941	28,242	29,591	31,479	35,394	41,744	48,772	49,224	49,553	50,598
Northern Ireland	23,656	19,890	20,177	20,878	21,455	23,012	25,743	27,773	29,875	30,280	31,849	35,352	37,775	38,878	38,685
United Kingdom	23,596	24,188	23,644	26,469	29,106	31,103	36,276	40,391	49,355	54,846	59,785	62,455	60,821	61,223	63,077

Source: Housing Finance, Council of Mortgage Lenders, derived from the DoE/BSA 5% sample survey.
Note: The average prices are not adjusted for changes in the mix of properties mortgaged to building societies.

Private housing

Table 42b Average regional house prices
Mix adjusted index (1990 = 100)

Year	1980	1981	1982	1983	1984	1985	1986	1987	1988	1989	1990	1991	1992	1993	1994
North	38	41	43	47	50	52	57	61	68	88	100	101	105	107	110
Yorks & Humberside	33	37	37	42	45	47	52	56	66	92	100	104	102	103	100
North West	36	38	39	43	45	47	52	55	65	87	100	101	103	99	101
East Midlands	33	36	37	41	45	48	53	60	77	100	100	98	96	93	94
West Midlands	35	36	37	40	43	45	49	56	75	98	100	100	97	96	96
East Anglia	35	36	38	41	45	51	59	71	96	112	100	97	92	88	88
Greater London	32	33	34	37	44	50	62	76	94	102	100	96	86	85	89
Rest of South East	34	35	36	40	46	51	60	73	94	109	100	95	88	84	87
South West	36	37	38	42	46	50	58	68	91	110	100	97	91	88	89
Wales	35	38	40	44	46	50	54	59	71	96	100	99	98	98	99
Scotland	42	46	50	56	59	62	66	70	76	90	100	108	113	117	118
Northern Ireland	63	62	64	69	72	77	81	87	90	95	100	107	109	114	118
United Kingdom	35	37	38	42	46	50	57	67	84	101	100	99	95	92	94

Source: Housing Finance, Council of Mortgage Lenders, derived from the DoE/BSA 5% sample survey.
Note: The indexes are adjusted for changes in the mix of properties mortgaged to building societies.

Table 43 **Average regional mortgage repayments**
£ per week

Year	1980	1981	1982	1983	1984	1985	1986	1987	1988	1989	1990	1991	1992	1993
North	16.30	20.08	19.98	18.82	19.07	21.27	26.07	28.81	28.29	33.50	40.14	44.34	38.81	35.37
North West	15.48	17.73	20.79	18.03	20.11	23.13	25.42	29.51	26.54	35.20	45.05	49.68	46.91	37.93
Yorks & Humberside	14.14	18.78	20.00	18.53	17.62	24.22	25.45	25.28	26.46	33.24	42.97	47.49	44.24	37.22
West Midlands	18.82	19.49	23.23	18.43	19.84	25.85	27.49	29.00	29.92	40.46	46.92	51.46	48.42	43.46
East Midlands	15.89	18.60	20.67	18.18	18.74	22.32	25.77	25.06	30.72	39.21	50.30	48.34	54.41	42.61
East Anglia	19.63	20.61	26.12	21.07	21.48	27.13	31.49	35.89	38.80	50.50	61.83	50.36	55.22	50.56
Greater London	23.00	27.97	31.32	30.55	32.31	38.48	43.53	51.86	56.37	79.66	89.56	89.35	78.70	76.05
Rest of South East	23.70	29.76	30.25	27.98	27.55	36.85	39.53	46.15	50.79	66.52	81.76	76.08	75.19	65.10
South West	18.58	23.40	24.97	22.20	25.10	28.29	32.41	35.47	38.79	49.46	67.80	62.97	61.97	47.11
Wales	17.74	19.64	21.37	17.40	17.41	24.07	27.26	29.57	27.15	37.63	49.79	43.37	42.37	42.65
Scotland	24.18	26.51	28.32	24.91	25.43	31.11	32.12	33.50	37.17	43.72	48.65	52.69	49.05	39.79
Northern Ireland	18.00	22.97	21.77	16.99	21.16	27.61	23.36	24.69	26.36	42.20	36.89	44.09	35.01	32.15
United Kingdom	19.50	22.97	25.16	22.43	23.22	29.07	31.94	35.81	37.83	49.82	60.39	60.27	57.65	49.49

Source: Family Expenditure Surveys; data for years to 1992 extracted from FES database by Anthony Murphy, Northern Ireland Economic Research Centre.
Note: Repayments include both capital and interest, and are the average for all home buyers with outstanding mortgages.

Private housing

Table 44 Mortgage arrears and repossessions

Year	1980	1981	1982	1983	1984	1985	1986	1987	1988	1989	1990	1991	1992	1993	1994	1995 1st half
Number of mortgages at year end (000s)	6,210	6,336	6,518	6,846	7,313	7,717	8,138	8,283	8,564	9,125	9,415	9,815	9,922	10,137	10,410	10,443
Repossessions during year	3,480	4,870	6,860	8,420	12,400	19,300	24,090	26,390	18,510	15,810	43,890	75,540	68,540	58,540	49,190	25,200
Cases in mortgage arrears																
12+ months arrears	-	-	5,540	7,530	9,510	13,120	13,020	14,960	10,280	13,840	36,100	91,740	147,040	151,810	117,110	94,710
6-12 months arrears	15,530	21,540	27,380	29,440	48,270	57,110	52,080	55,490	42,810	66,800	123,110	183,610	205,010	164,620	133,700	114,890
3 - 5 months arrears	-	-	-	-	-	97,000	125,400	121,000	124,800	122,000	206,600	305,500	275,400	242,050	191,590	-
2 months arrears	-	-	-	-	-	140,000	145,200	164,400	171,600	153,900	237,500	269,800	207,800	198,400	135,840	-

Sources: Housing Finance, Council of Mortgage Lenders; Janet Ford, Roof (figures for 2 & 3-5 months arrears).
Notes: Properties taken into possession include those voluntarily surrendered. 6-12 month arrears figures are for the end of the year. 2 and 3-5 month arrears figures are for the March of the year. Changes in the mortgage rate have the effect of changing monthly repayments and hence the number of months in arrears which a given amount represents. 1995 figures are for the first half of the year only

Table 45a Regional court orders for mortgage repossession in England and Wales

	Actions entered					Suspended orders					Orders made				
Region	1990	1991	1992	1993	1994	1990	1991	1992	1993	1994	1990	1991	1992	1993	1994
North	4,943	6,917	6,064	4,639	3,742	1,997	3,368	4,216	3,385	2,820	1,549	2,192	2,138	1,652	1,322
Yorks & Humberside	10,434	14,146	10,280	8,447	7,619	3,002	5,103	4,763	4,540	3,154	3,792	5,741	4,171	2,892	2,320
East Midlands	11,036	13,468	10,110	7,672	6,045	3,610	4,480	4,946	4,233	3,185	3,828	5,224	4,346	2,752	2,361
East Anglia	5,558	6,237	5,012	3,884	2,974	1,420	1,991	1,752	2,237	1,291	2,299	3,060	2,328	1,804	1,141
Greater London	29,291	35,265	25,681	21,250	15,545	12,076	13,051	12,444	10,640	8,399	11,146	14,400	11,409	8,825	6,797
South East	35,673	44,610	33,780	27,698	19,896	11,112	17,223	16,832	15,154	10,797	15,422	18,561	14,222	10,484	7,956
South West	12,209	16,694	12,544	11,742	7,355	3,406	5,786	5,182	5,189	3,473	4,812	6,468	5,085	4,056	2,537
West Midlands	13,596	17,693	13,974	10,299	8,614	4,456	6,475	6,384	5,488	4,372	4,582	6,940	5,235	3,358	2,600
North West	14,974	21,384	17,158	14,103	11,726	5,329	8,112	8,123	7,802	5,800	4,708	7,312	6,331	4,897	3,618
Wales	7,636	10,235	7,588	6,447	4,442	2,382	3,457	3,673	3,598	2,253	2,580	3,958	3,403	2,297	1,485
England and Wales	145,350	186,649	142,191	116,181	87,958	48,790	69,046	68,315	62,266	45,544	54,718	73,856	58,668	43,017	32,137

Source: Answers to Parliamentary Questions - 12/12/91 & 13/2/92; Mortgage possession statistics, Lord Chancellors Department.

Table 45b Regional court orders as a percentage of the total for England and Wales

Region	Actions entered					Suspended orders					Orders made				
	1990	1991	1992	1993	1994	1990	1991	1992	1993	1994	1990	1991	1992	1993	1994
North	3.4	3.7	4.3	4.0	4.3	4.1	4.9	6.2	5.4	6.2	2.8	3.0	3.6	3.8	4.1
Yorks & Humberside	7.2	7.6	7.2	7.3	8.7	6.2	7.4	7.0	7.3	6.9	6.9	7.8	7.1	6.7	7.2
East Midlands	7.6	7.2	7.1	6.6	6.9	7.4	6.5	7.2	6.8	7.0	7.0	7.1	7.4	6.4	7.3
East Anglia	3.8	3.3	3.5	3.3	3.4	2.9	2.9	2.6	3.6	2.8	4.2	4.1	4.0	4.2	3.6
Greater London	20.2	18.9	18.1	18.3	17.7	24.8	18.9	18.2	17.1	18.4	20.4	19.5	19.4	20.5	21.2
South East	24.5	23.9	23.8	23.8	22.6	22.8	24.9	24.6	24.3	23.7	28.2	25.1	24.2	24.4	24.8
South West	8.4	8.9	8.8	10.1	8.4	7.0	8.4	7.6	8.3	7.6	8.8	8.8	8.7	9.4	7.9
West Midlands	9.4	9.5	9.8	8.9	9.8	9.1	9.4	9.3	8.8	9.6	8.4	9.4	8.9	7.8	8.1
North West	10.3	11.5	12.1	12.1	13.3	10.9	11.7	11.9	12.5	12.7	8.6	9.9	10.8	11.4	11.3
Wales	5.3	5.5	5.3	5.5	5.1	4.9	5.0	5.4	5.8	4.9	4.7	5.4	5.8	5.3	4.6
Total	100	100	100	100	100	100	100	100	100	100	100	100	100	100	100

Source: As Table 45a.

Table 46 Court actions for mortgage repossessions in England and Wales

Year & Quarter	1991				1992				1993				1994				1995	
	Q1	Q2	Q3	Q4	Q1	Q2	Q3	Q4	Q1	Q2	Q3	Q4	Q1	Q2	Q3	Q4	Q1	Q2
Actions entered	43,507	49,358	51,037	42,747	42,267	35,777	34,540	29,583	31,731	33,371	32,276	18,803	21,983	22,171	22,884	21,046	21,345	19,560
Suspended orders	14,122	16,407	19,588	18,717	19,155	17,666	16,308	15,319	15,246	15,764	17,160	14,096	10,664	11,293	11,983	11,659	11,063	11,076
Orders made	17,192	18,211	20,218	18,171	16,558	15,504	14,353	12,337	11,664	10,762	11,041	9,550	7,125	8,113	8,828	8,133	7,767	7,725

Source: Mortgage Possession Statistics, Lord Chancellors Department.

Private housing

Table 47 Types of letting in the private rented sector

Type of letting	1988 000s	1990 000s	1993 000s	1988 %	1990 %	1993 %
All assured (A)	60	540	1,204	4	30	56
Assured	-	360	378	-	20	17
Assured shorthold	-	140	826	-	8	38
Protected shorthold & pre-89 assured	60	40	-	4	2	-
All regulated (B)	1,070	590	407	59	33	19
Regulated, registered rent	470	320	245	26	18	11
Regulated, unregistered rent	600	270	162	33	15	8
All not accessible to the public (C)	510	480	375	28	27	17
Not accessible to the public, rent paid	240	230	146	13	13	7
Not accessible to the public, rent free	270	250	230	15	14	11
Resident landlord (D)	110	90	158	6	4	7
No security (E)	60	90	22	4	5	1
Total (A)+(B)+(C)+(D)+(E)	1,810	1,790	2,166	100	100	100

Source: Private Renting in England, 1993/94: Survey of English Housing, HMSO, 1995. Department of the Environment.
Notes: Resident landlord lettings in 1993 include lodgers who are members of owner occupier or social rented sector households; such lodgers were not identified in the earlier surveys. Lettings not accessible to the public include tied tenancies, lettings of student residences, and lettings at low rents to friends and relatives. Pre-1989 protected shorthold lettings have been grouped with the various forms of assured tenancies, but legally they are a form of regulated tenancy.

Table 48 Investment in Business Expansion Scheme Assured Tenancy Companies

	1988/89	1989/90	1990/91	1991/92	1992/93	1993/94	Total for all years
Number of schemes	1,962	484	455	465	530	550	4,446
Amount of investment (£ million)	368	162	284	368	880	937	2,999
Value of income tax relief (£ million) (A)	130	55	105	135	315	335	1,075
Number of lettings (B)	6,400	3,100	5,700	9,300	21,400	28,000	73,900
Value of income tax relief per letting (£) (A)/(B)	20,313	17,742	18,421	14,516	14,720	11,964	16,279

Source: Inland Revenue Statistics, Inland Revenue
Note: The figures for the initial value of income tax relief do not take account of any subsequent eligibility for Capital Gains tax relief.

Housing expenditure plans

Table 49 Territorial analysis of identifiable General Government Expenditure
£ million

	1985-86	1986-87	1987-88	1988-89	1989-90	1990-91	1991-92	1992-93	1993-94
Housing expenditure (A)									
England	3,099	2,932	2,957	2,055	3,926	3,548	4,330	4,835	4,094
Wales	135	183	231	185	249	323	347	428	390
Scotland	624	586	562	441	589	649	696	646	649
Northern Ireland	346	335	337	335	268	245	255	261	237
United Kingdom	4,204	4,036	4,086	3,015	5,033	4,765	5,627	6,169	5,371
All government expenditure (B)									
England	84,557	90,646	96,908	101,681	112,795	124,569	143,030	157,865	167,848
Wales	5,565	6,192	6,627	7,121	7,671	8,557	9,553	10,944	11,372
Scotland	11,682	12,528	13,277	13,975	14,973	16,300	17,881	20,323	21,926
Northern Ireland	4,318	4,620	4,910	5,633	5,930	6,121	6,704	7,295	7,802
United Kingdom	106,122	113,986	121,721	128,410	141,368	155,527	177,169	196,427	208,448
Housing share of government expenditure (A/B) (percentages)									
England	3.7	3.2	3.1	2.0	3.5	2.8	3.0	3.1	2.4
Wales	2.4	3.0	3.5	2.6	3.2	3.8	3.6	3.9	3.4
Scotland	5.3	4.7	4.2	3.2	3.9	4.0	3.9	3.2	3.0
Northern Ireland	8.0	7.2	6.9	5.9	4.5	4.0	3.8	3.6	3.0
United Kingdom	4.0	3.5	3.4	2.3	3.6	3.1	3.2	3.1	2.6

Sources: Public Expenditure Analyses, Cm 1520, Cm 1920, Cm 2219, Cm 2519 & Cm 2821
Notes: General Government Expenditure is net of housing capital receipts, which are treated as 'negative expenditure' rather than income. This covers the use of receipts to redeem debt by local authorities in England and Wales. Housing expenditure excludes housing benefit subsidy.

Table 50a Gross social housing investment in Great Britain
£ billions (cash)

Year	1979/80	1980/81	1981/82	1982/83	1983/84	1984/85	1985/86	1986/87	1987/88	1988/89	1989/90	1990/91	1991/92	1992/93	1993/94	1994/95
England	3,504	3,400	3,269	4,065	4,405	4,285	3,792	3,773	4,073	4,440	6,097	4,431	4,580	5,170	4,989	4,790
Wales	153	146	128	185	257	210	180	239	293	295	376	371	370	457	431	403
Scotland	382	477	513	577	706	583	594	655	836	889	952	942	958	941	992	985
Great Britain	4,039	4,023	3,910	4,827	5,368	5,078	4,566	4,667	5,202	5,624	7,425	5,744	5,908	6,568	6,412	6,178

Sources: See Tables 54a, 65, 66 and 70.
Note: Figures exclude private finance. See source tables for further notes.

Table 50b Gross social housing investment in Great Britain at constant prices
£ billions (1993-94 prices)

Year	1979/80	1980/81	1981/82	1982/83	1983/84	1984/85	1985/86	1986/87	1987/88	1988/89	1989/90	1990/91	1991/92	1992/93	1993/94	1994/95
England	8,609	7,054	6,180	7,182	7,441	6,889	5,780	5,581	5,721	5,842	7,499	5,047	4,909	5,330	4,989	4,696
Wales	375	302	242	327	434	338	274	354	412	388	462	423	397	471	431	395
Scotland	939	990	970	1,019	1,193	937	905	969	1,174	1,170	1,171	1,073	1,027	970	992	966
Great Britain	9,924	8,346	7,391	8,528	9,068	8,164	6,960	6,904	7,306	7,400	9,133	6,542	6,332	6,771	6,412	6,057

Sources: As Table 50a.

Housing expenditure plans

Table 51 Local authority gross investment plans in Great Britain
£ million

		1986/87	1987/88	1988/89	1989/90	1990/91	1991/92	1992/93	1993/94	1994/95	1995/96	1996/97	1997/98
	England												
	Capital provision[1]	1,568	1,513	1,374	1,234	1,697	1,798	1,622	1,438	1,165	1,166	1,253	1,247
+	Estate Action	45	75	140	190	180	268	348	357	373	314	-	-
+	Local resources[2]	1,380	1,659	2,057	3,674	1,289	774	784	1,278	1,563	1,150	1,000	950
=	Total	2,993	3,247	3,571	5,098	3,166	2,840	2,754	3,073	3,101	2,630	2,253	2,197
	Wales												
	Capital provision[1,3]	142	155	122	132	198	212	274	264	266	268	-	-
+	Local resources[2]	45	75	107	171	71	44	21	36	29	24	-	-
=	Total	187	230	229	303	269	256	295	300	295	292	-	-
	Scotland												
	Capital provision[1]	312	411	351	312	322	311	273	285	315	291	286	287
+	Local resources[2]	141	193	281	332	299	276	307	309	286	290	281	273
=	Total	453	604	632	643	621	587	580	594	601	581	567	560
	Great Britain												
	Capital provision[1]	2,068	2,154	1,987	1,868	2,397	2,589	2,517	2,344	2,119	2,039	-	-
+	Local resources[2]	1,566	1,927	2,445	4,177	1,659	1,094	1,112	1,623	1,878	1,464	-	-
=	Total	3,634	4,081	4,432	6,044	4,056	3,683	3,629	3,967	3,997	3,503	-	-

Sources: See tables 55, 66, 72.
Notes: 1. Capital provision includes all credit approvals, and capital grants, excluding provision for the Estate Action programme, which is shown seperately, and the Urban Programme.
2. Local resources comprise use of capital receipts and RCCOs (revenue contributions to capital outlay). Estimates of use of local resources are included for 1995/96 and subsequent years.
3. Welsh capital provision figures include capital vired to Housing for Wales for local housing association schemes.

Table 52 Housing associations' gross investment plans, including use of private finance, in Great Britain
£ million

	1986/87	1987/88	1988/89	1989/90	1990/91	1991/92	1992/93	1993/94	1994/95	1995/96	1996/97	1997/98
England[1]												
Housing Corporation	809	864	881	1,034	1,234	1,703	2,370	1,843	1,527	1,197	1,178	1,182
Local authorities	145	156	128	308	193	179	286	393	353	325	250	225
Private finance	0	0	100	150	175	240	950	1,000	1,050	1,000	950	925
Total	954	1,020	1,109	1,492	1,602	2,122	3,606	3,236	2,930	2,522	2,378	2,332
Housing for Wales[2]												
Capital programme	52	63	66	73	102	115	162	131	121	101	-	-
Local authorities	0	2	7	17	14	17	11	10	6	6	-	-
Private finance	0	8	8	22	33	53	73	70	69	65	-	-
Total	52	73	81	112	149	185	246	211	196	172	-	-
Scottish Homes[2,3]												
Capital programme	114	132	164	203	195	221	255	263	269	269	-	-
Local authorities	-	-	-	-	11	8	3	10	-	-	-	-
Private finance	0	0	0	10	37	42	55	54	81	94	-	-
Total	114	132	164	213	243	271	313	327	350	363	-	-
Great Britain												
'Housing corporations'[4]	975	1,059	1,111	1,310	1,531	2,039	2,787	2,237	1,917	1,567	-	-
Local authority	145	158	135	325	218	204	300	413	359	331	-	-
Private finance	0	8	108	182	245	335	1,078	1,124	1,200	1,159	-	-
Total	1,120	1,225	1,354	1,817	1,994	2,578	4,165	3,774	3,476	3,057	-	-

Sources: Welsh private finance figures from Cm 1916, 2215, 2515 &2815, Scottish figures from Scottish Homes. English private finance figures are author's estimates based on various NFHA, DoE and other sources.

Notes: 1. English figures include HAG on deferred interest.
2. In Scotland and Wales local authorities provide funding for housing associations through Scottish Homes and Housing for Wales.
3. Scottish figures exclude provision for NLF repayments, expenditure on Scottish Homes properties and 'GRO' grants to private developers.
4. 'Housing Corporations' includes Housing for Wales (Tai Cmyru) and Scottish Homes.

Housing expenditure plans

Table 53 UK local authority housing revenue accounts
£ million

	1980	1981	1982	1983	1984	1985	1986	1987	1988	1989	1990	1991	1992	1993
Income														
Rent on dwellings:														
Paid by tenants [1]	1,778	2,719	3,057	2,019	2,012	2,063	2,187	2,239	2,389	2,477	2,813	3,085	3,275	3,019
Rent rebates[1]	541	473	782	1,881	2,005	2,190	2,285	2,389	2,547	2,773	3,003	3,442	4,171	4,768
Rent on other properties	75	83	96	65	60	108	125	130	144	173	183	192	230	268
Subsidies:														
Central government[2]	1,715	1,258	644	434	432	537	521	501	577	688	1,132	1,175	1,055	947
Local authorities[2]	516	554	571	637	632	578	538	502	537	503	129	-	-	1
Other income	133	188	267	317	353	393	306	305	336	402	409	419	436	445
Total	4,758	5,275	5,417	5,353	5,494	5,869	5,962	6,066	6,530	7,016	7,669	8,313	9,167	9,448
Expenditure														
Supervision and management	649	783	861	941	1,005	1,084	1,172	1,251	1,401	1,551	1,631	1,741	1,966	1,921
Repairs	1,015	1,141	1,261	1,420	1,506	1,558	1,616	1,686	1,845	1,982	2,253	2,373	2,590	2,566
Debt interest (net)	2,715	2,774	2,586	2,309	2,276	2,447	2,389	2,270	2,347	2,280	2,480	2,550	2,562	2,562
Capital repayments	306	341	377	405	433	449	476	520	546	583	558	544	541	540
Other current expenditure	63	72	118	135	144	184	118	107	142	245	326	391	427	394
Balance	10	164	214	143	130	147	191	232	249	375	421	714	1,081	1,465
Total	4,758	5,275	5,417	5,353	5,494	5,869	5,962	6,066	6,530	7,016	7,669	8,313	9,167	9,448

Source: United Kingdom National Accounts (1991 - 1994 editions), CSO.
Notes: 1. Prior to April 1983 Supplementary Benefit in respect of rent was generally paid direct to tenants. After that date it became housing benefit automatically paid direct to the local authority. As a result of that change those payments transfer from the rent paid by tenants to the rent rebate line.
2. From April 1990 local authority subsidies were ended. In England and Wales equivalent amounts were then included in the calculation of central government subsidy under transitional arrangements. Restrictions on local authority subsidies, leading to their phased reduction, applied from 1981/82 onwards in Scotland.

Table 54a Housing capital investment in England
£ million (cash)

Year	1979/80	1980/81	1981/82	1982/83	1983/84	1984/85	1985/86	1986/87	1987/88	1988/89	1989/90	1990/91	1991/92	1992/93	1993/94	1994/95
Gross housing investment																
Local authority investment:																
+ New build & acquisitions	1,168	1,008	760	736	743	792	704	612	625	782	932	544	431	211	238	142
+ HRA stock renovation	723	670	620	962	1,148	1,280	1,315	1,521	1,742	1,904	2,953	1,721	1,483	1,561	1,684	1,929
+ Housing association	189	170	142	134	138	147	120	145	156	128	308	193	179	286	393	353
+ Private renovation	227	263	321	550	1,040	869	581	519	535	458	489	488	545	527	587	590
+ Home-ownership	626	611	776	830	477	391	276	196	188	300	417	176	174	136	111	106
+ Urban programme	14	9	14	23	25	22	27	24	25	34	26	42	29	33	45	35
= Local authority total	2,948	2,730	2,632	3,234	3,572	3,501	3,023	3,017	3,272	3,605	5,125	3,164	2,841	2,754	3,058	3,155
+ New towns	161	165	115	71	85	81	56	40	50	46	39	32	27	18	12	17
+ Housing Corporation	400	508	521	755	734	697	711	715	752	791	935	1,234	1,703	2,371	1,843	1,527
+ HATS													10	27	78	91
+ Other (net)	-5	-3	2	4	14	6	3	1	-1	-2	-2	1	-1	0	-2	0
= Total gross investment (A)	3,504	3,400	3,269	4,065	4,405	4,285	3,792	3,773	4,073	4,440	6,097	4,431	4,580	5,170	4,989	4,790
Capital receipts																
Local authority	799	1,037	1,684	2,491	2,156	1,941	1,838	2,034	2,369	3,423	3,319	2,395	1,549	1,432	1,829	1,591
+ New towns	20	19	38	63	84	88	64	98	143	226	207	111	195	47	166	62
+ Housing Corporation	4	13	29	76	110	86	101	129	117	139	125	79	64	66	48	48
= Total capital receipts (B)	822	1,069	1,751	2,629	2,350	2,116	2,002	2,260	2,629	3,788	3,651	2,585	1,808	1,545	2,043	1,701
Net housing investment																
Local authority	2,149	1,692	948	743	1,416	1,560	1,185	984	903	182	1,806	769	1,292	1,322	1,229	1,564
+ New towns	141	146	77	8	1	-7	-8	-58	-93	-180	-169	-79	-168	-29	-154	-45
+ Housing Corporation	397	495	491	680	624	610	610	586	635	652	810	1,155	1,639	2,305	1,795	1,479
+ HATS													10	27	78	91
+ Other (net)	-5	-3	2	4	14	6	3	1	-1	-2	-2	1	-1	0	-2	0
= Total net investment (A-B)	2,682	2,330	1,518	1,435	2,055	2,170	1,790	1,513	1,444	652	2,446	1,846	2,772	3,625	2,946	3,089

Sources: Public Expenditure Plans, Department of the Environment.
Notes: Local authority capital receipts are shown gross of loans to purchasing council tenants, which are also included as expenditure in the home-ownership row.
Housing Corporation expenditure figures for 1989/90 and earlier years exclude capitalised interest, which has only in recent years been added to the Corporation's expenditure total. Other expenditure includes the now abolished 'homeloan' scheme. Local authority stock renovation includes the Estate Action programme. 1994/95 figures are provisional.

Table 54b Housing capital investment in England at constant prices
£ million (1993/94 prices)

Year	1979/80	1980/81	1981/82	1982/83	1983/84	1984/85	1985/86	1986/87	1987/88	1988/89	1989/90	1990/91	1991/92	1992/93	1993/94	1994/95
Gross housing investment																
Local authority investment:																
+ New build & acquisitions	2,870	2,090	1,436	1,299	1,256	1,273	1,073	906	878	1,029	1,146	620	462	218	238	139
+ HRA stock renovation	1,777	1,389	1,173	1,700	1,940	2,058	2,004	2,250	2,447	2,505	3,632	1,960	1,589	1,609	1,684	1,891
+ Housing association	465	352	268	237	233	237	183	214	219	169	379	220	192	295	393	346
+ Private renovation	559	545	607	971	1,756	1,398	885	768	751	603	602	556	584	543	587	578
+ Home-ownership	1,537	1,267	1,466	1,466	806	628	421	290	264	394	513	200	186	140	111	104
+ Urban programme	34	19	26	41	42	35	41	36	35	45	32	48	31	34	45	34
= Local authority total	7,242	5,663	4,976	5,714	6,033	5,629	4,608	4,464	4,595	4,743	6,303	3,604	3,045	2,839	3,058	3,093
+ New towns	395	343	217	125	143	130	85	59	71	61	48	36	29	19	12	17
+ Housing Corporation	983	1,054	984	1,334	1,239	1,120	1,084	1,057	1,056	1,041	1,150	1,405	1,825	2,444	1,843	1,497
+ HATS													11	28	78	89
+ Other (net)	-11	-7	3	8	24	10	4	1	-2	-3	-2	1	-1	0	-2	0
= Total gross investment (A)	8,609	7,053	6,179	7,182	7,440	6,889	5,780	5,581	5,720	5,843	7,499	5,047	4,909	5,330	4,989	4,696
Capital receipts																
Local authority	1,963	2,152	3,184	4,401	3,642	3,121	2,802	3,008	3,327	4,504	4,082	2,728	1,660	1,476	1,829	1,560
+ New towns	49	39	71	111	142	141	97	144	201	297	255	126	209	48	166	61
+ Housing Corporation	9	27	55	134	185	139	154	190	164	183	154	90	69	68	48	47
= Total capital receipts (B)	2,021	2,218	3,310	4,646	3,970	3,401	3,052	3,343	3,692	4,984	4,490	2,944	1,938	1,593	2,043	1,668
Net housing investment																
Local authority	5,279	3,511	1,792	1,314	2,391	2,508	1,806	1,455	1,268	240	2,221	876	1,385	1,363	1,229	1,533
+ New towns	346	304	146	14	1	-11	-12	-86	-131	-237	-208	-90	-180	-30	-154	-44
+ Housing Corporation	974	1,027	929	1,201	1,054	981	930	867	892	858	996	1,315	1,757	2,376	1,795	1,450
+ HATS													11	28	78	89
+ Other (net)	-11	-7	3	8	24	10	4	1	-2	-3	-2	1	-1	0	-2	0
= Total net investment (A-B)	6,588	4,835	2,869	2,536	3,471	3,488	2,728	2,238	2,028	858	3,008	2,103	2,971	3,737	2,946	3,028

Sources and Notes: As Table 54a.

Table 55 **Housing capital provision in England**
£ million

	1985/86 outturn	1986/87 outturn	1987/88 outturn	1988/89 outturn	1989/90 outturn	1990/91 outturn	1991/92 outturn	1992/93 outturn	1993/94 outturn	1994/95 estimated outturn	1995/96 plans	1996/97 plans	1997/98 plans
Housing Corporation													
Gross (A)	841	809	864	881	1,034	1,234	1,704	2,372	1,843	1,527	1,197	1,178	1,192
- Capital receipts	105	132	124	143	127	79	65	66	48	48	48	50	50
= Net Housing Corporation (B)	737	677	740	738	907	1,154	1,639	2,306	1,795	1,479	1,149	1,128	1,142
Local authorities													
Credit approvals	1,586	1,423	1,362	1,178	908	1,386	1,441	1,194	1,020	873	869	972	959
+ Capital grants	135	145	151	196	326	311	357	428	418	292	297	281	288
+ Estate Action		45	75	140	190	180	268	348	357	373	314		
= Total capital provision (C)	1,721	1,613	1,588	1,514	1,424	1,877	2,066	1,970	1,795	1,538	1,480	1,253	1,247
+ LA 'self financed'	970	1,380	1,659	2,057	3,674	1,289	774	784	1,278	1,563	1,150	1,000	950
= Gross LA capital (D)	2,691	2,993	3,247	3,571	5,098	3,166	2,840	2,754	3,073	3,101	2,630	2,253	2,197
HATS (E)	0	0	0	0	0	0	10	27	78	88	90	90	90
Other (F)	3	1	-1	1	1	0	-1	0	0	0	0	0	0
Total central government capital provision (B+C+E+F)	2,460	2,290	2,327	2,253	2,332	3,031	3,714	4,303	3,668	3,105	2,719	2,471	2,479
Total gross capital (A+D+E+F)	3,535	3,803	4,109	4,452	6,133	4,400	4,553	5,153	4,994	4,716	3,917	3,521	3,479

Sources: Cm 1508, Cm 1908, Cm 2207, Cm 2507 & Cm 2807, Department of the Environment.
Notes: Author's estimates of local authority 'self financed' capital spending for 1993/94 and subsequent years. These are based on estimates for capital receipts and revenue financed investment (RCCOs). Credit approvals are shown net of provision for the Estate Action programme. This is shown separately, as from 1994/95 the programme has been switched to the Single Regeneration Budget. No figures have been given for provision for the Estate Action programme in 1996/97 and 1997/98.

Table 56 Housing Corporation Approved Development Programme
£ million

Item	1989-90 outturn	1990-91 outturn	1991-92 outturn	1992-93 outturn	1993-94 outturn	1994-95 estimate	1995-96 plans	1996-97 plans	1997-98 plans
Housing for rent	826	1,008	1,496	2,203	1,539	1,248	907	856	857
+ Housing for sale	107	65	87	124	290	273	282	315	328
+ HAG on deferred interest	99	158	118	42	14	4	1	0	0
+ Other capital expenditure	2	3	2	1	1	2	7	7	7
= Gross capital expenditure	1,034	1,234	1,703	2,370	1,844	1,527	1,197	1,178	1,192
- Capital receipts	127	79	65	66	48	48	48	50	50
= Net capital expenditure	907	1,156	1,638	2,304	1,795	1,479	1,149	1,128	1,142

Sources: Cms 1508, 1908, 2207, 2507 & 2807.
Notes: Housing for rent figures include major repairs, mini-HAG and Tenants Incentive Scheme.

Table 57 Housing Corporation planned revenue expenditure
£ million

Item	1989-90 outturn	1990-91 outturn	1991-92 outturn	1992-93 outturn	1993-94 outturn	1994-95 estimate	1995-96 plans	1996-97 plans	1997-98 plans
Hostel Deficit Grant/Special Needs Management Allowance	29	39	62	95	97	128	128	129	129
+ Other grants and subsidies	25	29	39	37	40	68	55	59	59
+ Running costs	20	24	25	28	30	30	30	30	30
= Total revenue expenditure	74	92	127	160	176	221	216	221	221

Sources: Cms 1508, 1908, 2207, 2507 & 2807, Housing Corporation
Notes: Hostel Deficit Grant has now been replaced by the 'Special Needs Management Allowance'. The outturn increase in the costs of 'Other grants and subsidies' in 1994/95 is the result of increased grants for Corporation tax relief. This has not been reflected in the budget forecasts for future years.

Table 58a Regional local authority housing capital expenditure in England
£ million

Region	1982/83	1983/84	1984/85	1985/86	1986/87	1987/88	1988/89	1989/90	1990/91	1991/92	1992/93	1993/94
North (excl Cumbria)	197	197	174	145	153	174	166	186	142	151	143	161
Yorkshire & Humberside	287	302	251	234	222	265	289	361	271	252	259	270
North West	452	500	441	407	383	432	434	532	386	363	399	437
East Midlands	242	254	219	180	197	201	212	292	185	185	171	202
West Midlands	300	355	314	275	275	286	309	423	313	282	301	323
Eastern	282	314	343	309	302	327	428	572	347	331	247	363
Greater London	848	913	983	780	838	890	909	1,504	791	650	670	736
South East	338	406	418	354	364	430	533	663	416	325	320	336
South West	214	250	227	194	197	213	258	412	250	228	202	236
Unallocated [1]	75	80	131	145	86	52	66	181	63	51	38	46
England	3,235	3,571	3,501	3,023	3,017	3,270	3,604	5,126	3,164	2,818	2,750	3,111

Sources: Answer to Parliamentary Question, 14/12/92, Department of the Environment.
Note: 1. This includes items, such as the housing element of the Urban Programme, for which regional figures are not available

Table 58b Local authority regional shares of housing capital expenditure in England
Percentages

Region	1982/83	1983/84	1984/85	1985/86	1986/87	1987/88	1988/89	1989/90	1990/91	1991/92	1992/93	1993/94	Shares of 'GNI' [1]
North (excl Cumbria)	6.2	5.6	5.2	5.0	5.2	5.4	4.7	3.8	4.6	5.5	5.3	5.3	4.5
Yorkshire & Humberside	9.1	8.7	7.4	8.1	7.6	8.2	8.2	7.3	8.7	9.1	9.6	8.8	8.1
North West	14.3	14.3	13.1	14.1	13.1	13.4	12.3	10.8	12.4	13.1	14.7	14.2	9.7
East Midlands	7.7	7.3	6.5	6.3	6.7	6.2	6.0	5.9	6.0	6.7	6.3	6.6	6.0
West Midlands	9.5	10.2	9.3	9.6	9.4	8.9	8.7	8.6	10.1	10.2	11.1	10.6	9.1
Eastern	8.9	9.0	10.2	10.7	10.3	10.2	12.1	11.6	11.2	12.0	9.1	11.8	8.4
Greater London	26.8	26.2	29.2	27.1	28.6	27.7	25.7	30.4	25.5	23.5	24.7	4.0	36.2
South East	10.7	11.6	12.4	12.3	12.4	13.4	15.1	13.4	13.4	11.7	11.8	11.0	10.9
South West	6.8	7.2	6.7	6.7	6.7	6.6	7.3	8.3	8.1	8.2	7.4	7.7	9.9
England	100	100	100	100	100	100	100	100	100	100	100	100	100

Sources: Answer to Parliamentary Question, 14/12/92, Department of the Environment.
Notes: 1. The 'GNI' is the General Needs Index of statistical indicators used in the regional allocation of local authority housing capital guidelines. The regional shares shown as given by the Index are those for 1994/95.

Housing expenditure plans

Table 59 **Estate Action Programme in England**

	1986-87	1987-88	1988-89	1989-90	1990-91	1991-92	1992-93	1993-94	1994-95
Financial provision (£m)	45	75	140	190	180	268	348	357	373
Continuing schemes	0	85	130	213	212	210	236	245	285
New schemes started of which:	138	106	190	162	118	163	162	163	115
involving private finance	18	22	14	30	41	77	107	105	88
dwellings improved		47,000	79,400	63,700	49,500	62,600	69,200	66,000	58,800
disposals to the private sector	3,400	3,200	4,000	4,200	2,500	3,800	3,000	3,900	2,000
Estates where tenants participate in management	3	7	8	30	47	46	53	39	29

Sources: Cms 1508, 1908, 2207, 2507 & 2807.
Notes: Disposals of dwellings do not include Right-to-Buy sales. From 1994/95 the Estate Action Programme has formed part of the Single Regeneration Budget (SRB). £314 million has been provided in 1995/96 for expenditure on continuing schemes. No more new Estate Action schemes will now be established.

Table 60a Large-scale voluntary transfers of council housing in England December 1988-March 1993

Authority	Date of transfer	Number of dwellings	Transfer price £m	Price per dwelling £	Loan facilities at transfer £m	Housing debt (HRA) £m	Set up costs £m	Treasury 'levy' £m	Useable receipt £m	Net balance £m
Chiltern	15/12/88	4,650	32.9	6,926	62.7	21.0	1.1	-	8.2	2.6
Sevenoaks	29/ 3/89	6,526	65.5	10,037	68.0	25.0	1.8	-	16.4	22.3
Newbury	30/11/89	7,053	47.0	6,664	48.5	43.0	1.4	-	2.6	0.0
Swale	28/ 3/90	7,352	55.2	7,501	75.0	23.0	1.6	-	13.8	16.8
Broadland	4/ 4/90	3,721	25.1	6,739	40.5	12.1	1.8	-	6.3	4.9
North Bedfordshire	13/ 6/90	7,472	64.3	8,605	130.0	39.7	3.1	-	16.1	5.4
Medina	27/ 7/90	2,825	27.9	9,858	35.3	12.6	1.4	-	7.0	6.9
Rochester upon Medway	27/ 7/90	8,029	77.0	9,590	90.0	11.5	4.5	-	19.3	41.8
South Wight	30/ 7/90	2,119	22.8	10,776	36.5	11.3	1.2	-	5.7	4.6
Mid Sussex	9/11/90	4,426	44.2	9,984	90.0	25.0	2.3	-	11.1	5.9
East Dorset	3/12/90	2,245	21.6	9,620	41.0	11.8	1.2	-	5.4	3.2
Tonbridge & Malling	15/ 1/91	6,382	53.8	8,524	97.0	18.3	2.2	-	13.5	19.9
Ryedale	28/ 2/91	3,353	28.3	8,436	54.0	10.7	1.6	-	7.1	8.9
South Buckinghamshire	26/ 3/91	3,319	34.0	10,244	60.0	19.2	1.5	-	8.5	4.8
Christchurch	28/ 3/91	1,621	15.4	9,144	34.1	4.4	1.1	-	3.9	6.1
Suffolk Coastal	22/ 5/91	5,272	34.0	6,508	74.5	11.1	2.1	-	8.5	12.3
Tunbridge Wells	29/ 1/92	5,519	58.1	10,221	102.0	40.0	2.8	-	14.5	0.8
Bromley	6/ 4/92	12,393	117.6	9,489	136.0	0.0	5.8	-	29.4	82.4
Surrey Heath	15/ 1/93	2,885	28.7	9,962	45.0	0.0	1.7	-	7.2	19.8
Breckland	30/ 3/93	6,781	60.2	8,879	90.0	19.8	2.5	-	15.1	22.9
East Cambridgeshire	31/ 3/93	4,266	31.5	7,384	48.0	0.0	2.2	-	7.9	21.4
Total		108,209	945.1	-	1458.1	359.5	44.9	-	227.1	313.6

Table 60b Large-scale voluntary transfers of council housing in England April 1993-March 1995

Authority	Date of transfer	Number of dwellings	Transfer price £m	Price per dwelling £	Loan facilities at transfer £m	Housing debt (HRA) £m	Set up costs £m	Treasury 'levy' £m	Useable receipt £m	Net balance £m
Hambleton	29/ 4/93	4,268	33.5	7,873	55.0	8.0	1.8	-	8.4	15.3
West Dorset	27/ 5/93	5,279	40.3	7,629	72.5	6.0	1.8	-	10.1	22.4
Havant	31/ 1/94	3,561	35.2	9,893	65.0	25.2	1.9	2.0	6.1	0.0
Epsom & Ewell	14/ 2/94	1,740	20.0	11,665	23.5	1.9	1.1	3.6	4.1	9.3
Hart	5/ 3/94	2,408	23.1	9,593	49.0	10.0	1.3	2.6	5.1	4.1
South Shropshire	23/ 3/94	1,500	14.1	9,400	25.0	4.5	0.7	1.9	3.0	3.9
Leominster	25/ 3/94	1,832	15.5	8,460	34.0	7.7	1.5	1.6	3.5	1.3
South Ribble	30/ 3/94	3,445	32.3	9,097	57.0	16.3	1.5	3.2	7.3	4.1
Hertsmere	31/ 3/94	6,070	56.5	8,688	74.3	17.2	2.3	7.9	12.2	17.0
Penwith	16/ 5/94	3,354	30.5	8,892	55.0	17.3	2.0	2.7	7.0	1.6
North Dorset	6/ 9/94	2,881	25.3	8,775	52.5	6.0	1.4	3.9	5.4	8.7
Wychavon	3/10/94	6,563	62.9	9,583	111.0	19.5	2.8	8.7	13.6	18.4
Mid Bedforshire	4/10/94	2,971	24.1	8,100	52.3	2.5	1.9	4.3	4.9	10.4
Thanet	19/12/94	2,658	21.5	8,087	34.0	10.3	1.8	1.8	4.9	2.7
Vale of White Horse	9/ 2/95	5,028	57.7	11,543	120.0	15.8	2.5	7.6	12.5	19.3
Cherwell	20/ 2/95	1,046	10.7	10,250	25.0	3.7	0.8	1.2	2.4	2.6
Basingstoke & Deane	20/ 3/95	8,910	101.7	11,016	171.1	23.6	5.5	14.5	21.8	36.3
Malvern Hills	21/ 3/95	4,817	47.0	9,747	77.0	13.0	2.0	6.4	10.2	15.5
Maldon	27/ 3/95	2,006	21.6	10,780	44.0	2.3	1.4	3.6	4.5	9.8
Total		70,337	673.5	-	1,197.2	210.6	36.0	77.5	146.8	202.7
Total (1988/89 - 1994/95)		178,546	1,618.6	-	2,655.3	570.1	80.9	77.5	373.9	516.2

Sources: Department of the Environment, author's calculations.
Notes: The useable receipt is the lower of either 25% of the gross transfer price, or the balance left after the HRA debt and the set up costs have been covered. The net balance is the sum available after the HRA debt, the set up costs and the useable recipt have all been covered. For stock transfers approved by the Department of the Environment following the 1993/94 LSVT Review, a 20% Treasury 'levy' is imposed on the receipt net of the outstanding HRA debt. The 'levy' is also deducted before calculating the 25% useable receipt. The net balance must first be set against any outstanding General Fund debt. Any subsequently remaining receipt can then also be used for capital investment. Some housing debt and Treasury levy figures for the transfers in the first quarter of 1995 are provisional.

Table 61 Local authority housing revenue accounts in England
£ million

		1990-91	1991-92	1992-93	1993-94	1994-95
	Income					
	Gross rent from dwellings	4,887.8	5,449.2	6,021.8	6,423.6	6,723.3
+	Other rents	164.2	168.7	189.5	205.4	195.0
+	Housing subsidy	3,486.4	3,687.4	3,958.2	4,059.3	3,923.3
+	Interest income	259.3	207.3	182.4	145.8	119.4
+	LA subsidy (sums directed)	0.8	2.9	1.7	0.6	0.4
+	Other income	323.4	418.7	323.4	339.2	412.1
=	Total income	9,121.9	9,934.2	10,677.0	11,173.9	11,373.5
	Expenditure					
	Supervision and management	1,470.9	1,593.7	1,682.5	1,781.1	1,812.1
+	Repairs	1,971.2	2,009.7	2,119.4	2,174.0	2,314.1
+	Revenue to capital	268.7	437.5	390.4	333.5	505.6
+	Charge for capital	2,706.6	2,461.4	2,437.2	2,515.2	2,571.8
+	Gross rebates	2,468.1	2,945.8	3,526.1	3,947.3	4,178.2
+	Transfers	22.9	20.7	38.8	18.4	20.5
+	Other expenditure	278.6	381.2	415.8	310.0	321.6
=	Total expenditure	9,187.0	9,850.0	10,610.2	11,079.5	11,723.9
	Balances					
	End of year balances	317.4	462.5	595.2	730.0	410.5
-	Beginning of year balances	382.9	329.2	452.7	624.5	708.6
=	Changes in balances	(65.5)	131.3	142.6	105.6	(298.1)
	Average number of dwellings (000s)	4,047	3,891	3,813	3,754	3,655

Source: Department of the Environment, taken from local authority subsidy claim forms, grossed up for missing authorities.
Notes: Repair expenditure includes net transfers to repair accounts. Housing subsidy comprises basic housing subsidy plus housing benefit subsidy.
For a breakdown of housing subsidy into its component parts see Table 62. The balance figures for each year do not tally as they are derived from estimates for each year.

Housing expenditure plans

Table 62 **Rent 'surpluses', housing subsidy and housing benefit subsidy in England**
£ million

	1990-91 outturn	1991-92 outturn	1992-93 outturn	1993-94 outturn	1994-95 estimate	1995-96 forecast	1996-97 projection	1997-98 projection
Gross rent rebates	2,505	2,877	3,453	4,005	4,427	4,345	4,528	4,638
− Rent 'surpluses'	201	283	495	706	885	1,030	1,260	1,400
= Net rebate subsidy	2,304	2,594	2,958	3,299	3,542	3,315	3,268	3,238
+ Housing subsidy	1,357	1,156	1,003	827	801	804	735	726
= Total HRA subsidy	3,661	3,750	3,961	4,126	4,343	4,119	4,003	3,964

Source: Figure 22, Department of the Environment Annual Report 1995, Cm 2807, Department of the Environment.
Notes: Rent surpluses are technically described as 'negative housing subsidy entitlements'. The projections for 1996/97 and 1997/68 are based on an assumed 3% and 2% increase, in real terms, for guideline rents in each year, and an assumed 0.5% real increase in the management and maintenance allowances for 1996/97 only. It should be understood, however, that no decisions have yet been made for those future years.

Table 63 **Rents and earnings in England**
£ per week

	1980	1981	1982	1983	1984	1985	1986	1987	1988	1989	1990	1991	1992	1993	1994
Local authorities:															
Subsidy guideline	8.47	11.42	13.92	14.77	15.52	16.12	16.77	17.42	19.02	20.97	23.05	24.89	27.34	29.40	31.60
Average rent	7.70	11.42	13.48	13.97	14.66	15.54	16.36	17.70	18.82	20.70	23.76	27.28	30.57	33.52	35.90
Housing associations:															
Fair rents	12.52	13.98	15.63	17.19	18.69	19.75	21.44	22.86	25.00	26.83	29.94	32.73	36.48	38.50	41.38
Assured rents										24.50	28.97	33.93	39.03	44.87	45.90
Private tenants:															
Unfurnished fair rents	10.85	12.40	14.05	14.85	16.71	17.44	19.84	20.60	24.00	24.38	28.63	32.02	35.96	38.83	42.56
Unfurnished market rents										37.42	44.8	54.1	56.96	61.15	64.56
Average male earnings	111.4	121.6	133.4	143.5	152.6	163.8	175.0	186.4	201.7	219.2	238.6	254.2	268.9	275.7	282.6
Rents as a % earnings:															
Local authority rents	6.9	9.4	10.1	9.7	9.6	9.5	9.3	9.5	9.3	9.4	10.0	10.7	11.4	12.2	12.7
H.A. fair rents	11.2	11.5	11.7	12.0	12.2	12.1	12.3	12.3	12.4	12.2	12.5	12.9	13.6	14.0	14.6
H.A. assured rents										11.2	12.1	13.3	14.5	16.3	16.2
Private fair rents	9.7	10.2	10.5	10.3	11.0	10.6	11.3	11.1	11.9	11.1	12.0	12.6	13.4	14.1	15.0
Private market rents										17.1	18.8	21.3	21.2	22.2	22.0

Sources: Cmnd 1908, Cmnd 288-II, Regional Trends, Determination of Reckonable Income 1988/89, Rent Officer Statistics, answer to Parliamentary Question 26/7/93, Housing and Construction Statistics, New Earnings Surveys 1993 & 1994, NFHA Core Quarterly Bulletin (assured rents only).
Notes: Local authority rents are for the April of each year; the guideline rents refer to the financial year. Housing association assured rents exclude service charges, which average about £6 per week. Private market rents are those determined by the rent officer when referred for the purposes of housing benefits. Earnings figures are average England manual male earnings. 1994 housing association fair rents, and private fair rent figures, are for the 2nd quarter.

Table 64 Housing association and private sector rents in England in 1993[1]

£ per week

Letting type & size of dwelling[2]	North West	Northern	Yorkshire & Humberside	West Midlands	East Midlands	East Anglia	London	South East	South West
Housing associations[3]:	£	£	£	£	£	£	£	£	£
Relets:									
Bedsit	31.30	32.59	31.89	34.76	38.64	32.13	40.41	40.71	37.15
One bedroom	36.08	34.44	37.82	39.83	39.90	38.12	45.05	45.53	42.59
Two bedroom	35.92	35.61	39.39	42.43	42.18	41.95	53.00	49.70	47.36
Three bedroom	40.71	40.19	42.26	46.89	45.63	46.07	62.82	53.50	52.19
Four (+) bedroom	45.41	41.23	48.87	54.86	49.20	53.07	69.89	56.30	58.21
New lets:									
Bedsit	40.13	47.43	35.81	40.57	39.76	38.19	46.16	43.85	37.00
One bedroom	43.18	40.36	44.26	44.39	43.99	42.39	51.58	50.82	46.98
Two bedroom	47.52	46.19	47.37	49.92	48.79	49.05	62.57	57.00	51.40
Three bedroom	51.43	51.25	50.43	52.93	52.10	53.77	70.26	64.25	56.74
Four (+) bedroom	59.31	55.60	58.64	63.48	58.56	61.62	77.50	70.10	60.41
Private unfurnished letting:									
Bedsit	40.04	35.27	34.73	37.58	33.17	40.90	68.13	51.92	44.21
One bedroom	47.15	40.06	43.25	44.73	43.77	48.71	76.08	64.52	54.62
Two bedroom	55.12	42.33	48.38	55.94	50.40	57.65	90.50	63.94	66.08
Three bedroom	58.67	48.17	51.75	60.71	53.62	61.00	101.40	87.08	69.73
Four (+) bedroom	67.10	52.98	57.31	68.28	56.85	64.88	109.59	93.84	74.93

Sources: Competitive Local Rents, HACAS 1995; data from NFHA and Department of the Environment databases.

Notes: 1. Private rents are the average determined by rent officers for housing benefit purposes. They are not, therefore, representative of the overall private rented market. Nor are they at all comparable in qualatative terms with housing association lettings of the same size. A large proportion of private sector bedsit and one bedroom lettings, for example, are of rooms with shared amenities, rather than of self contained dwellings.

2. Rents for private lettings are categorised by numbers of habitable rooms. In constructing the table it has been assumed that all private lets comprise one living room, and that all other habitable rooms are bedrooms

3. Housing association lets exclude those in sheltered and warden schemes.

Table 65 Welsh housing capital expenditure
£ million

	1981/82	1982/83	1983/84	1984/85	1985/86	1986/87	1987/88	1988/89	1989/90	1990/91	1991/92	1992/93	1993/94
Gross investment													
Local authorities:													
HRA acquisitions and newbuild	44.5	41.5	47.3	36.0	26.2	28.5	39.7	32.2	28.5	20.4	11.7	11.9	9.7
+ HRA renovation	24.3	47.6	48.2	44.2	49.7	78.3	98.0	99.7	147.2	105.8	85.1	78.7	87.2
+ Enveloping and environmental works	0.3	0.4	1.6	4.6	4.8	9.1	13.6	15.9	22.0	26.2	6.8	8.5	15.1
+ Slum clearance	2.0	0.9	0.9	1.0	0.6	0.6	0.4	0.5	0.5	0.7	0.5	0.7	0.9
+ Low cost home-ownership	0.6	1.1	0.8	0.7	0.4	1.3	1.7	2.1	3.2	3.4	2.7	1.2	0.9
+ Improvement grants etc	18.5	42.5	109.3	80.3	55.3	65.4	70.7	68.5	70.5	93.5	129.9	181.5	175.9
+ Private housing loans	5.7	6.5	8.0	4.5	2.4	4.0	3.9	3.3	2.0	5.1	1.1	1.0	0.6
+ Loans/grants to housing associations								0.2	0.5	11.7			
= Total local authorities	95.9	140.5	216.1	171.3	139.4	187.3	228.1	222.7	285.6	255.1	237.8	283.5	290.3
+ Housing for Wales	32.3	44.9	41.0	39.0	40.6	51.5	64.5	72.7	90.4	116.0	132.5	173.9	140.9
+ Total gross investment (A)	128.2	185.4	257.1	210.3	180.0	238.8	292.6	295.4	376.0	371.1	370.3	457.4	431.2
Capital receipts:													
Local authorities	65.5	86.0	79.2	91.1	72.0	82.3	84.7	137.8	179.2	87.3	63.9	55.6	70.8
+ Housing for Wales	1.0	1.5	7.8	4.4	3.8	5.1	7.1	6.9	8.0	9.5	7.8	10.9	9.3
= Total receipts (B)	66.5	87.5	87.0	95.5	75.8	87.4	91.8	144.7	187.2	96.8	71.7	66.5	80.1
Total net investment (A-B)	61.7	97.9	170.1	114.8	104.2	151.4	200.8	150.7	188.8	274.3	298.6	390.9	351.1

Sources: Welsh Housing Statistics, Volumes 7, 12, 13 & 14, Welsh Office
Notes: Housing for Wales took over from the Housing Corporation from 1989/90. Housing for Wales figures include credit approvals vired from Welsh local authorities.

Table 66 Welsh housing capital plans and investment
£ million

	1986/87	1987/88	1988/89	1989/90	1990/91	1991/92	1992/93	1993/94	1994/95	1995/96
Local authorities:										
Grants and credit approvals	141.9	153.2	115.2	115.0	183.9	194.3	262.6	254.4	265.7	267.6
+ 'Local' finance	45.4	74.9	107.5	170.6	71.2	43.5	20.9	35.9	29.3	24.3
= Gross investment (A)	187.3	228.1	222.7	285.6	255.1	237.8	283.5	290.3	295.0	291.9
Housing for Wales:										
Net provision	46.4	57.1	59.2	65.2	92.2	107.4	151.7	122.1	111.9	93.5
+ Local authority transfers	0.0	1.7	6.6	17.2	14.3	17.3	11.3	9.5	0.0	0.0
+ Capital receipts	5.1	5.7	6.9	8.0	9.5	7.8	10.9	9.3	9.5	7.2
= Gross provision	51.5	64.5	72.7	90.4	116.0	132.5	173.9	140.9	121.4	100.7
+ Private finance	0.0	7.8	7.5	22.0	33.0	53.0	73.4	70.4	68.5	65.0
= Gross investment (B)	51.5	72.3	80.2	112.4	149.0	185.5	247.3	211.3	189.9	165.7
Total gross investment (A+B)	238.8	300.4	302.9	398.0	404.1	423.3	530.8	501.6	484.9	457.6

Sources: Departmental reports by the Welsh Office; Cms 1916, 2215, 2515 & 2815, Welsh Housing Statistics.
Notes: Welsh Office estimates of 1994/95 and 1995/96 local authority outturn investment. Housing for Wales figures for 1994/95 onwards do not include credit approvals vired from local authorities. Vired credit approvals in earlier years have been netted off from the local authority figures. Welsh Office estimates of council local resources for 1994/95 and 1995/96.

Table 67a Welsh local authority housing revenue accounts
£ thousands

	1981/82	1982/83	1983/84	1984/85	1985/86	1986/87	1987/88	1988/89	1989/90
Income									
Net rents from dwellings	143,327	151,426	89,287	86,082	91,054	94,030	86,908	100,525	104,433
+ Rent rebates	24,802	42,442	106,011	118,912	127,088	133,068	131,830	146,591	153,222
= Total rent from dwellings (A)	168,129	193,868	195,298	204,994	218,142	227,098	218,738	247,116	257,655
Rate fund contributions:									
Rent rebate administration	768	1,001	1,431	1,317	1,683	2,318	1,918	2,357	3,246
+ Other rate fund	11,171	11,104	7,336	4,742	3,495	2,998	5,994	7,852	3,994
= Total from rate funds (B)	11,939	12,105	8,767	6,059	5,178	5,316	7,912	10,209	7,240
+ Rents from land etc	1,751	1,891	1,926	1,990	2,089	2,314	2,241	2,588	3,041
+ Government subsidy	34,624	10,102	8,832	7,104	10,024	8,698	10,995	11,987	14,808
+ Mortgage interest from former tenants	6,562	13,414	15,374	15,805	15,108	13,311	11,210	11,435	13,469
+ Interest from capital receipts	4,593	8,546	11,034	13,507	18,062	19,205	18,039	24,043	33,020
+ Other income	7,098	7,202	8,048	8,573	11,346	12,054	11,978	15,759	15,130
= Total all other income (C)	54,628	41,155	45,214	46,979	56,629	55,582	54,463	65,812	79,468
Total income (A+B+C)	234,696	247,128	249,279	258,032	279,949	287,996	281,113	323,137	344,363
Expenditure									
Supervision & management	30,241	32,486	33,967	35,131	38,273	41,384	43,293	51,993	58,833
+ Repairs and maintenance	57,860	67,467	72,979	76,500	77,822	88,213	87,883	92,250	105,816
+ Debt charges	135,566	135,104	132,699	140,479	149,398	146,059	142,441	153,809	160,863
+ Capital expenditure met from revenue	3,742	3,633	3,848	4,034	3,255	4,453	4,260	6,479	5,699
+ Transfers to rate funds	-	-	1,090	910	1,457	1,448	300	2,317	8,770
+ Other expenditure	1,894	2,045	1,844	2,059	2,844	4,405	5,819	5,681	7,627
= Total expenditure	229,303	240,735	246,427	259,113	273,049	285,962	283,996	312,529	347,608
Dwellings in HRA (000s)	279	277	259	255	251	255	230	235	226

Source: Welsh Housing Statistics, Volumes 7, 11 & 12.
Notes: From 1983/84 the introduction of the Unified Housing Benefit Scheme transferred the payment of housing benefit from the D(H)SS to local authorities.
As a result from that date there is a large change in the balance between net rents and rent rebates.

Table 67b Welsh local authority housing revenue accounts
£ thousands

		1990/91	1991/92	1992/93	1993/94	1994/95
	Income					
	Net rents from dwellings	115,295	123,899	124,512	124,089	127,885
+	Rebates	165,042	183,517	208,729	227,903	243,371
=	Total rent from dwellings	280,337	307,416	333,241	351,992	371,256
+	Rents from land etc	2,934	3,407	3,674	3,750	3,932
+	Government subsidy	164,945	175,843	188,590	195,639	193,028
+	Sums transferred into the HRA	5,854	86	136	131	116
+	Credit to the HRA	14,867	11,036	8,084	7,194	5,356
+	Other transfers	7,491	1,442	159	159	2,329
+	Other income	5,711	8,705	10,646	10,218	10,732
+	Credit balance from previous year	24,591	21,439	25,513	33,476	30,035
=	Total income	506,730	529,374	570,043	602,559	616,784
	Expenditure					
	Supervision & management	59,992	67,017	72,698	78,429	77,713
+	Repairs and maintenance	114,214	112,164	113,606	119,429	117,429
+	Expenditure for capital purposes	46,701	31,753	30,911	33,605	24,066
+	Net debit to HRA	96,539	106,265	107,973	110,964	110,916
+	Other expenditure/transfers	2,803	2,586	2,650	2,043	8,599
+	Rent rebates	165,042	183,517	208,729	227,903	243,371
+	Debit balance from previous year	0	559	0	151	225
+	Balance at year end	21,439	25,513	33,476	30,035	34,465
=	Total expenditure	506,730	529,374	570,043	602,559	616,784

Source: Welsh Housing Statistics, Volume 14.
Note: In the main this analysis follows the same format as Table 67a. However, some changes are inevitable due to the introduction of the 1989 Act housing finance regime.

Table 68 Housing subsidy and housing benefit subsidy in Wales
£ million

	1990/91	1991/92	1992/93	1993/94	1994/95	1995/96	1996/97	1997/98
Basic housing subsidy:								
Positive entitlements (A)	17.8	7.6	7.4	3.8	3.2	2.3	2.0	2.0
- Negative entitlements	10.5	17.4	23.2	41.2	53.5	66.5	76.3	84.3
= Net housing subsidy	7.3	-9.8	-15.8	-37.4	-50.3	-64.1	-74.3	-82.3
Gross rent rebate subsidy	165.9	184.4	210.8	228.2	246.2	292.0	310.6	325.1
- Negative basic housing subsidy entitlements	10.5	17.4	23.2	41.2	53.5	66.5	76.3	84.3
= Net rent rebate subsidy (B)	155.4	167.0	187.6	187.0	192.7	225.5	234.3	240.8
Combined housing subsidy (A)+(B)	173.2	174.6	195.0	190.8	195.9	227.8	236.3	242.8

Source: Welsh Office.
Notes: The combined housing subsidy is conventionally presented as the sum of positive basic housing subsidy entitlements and net rent rebate subsidy. Alternatively it could be expressed as the sum of net basic housing subsidy entitlements and gross rent rebate subsidy. The latter approach would make the role of negative housing subsidy entitlements more explicit. The forecasts for 1995/96 and subsequent years are made on the same assumptions as the Welsh Office Departmental Report (Cm 2815). They are therefore subject to the caveat that decisions by the Secretary of State for Wales on subsidy guidelines have not yet been made for 1996/97 and 1997/98.

Table 69 Rents and earnings in Wales
£ per week

Year	1981	1982	1983	1984	1985	1986	1987	1988	1989	1990	1991	1992	1993	1994
Local authorities:														
Subsidy guideline										22.98	24.73	27.31	29.11	31.32
Average rent	11.43	13.93	14.55	15.51	16.53	17.23	17.91	19.74	22.35	23.49	26.44	30.19	31.80	34.11
Housing associations:														
Fair rents	13.53	15.19	16.17	17.77	18.67	20.86	22.15	24.58	26.06	30.08	32.02	34.60	35.37	37.50
Assured rents									26.00	30.04	34.30	37.92	42.50	43.00
Private tenants:														
Unfurnished fair rents	10.10	11.15	11.77	13.29	14.12	16.40	17.48	20.96	21.98	23.87	26.67	29.29	31.51	34.96
Unfurnished market rents										29.75	35.38	42.25	46.37	51.13	54.07
Average male earnings	120.3	134.7	140.2	148.9	159.6	167.9	180.4	193.1	209.8	224.7	239.3	254.3	258.6	272.3
Rent as a % earnings														
Local authority rents	9.5	10.3	10.4	10.4	10.4	10.3	9.9	10.2	10.7	10.5	11.0	11.9	12.3	12.5
H.A. fair rents	11.2	11.3	11.5	11.9	11.7	12.4	12.3	12.7	12.4	13.4	13.4	13.6	13.7	13.8
H.A. assured rents									12.4	13.4	14.3	14.9	16.4	15.8
Private fair rents	8.4	8.3	8.4	8.9	8.8	9.8	9.7	10.9	10.5	10.6	11.1	11.5	12.2	12.8
Private market rents										14.2	15.7	17.7	18.2	19.8	19.9

Sources: Welsh Office, Welsh Housing Statistics, Housing & Construction Statistics, Regional Trends, New Earnings Surveys, Welsh Federation of Housing Associations.
Notes: The housing association assured tenancy rents derived from the WFHA 'Core' data are median, rather than mean rents, and are not therefore entirely comparable with the mean fair rent figures derived from Housing and Construction Statistics. Private market rents are those determined by the rent officer when referred for the purposes of housing benefit. Earnings figures are average Welsh male manual earnings. 1994 fair rent figures are for the second quarter of the year.

Table 70 Scottish gross housing investment
£ million

	1980/81	1981/82	1982/83	1983/84	1984/85	1985/86	1986/87	1987/88	1988/89	1989/90	1990/91	1991/92	1992/93	1993/94	1994/95 estimate	1995/96 plans	1996/97 plans	1997/98 plans
Cash	477	513	577	706	583	594	655	836	889	952	942	958	941	992	988	944	922	898
1993/94 prices	990	970	1,019	1,193	937	905	969	1,174	1,170	1,171	1,073	1,027	970	992	969	896	854	813
GDP deflator	48.2	52.9	56.6	59.2	62.2	65.6	67.6	71.2	76.0	81.3	87.8	93.3	97.0	100.0	102.0	105.3	107.9	110.4

Sources: The Government's Expenditure Plans 1995/96 to 1997/98, The Scottish Office, Cm 2814, The Scottish Office Statistical Bulletin Housing 1995/1
Notes: Gross outturn capital expenditure by local authorities, new towns, Scottish Homes and its predecessors.
Exludes NLF repayments, Corporation tax provision and housing association use of private finance.

Table 71 Scottish housing investment by agency
£ million

	1985/86	1986/87	1987/88	1988/89	1989/90	1990/91	1991/92	1992/93	1993/94	1994/95	1995/96	1996/97	1997/98
Gross investment:													
Local authorities	408	453	604	632	643	621	587	580	594	601	581	567	560
+ New towns	26	28	31	37	45	43	33	34	35	33	22	7	0
+ Housing Corporation	104	114	127	164									
+ SSHA	51	54	67	62									
+ Scottish Homes					294	288	470	581	367	356	343	350	340
= Total	589	649	829	895	982	952	1,090	1,195	996	990	946	924	900
- Capital receipts	210	204	288	419	490	411	371	384	389	347	367	344	324
- Loan repayments					30	10	132	254	4	2	2	2	2
= Net investment	379	445	541	476	462	531	587	557	603	641	577	578	574

Sources: The Government's Expenditure Plans, Cms 1515, 1919, 2214, 2514 and 2814, Scottish Office.
Notes: Detailed Scottish Homes budgets for 1996/97 and 1997/98 have yet to be agreed with the Scottish Office. The figures given for those years assume that the revenue budgets remain at the same level as in 1995/96 (i.e. £35 million).Local authority investment includes estimated use of HRA revenue to fund capital investment.

Table 72 **Provision for local authority housing investment in Scotland**
£ million

	1984/85	1985/86	1986/87	1987/88	1988/89	1989/90	1990/91	1991/92	1992/93	1993/94	1994/95 estimate	1995/96 plans	1996/97 plans	1997/98 plans
HRA investment	254	291	341	452	476	486	492	476	448	475	473	464	427	420
Financed by:														
Borrowing	121	169	211	267	202	162	200	205	145	171	191	177	179	180
Capital receipts	132	122	128	185	274	325	290	265	289	279	250	256	248	240
Revenue	1		2				2	6	14	25	32	31		
Non HRA investment	167	117	112	152	156	157	129	111	132	119	128	117	110	110
Financed by:														
Borrowing	141	88	101	144	149	150	122	106	128	114	124	114	107	107
Capital receipts	26	29	11	8	7	7	7	5	4	5	4	3	3	3

Source: Scottish Office, Cm 2814.
Note: Figures for HRA investment for 1996/97 and 1997/98 do not include estimates of the use of HRA revenue to finance investment.

Table 73 Scottish Homes capital grants and private finance
£ million

Programme	1989/90	1990/91	1991/92	1992/93	1993/94	1994/95	1995/96 estimate
Housing associations:							
Capital programme (A)	202.6	194.5	220.6	255.1	263.1	268.6	268.6
+ Private finance (B)	9.9	37.4	41.9	54.9	54.4	81.4	94.3
= Total housing associations (Y)	212.5	231.9	262.5	310.0	317.5	350.0	362.9
Private developers:							
Capital programme (C)	2.0	8.5	14.4	27.5	39.5	33.1	36.2
+ Private finance (D)	-	42.5	45.2	76.1	94.1	102.7	80.7
= Total private developers (Z)	2.0	51.0	59.6	103.6	133.6	135.8	116.9
Total capital programme (A+C)	204.6	203.0	235.0	282.6	302.6	301.7	304.8
Total private finance (B+D)	9.9	79.9	87.1	131.0	148.5	184.1	175.0
Total capital investment (Y+Z)	214.5	282.9	322.1	413.6	451.1	485.8	479.8

Source: Scottish Homes.
Note: Grants to housing associations and private developers are for both rent and sale schemes. Capital programme figures exclude investment in Scottish Homes dwellings, PES transfers from Scottish local authorities (see table 52). They also exclude revenue grants, and grants for social, recreational and environmental improvement schemes.

Table 74 **Scottish local authorities consolidated housing revenue account**
£ 000s

Item	1987/88 outturn	1988/89 outturn	1989/90 outturn	1990/91 outturn	1991/92 outturn	1992/93 outturn	1993/94 outturn	1994/95 estimated outturn	1995/96 budgeted
Expenditure:									
Loan charges	429,413	463,313	496,460	519,206	526,672	514,152	488,559	489,700	505,100
+ Supervision & management	78,349	88,159	101,387	113,759	117,874	124,734	136,826	142,200	145,400
+ Repairs & maintenance	211,929	219,919	231,180	255,074	271,924	288,125	302,823	327,500	338,800
+ Other	23,171	29,625	47,420	46,090	52,818	64,760	72,768	75,600	73,900
= Total	742,862	801,016	876,447	934,129	969,288	991,771	1,000,976	1,035,000	1,063,200
Income:									
Rental income	630,483	685,458	760,323	812,340	870,870	894,465	925,253	937,400	941,100
+ Housing support grant	41,900	54,521	65,373	58,317	55,570	47,470	35,852	24,200	22,300
+ General fund contributions	41,033	25,384	10,267	8,315	(892)	(679)	(1,814)	(1,658)	(2,324)
+ Other	30,903	36,081	45,316	60,056	61,631	84,313	83,848	99,442	103,676
= Total	744,319	801,444	881,279	939,028	987,179	1,025,569	1,043,139	1,059,384	1,064,752

Source: Scottish Office.
Notes: Excludes balances carried forward. General fund contributions are shown net of HRA transfers to general funds.

Table 75 Average costs, rents and subsidies in Scottish housing revenue accounts

	1980/81	1981/82	1982/83	1983/84	1984/85	1985/86	1986/87	1987/88	1988/89	1989/90	1990/91	1991/92	1992/93	1993/94	1994/95	1995/96
Average annual cost per house (£)	688	729	758	764	779	807	861	914	991	1,047	1,252	1,338	1,421	1,494	1,585	1,672
Percentage of costs met by:-																
Rents etc	50	59	66	71	74	79	83	88	90	92	93	94	95	97	98	98
+ Housing support grant	37	25	16	11	8	7	7	6	7	7	6	6	5	3	2	2
+ General Fund contributions	13	16	18	18	18	14	10	6	3	1	1	-	-	-	-	-
= Total	100	100	100	100	100	100	100	100	100	100	100	100	100	100	100	100

Source: Convention of Scottish Local Authorities, Scottish Office Housing Statistical Bulletin.
Note: COSLA figures to 1989/90; subsequent figures derived from Table 74.

Table 76 Rents and earnings in Scotland
£ per week

Year	1981	1982	1983	1984	1985	1986	1987	1988	1989	1990	1991	1992	1993	1994
Local authorities:														
Subsidy guideline							15.85	17.45	18.93	21.30	23.97	26.36	30.32	34.86
Average rent	7.67	9.01	9.86	10.47	11.53	12.99	14.59	16.29	18.85	20.91	23.13	24.64	26.56	27.79
Housing associations:														
Fair rents	9.38	13.63	14.73	16.88	18.79	16.94	20.56	22.73	23.37	18.60	19.25	21.44	23.57	25.48
Assured rents										21.00	23.70	25.53	27.37	27.85
Private tenants:														
Unfurnished fair rents	8.06	10.17	12.15	12.54	15.17	16.29	17.44	19.85	21.35	23.53	25.76	29.60	29.18	-
Average male earnings	124.8	136.9	145.8	156.2	164.2	173.0	179.7	194.9	209.9	231.7	251.1	270.6	269.7	269.5
Rent as a % earnings														
Local authority rents	6.1	6.6	6.8	6.7	7.0	7.5	8.1	8.4	9.0	9.0	9.2	9.1	9.8	10.3
H.A. fair rents	7.5	10.0	10.1	10.8	11.4	9.8	11.4	11.7	11.1	8.0	7.7	7.9	8.7	9.5
H.A. assured rents										9.1	9.4	9.4	10.1	10.3
Private fair rents	6.5	7.4	8.3	8.0	9.2	9.4	9.7	10.2	10.2	10.2	10.3	10.9	10.8	-

Sources: Housing & Construction Statistics, Regional Trends, New Earnings Surveys, Scottish Office, Scottish Federation of Housing Associations.
Notes: Local authority rents are for the April of each year; guideline rents refer to the financial year. The housing association assured and fair rent figures from 1990 onwards are derived from the SFHA CORE data, are median rather than mean rents, and are not therefore comparable with the mean fair rent figures derived from Housing and Construction Statistics for earlier years. The 1994 housing association rent figures are for the 2nd quarter of the year. Earnings figures are average Scottish male manual earnings. Scottish rent officer statistics are no longer collated by the Scottish Office.

Housing expenditure plans

Table 77 **Financial provision for housing in Northern Ireland**
£ million

	1985/86 outturn	1986/87 outturn	1987/88 outturn	1988/89 outturn	1989/90 outturn	1990/91 outturn	1991/92 outturn	1992/93 outturn	1993/94 outturn	1994/95 estimated outturn	1995/96 plans	1996/97 plans	1997/98 plans
Northern Ireland Housing Executive Grant	131	146	157	170	121	127	140	123	127	119	126	127	136
+ Net lending	118	96	99	86	80	60	54	60	49	47	48	56	52
= Total	249	242	256	256	201	187	194	183	176	166	174	183	188
+ Voluntary housing	35	34	34	34	28	25	27	42	28	29	35	32	32
+ Renovation grants and enveloping	60	56	45	42	36	32	32	34	32	33	35	36	40
+ Administration	2	2	2	2	2	2	2	2	2	2	2	2	2
= Total provision	346	335	337	334	268	245	255	261	237	230	246	253	263

Sources: Northern Ireland Expenditure Plans and Priorities, Cms 1517, 1917, 2216, 2516 and 2816.
Notes: The reduction in grant to the Northern Ireland Housing Executive (NIHE) in 1989/90 follows some £366 million of NIHE debt being written off. This had a neutral impact on the NIHE programmes. Provision for voluntary housing is net of capital receipts.

Table 78 Gross housing investment in Northern Ireland
£ Million

	1985/86 outturn	1986/87 outturn	1987/88 outturn	1988/89 outturn	1989/90 outturn	1990/91 outturn	1991/92 outturn	1992/93 outturn	1993/94 outturn	1994/95 estimated outturn	1995/96 plans	1996/97 plans	1997/98 plans
Northern Ireland Housing Executive													
New housebuilding	82	64	57	56	51	39	40	35	35	38	47	50	57
+ Land etc purchase	9	15	10	8	8	7	10	9	12	12	11	9	9
+ Estate renovation	79	68	80	83	76	71	66	71	75	74	71	80	85
+ Other	3	4	4	5	6	4	3	6	2	3	2	2	2
= Total	173	151	151	152	141	121	120	121	124	127	131	141	153
+ Voluntary housing	40	41	44	46	38	37	41	58	49	45	50	46	46
+ Renovation grants and enveloping	60	56	45	42	36	32	32	34	32	32	38	39	40
= Gross public investment (A)	273	248	240	240	215	190	193	213	205	204	219	226	239
Capital receipts:													
Northern Ireland Housing Executive	42	34	30	36	47	43	34	36	45	48	50	47	48
+ Voluntary housing	5	7	9	12	10	12	14	16	19	16	14	14	14
= Total (B)	47	41	39	48	57	55	48	52	64	64	64	61	62
Net Public Investment (A-B)	226	207	201	192	158	135	145	161	141	140	155	165	177

Sources: Northern Ireland Expenditure Plans and Priorities, Cms 1517, 1917, 2216, 2516 and 2816.
Note: Renovation grants and enveloping expenditure are financed from revenue in Northern Ireland.

Table 79 Northern Ireland Housing Executive rents and average earnings

Year	1981	1982	1983	1984	1985	1986	1987	1988	1989	1990	1991	1992	1993	1994
Average rent per week (£)	10.06	12.19	12.78	13.51	14.13	14.78	15.34	18.18	19.04	21.13	23.09	25.43	27.40	29.63
Average male earnings (£)	110.0	116.9	124.4	134.2	143.8	149.3	162.4	171.6	181.0	198.0	214.8	230.8	234.3	241.7
Rent as a % earnings	9.1	10.4	10.3	10.1	9.8	9.9	9.4	10.6	10.5	10.7	10.7	11.0	11.7	12.3

Sources: Northern Ireland Housing Statistics, Northern Ireland Housing Executive, Regional Trends, Northern Ireland New Earnings Survey 1994
Notes: Earnings figures are average Northern Ireland male manual earnings. The average weekly rent for 1995 is £31.56.

Housing needs and homelessness

Table 80 Local authority homeless acceptances
Number of households

	1979	1980	1981	1982	1983	1984	1985	1986	1987	1988	1989	1990	1991	1992	1993	1994
Not held to be intentionally homeless																
England	55,530	60,400	66,990	71,620	75,470	80,500	91,010	100,490	109,170	113,770	122,180	140,350	144,780	142,890	132,380	122,660
Scotland	7,122	7,038	7,332	8,360	7,770	8,787	10,992	11,056	10,417	10,463	12,396	14,233	15,508	17,062	15,462	-
Held to be intentionally homeless																
England	1,670	2,520	3,020	3,180	2,770	3,050	2,970	3,070	3,270	3,730	4,500	5,450	6,940	6,350	5,600	4,630
Scotland	1,040	938	773	847	808	977	980	1,144	1,030	1,128	1,271	1,580	1,796	2,114	1,827	-
All homeless acceptances																
England	57,200	62,920	70,010	74,800	78,240	83,550	93,980	103,560	112,440	117,500	126,680	145,800	151,720	149,240	137,980	127,290
Scotland	8,162	7,976	8,105	9,207	8,578	9,764	11,972	12,200	11,447	11,591	13,667	15,813	17,304	19,176	17,289	-
Wales	4,676	5,446	5,462	5,611	5,008	4,999	5,371	5,965	5,683	6,818	7,805	9,963	9,843	10,270	11,125	10,341
Great Britain	70,038	76,342	83,577	89,618	91,826	98,313	111,323	121,725	129,570	135,909	148,152	171,576	178,867	178,686	166,394	-

Sources: Department of the Environment, Scottish Office, Welsh Office.
Notes: The 1990 figures for Wales include 2,000 households made homeless in Colwyn Bay by flooding in the February of that year. Scottish figures are for priority need homeless and potentially homeless cases only.

Table 81 Homeless households in temporary accommodation
Number of households

	1980	1981	1982	1983	1984	1985	1986	1987	1988	1989	1990	1991	1992	1993	1994
Bed and breakfast	1,330	1,520	1,640	2,700	3,670	5,360	8,990	10,370	10,970	11,480	11,130	12,150	7,630	4,900	4,330
+ Hostels[1]	3,380	3,320	3,500	3,400	3,990	4,730	4,610	5,150	6,240	8,020	9,010	9,990	10,840	10,210	10,020
+ Private sector leasing												23,740	27,910	23,270	17,050
+ Other[2]			4,200	3,740	4,640	5,830	7,190	9,240	12,890	18,400	25,130	14,050	16,690	15,200	16,360
= Total	4,710	4,840	9,340	9,840	12,300	15,920	20,790	24,760	30,100	37,900	45,270	59,930	63,070	53,580	47,760

Sources: Homelessness Statistics, Department of the Environment, Hansard 18/4/91, Column 186.
Notes: 1. Includes women's refuges.
2. Other includes dwellings leased by local authorities from private landlords for years prior to 1991.

Table 82 Regional homelessness in England
Numbers of households

	Homeless acceptances:					In temporary accommodation:				
	1990	1991	1992	1993	1994	1990	1991	1992	1993	1994
London	36,480	37,310	38,570	31,890	28,810	27,820	37,130	39,580	33,260	27,820
Rest of South East	18,240	19,540	19,340	18,880	18,770	8,480	10,750	11,240	9,610	9,310
South West	8,640	9,330	9,060	9,470	9,170	1,980	2,630	3,020	2,610	2,660
East Anglia	3,550	3,700	3,360	3,340	3,290	840	1,080	1,070	920	940
East Midlands	9,810	10,300	10,720	10,370	9,090	1,500	1,810	1,560	1,380	1,500
West Midlands	18,290	18,400	17,440	17,060	16,800	1,240	2,120	1,660	1,470	1,280
Yorkshire & Humberside	13,800	13,080	14,540	13,650	11,640	1,080	1,620	1,890	1,640	1,380
North	9,310	9,050	8,290	7,620	6,740	410	580	650	660	640
North West	22,230	24,070	21,570	20,100	18,350	1,920	2,210	2,400	2,460	2,230
England	140,350	144,780	142,890	132,380	122,660	45,270	59,930	63,070	54,010	47,760

Source: Department of the Environment Homelessness Statistics.
Notes: Homeless acceptances figures exclude households found to be intentionally homeless. Temporary accommodation figures are for the end of the year.

Table 83 Reasons for homelessness
Percentages

	1987	1988	1989	1990	1991	1992	1993	1994
Parents, relatives or friends no longer willing or able to accommodate	41	43	43	43	42	42	38	34
Breakdown of relationship with partner	18	19	17	17	16	17	19	21
Loss of private dwelling, including tied accommodation	15	15	16	14	14	15	17	19
Mortgage arrears	9	7	6	9	12	10	8	8
Rent arrears	4	4	5	4	3	2	2	2
Other	13	12	13	13	14	16	16	16

Source: Department of the Environment Homelessness Statistics.
Note: Figures may not total 100 due to rounding.

Table 84 Homelessness: categories of need
Numbers of households

	Numbers of households:					Percentages:				
	1990	1991	1992	1993	1994	1990	1991	1992	1993	1994
Priority need housholds:										
Households with:										
Dependent children	84,120	88,950	85,300	76,390	69,300	60	61	60	58	58
+ Pregnant member	17,470	18,830	18,530	16,510	14,060	12	13	13	12	11
Vulnerable member:										
+ Old age	6,570	5,860	6,230	5,910	6,080	5	4	4	4	5
+ Physical handicap	3,950	4,430	5,440	5,400	6,160	3	3	4	4	5
+ Mental illness	4,220	4,750	6,070	6,490	6,960	3	3	4	5	6
+ Young	-	-	4,460	4,470	3,930	-	-	3	3	3
+ Domestic violence	-	-	6,470	7,060	7,260	-	-	5	5	6
+ Other	9,460	12,610	4,930	4,250	3,960	7	9	3	3	3
+ Homeless in emergency	2,300	1,820	1,270	1,140	990	2	1	1	1	1
= Total priority need	128,090	137,250	138,700	404,040	118,700	91	95	97	96	97
+ Non-priority need	12,260	7,530	4,190	4,750	3,960	9	5	3	4	3
= Total	140,350	144,780	142,890	132,380	122,660	100	100	100	100	100

Source: Department of Environment Homelessness Statistics.
Notes: Separate figures for domestic violence and young person cases are not available for 1991 or earlier years. Percentages do not always add to 100 as a result of roundings.

Table 85 Street homeless: people sleeping rough in 1991

	Greater London	Metropolitan Councils	District Councils	England	Scotland	Wales	Great Britain
Male	1,019	193	1,029	2,241	124	30	2,395
Female	178	32	224	434	21	2	457
Total	1,197	225	1,253	2,675	145	32	2,852

Source: 1991 Census, compiled from district data.
Notes: These totals are based on the Census survey, which was restricted to some 1,300 identified sites where people were known to have previously slept rough. They are commonly regarded as a substantial underestimate. For example the Census identifies only 5 people as sleeping rough in Birmingham, while a local survey in October 1992 found 61 people sleeping rough in the City. See Britain's Hidden Homeless, Louise Baker, Housing May 1993.

Housing needs and homelessness

Table 86 **Local authority dwelling stock, new dwellings and lettings in England**
Thousands

	1982-83	1983-84	1984-85	1985-86	1986-87	1987-88	1988-89	1989-90	1990-91	1991-92	1992-93	1993-94
Stock of dwellings[1]	4,660	4,560	4,510	4,440	4,410	4,320	4,180	4,040	3,900	3,840	3,760	3,666
Vacant dwellings[1]	114	113	117	113	112	103	101	99	83	75	71	70
Vacant dwellings as % of stock	2.4	2.5	2.6	2.5	2.5	2.4	2.4	2.5	2.1	1.9	1.9	1.9
Completions	27	28	27	21	18	15	16	14	13	7	2	1
Lettings[2]:	439	429	429	437	430	426	410	390	401	406	400	405
of which:												
to existing tenants	184	183	189	190	186	184	174	162	161	168	170	170
to new tenants	255	246	240	247	244	242	236	228	240	239	230	234
Homeless households as % of new tenants	19	20	23	26	27	31	31	35	40	46	45	40

Sources: Department of the Environment Annual Reports, Expenditure Plans, Housing and Construction Statistics
Notes: 1. Includes dwellings awaiting demolition, and from 1986/7 dwellings owned by authorities outside their own areas.
2. Includes non-secure lettings - 11,000 in 1984/85 rising to 31,000 in 1991/92. Also lettings to households displaced by slum clearance, averaging 4,000 a year over the period.

Table 87a Regional lettings to new tenants by local authorities in England
Thousands

Region	1979/80	1980/81	1981/82	1982/83	1983/84	1984/85	1985/86	1986/87	1987/88	1988/89	1989/90	1990/91	1991/92	1992/93	1993/94
London	52.2	50.1	48.0	40.5	37.1	33.6	33.5	31.8	32.7	33.1	35.1	43.9	49.4	45.2	44.2
South East	36.9	36.4	33.1	34.0	34.1	33.2	29.3	32.0	31.2	29.6	28.4	31.4	30.1	29.4	30.9
South West	17.3	15.5	14.6	15.6	15.3	15.6	15.6	15.1	14.4	13.4	13.3	14.1	14.0	13.1	14.3
East Anglia	9.8	9.6	7.6	7.9	8.1	9.1	11.8	7.3	7.1	6.4	6.7	7.4	6.9	6.5	6.2
East Midlands	24.9	23.1	20.8	22.8	22.0	22.4	21.6	22.0	20.2	20.5	18.8	19.0	18.0	18.2	20.5
West Midlands	32.2	34.0	30.0	31.8	30.3	30.9	32.0	32.9	34.1	31.7	29.7	29.1	29.0	28.0	29.1
Yorkshire & Humberside	35.5	37.7	32.7	32.9	32.9	31.8	36.1	35.3	34.2	34.6	32.1	31.5	30.8	30.5	29.7
North	25.2	26.2	23.3	25.5	24.2	22.4	24.4	24.5	23.6	24.0	24.2	23.0	21.3	22.5	22.1
North West	40.5	42.5	41.1	44.7	41.9	41.0	42.7	42.7	44.5	42.8	40.2	40.2	39.2	36.9	36.5
England	274.5	275.1	251.2	255.7	245.9	240.0	247.0	243.6	242.0	236.1	228.5	239.6	238.6	230.2	233.4

Sources: Housing and Construction Statistics, Department of the Environment.
Notes: Lettings figures are for lettings to new tenants only, including lettings for non-secure tenancies. The regional figures are compiled from local authority HIP returns, grossed up for incomplete responses. The 1993/94 figures are provisional.

Table 87b Lettings to homeless households
Percentage of all lettings to new tenants

Region	1979/80	1980/81	1981/82	1982/83	1983/84	1984/85	1985/86	1986/87	1987/88	1988/89	1989/90	1990/91	1991/92	1992/93	1993/94
London	26	27	29	32	36	40	47	52	53	51	46	48	42	48	45
South East	17	18	20	20	18	18	23	23	26	25	26	28	33	33	32
South West	20	23	22	22	20	23	27	29	34	32	34	34	36	38	36
East Anglia	15	18	11	11	11	11	15	22	25	26	27	30	33	31	27
East Midlands	9	10	11	10	10	11	15	16	20	20	20	28	37	37	30
West Midlands	12	16	18	19	17	22	27	28	29	30	32	39	39	41	35
Yorkshire & Humberside	10	10	11	12	14	14	15	15	18	18	20	23	28	31	28
North	10	10	9	10	11	11	11	15	18	18	20	22	26	23	20
North West	9	10	8	10	12	13	17	19	20	19	23	21	25	26	24
England	15	16	16	17	17	19	23	15	27	26	28	31	34	35	32

Sources: As Table 87a.
Notes: Percentages are for secure lettings to homeless households only. In addition some 10% or so lettings each year are of non-secure tenancies. Some 90% of non-secure tenancies are let to homeless households (see Table 88).

Table 88 Regional lettings to new tenants by size of dwelling in England 1993/94

Region	Local authority lettings: Homeless: Secure: 1 bed		Non-secure:		Other new tenants: Secure:		Non-secure:		Housing association nominations: Homeless:		Other new tenants:		Lettings to homeless as a percentage of all 2 bed+ lettings to new tenants Local authorities: Secure	Non-secure	Housing association
	1 bed	2+ bed	1 bed	2+ bed	1 bed	2+ bed	1 bed	2+ bed	1 bed	2+ bed	1 bed	2+ bed			
	000s	000s	000s	000s	000s	000s	000s	000s	000s	000s	000s	000s	%	%	%
London	6.9	12.9	3.7	4.7	10.0	5.8	0.0	0.1	1.8	6.4	2.6	3.9	69	98	62
South East	2.6	7.2	2.6	2.5	10.2	6.5	0.1	0.2	0.8	4.3	2.5	6.0	53	93	42
South West	1.4	3.6	0.3	1.0	3.6	4.2	0.2	0.0	0.4	1.4	1.1	2.5	46	100	36
East Anglia	0.3	1.4	0.1	0.2	2.3	1.8	0.0	0.0	0.2	1.0	0.5	1.1	44	100	48
East Midlands	1.4	4.7	0.6	0.9	7.6	5.2	0.1	0.0	0.3	1.7	1.0	2.2	47	100	44
West Midlands	2.5	7.5	0.4	0.4	8.2	9.6	0.2	0.3	0.5	1.9	1.6	2.0	44	57	49
Yorkshire & Humberside	1.5	6.8	0.4	0.8	11.0	9.0	0.0	0.2	0.4	1.3	3.0	4.1	43	80	24
North	1.0	3.3	0.5	0.2	5.8	11.3	0.0	0.1	0.2	0.8	1.2	1.4	23	67	36
North West	2.0	6.6	0.1	0.2	12.7	14.6	0.2	0.1	0.3	1.7	2.7	2.9	31	67	37
England	19.7	53.9	8.8	10.8	70.5	68.1	0.6	1.1	5.0	20.5	16.0	26.1	44	91	44

Source: Local authority HIP returns, Department of the Environment.
Note: Regional figures do not always sum to total for England due to rounding. Percentages are also only approximate as they are also based on the rounded figures.

Table 89 Housing association lettings in England
Thousands

	1979/80	1980/81	1981/82	1982/83	1983/84	1984/85	1985/86	1986/87	1987/88	1988/89	1989/90	1990/91	1991/92	1992/93	1993/94
Stock	428	410	423	432	447	464	483	495	512	534	567	608	646	714	779
Lettings	45	51	52	55	58	60	62	64	67	70	76	77	86	109	134
of which:															
New tenants	37	42	43	45	47	49	51	52	54	57	60	62	69	90	112
Existing tenants	8	9	9	10	11	11	11	12	13	13	16	15	17	19	22
Statutory homeless	-	-	-	-	-	-	-	-	-	-	-	9	15	23	28
Lettings to homeless as a % of all lettings to new tenants	-	-	-	-	-	-	-	-	-	-	-	14	21	25	25

Sources: Answers to Parliamentary Questions 16/7/91 and 2/2/94, Housing and Construction Statistics, Cm 2507 & Cm 2807
Note: For years prior to 1989/90 the lettings figures are Department of the Environment estimates. It should be noted that new housing association tenants include former council tenants transferring to a housing association letting.

Table 90a Projected output from the Housing Corporation's Approved Development Programme (ADP) - Approvals

	1990-91 outturn	1991-92 outturn	1992-93 outturn	1993-94 outturn	1994-95 estimated outturn	1995-96 forecast	1996-97 forecast	1997-98 forecast
Housing for rent:								
+ mixed and public funded	9,630	39,970	43,310	43,911	32,275	15,200	21,800	22,100
+ short life (Mini-HAG)	990	1,610	1,380	1,924	2,600	3,700	4,000	4,000
+ Housing Market Package			18,750					
= Total rent (A)	10,620	41,580	63,440	45,835	34,875	18,900	25,800	26,100
Sales and incentives:								
Tenants Incentive Scheme	1,650	3,240	4,800	6,687	7,000	7,300	7,600	8,000
+ Low cost home ownership	1,540	4,820	7,790	11,556	8,800	6,700	8,600	9,000
= Total sales/incentives (B)	3,190	8,060	12,590	18,243	15,800	14,000	16,200	17,000
Total all approvals (A+B)	13,810	49,640	76,030	64,078	50,675	32,900	42,000	43,100

Sources: Housing Corporation ADP for 1994/95 and earlier years, Cms 2207, 2507 & 2807.
Note: Mini-HAG and TIS figures include units financed through the special homeless programmes in 1990/91 and 1991/92.

Table 90b Projected output from the Housing Corporation's Approved Development Programme (ADP) - Completions

	1990-91 outturn	1991-92 outturn	1992-93 outturn	1993-94 outturn	1994-95 estimated outturn	1995-96 forecast	1996-97 forecast	1997-98 forecast
Housing for rent:								
+ mixed and public funded	17,610	21,190	32,160	40,136	41,725	32,700	20,600	20,600
+ short life (Mini-HAG)	990	1,610	1,380	1,924	2,500	3,300	3,900	4,000
+ Housing Market Package			18,430					
= Total rent (A)	18,600	22,800	51,970	42,060	44,225	36,000	24,500	24,200
Sales and incentives:								
Tenants Incentive Scheme	2,270	2,690	4,780	6,450	7,200	7,200	7,500	7,900
+ Low cost home ownership	780	1,280	5,380	7,990	10,000	9,300	9,200	9,000
= Total sales/incentives (B)	3,050	3,970	10,160	14,400	17,200	16,500	16,700	16,900
Total all approvals (A+B)	21,650	26,770	62,130	56,460	61,425	52,500	41,200	41,100

Sources & Notes: As Table 90a.

Table 91 Local authority and housing association lettings to new tenants

Thousands

Year	1979/80	1980/81	1981/82	1982/83	1983/84	1984/85	1985/86	1986/87	1987/88	1988/89	1989/90	1990/91	1991/92	1992/93	1993/94
Local authorities	275	275	251	256	246	240	247	244	242	236	229	240	239	230	234
Housing association	37	42	43	45	47	49	51	52	54	57	60	62	69	90	112
Total	312	317	294	301	293	289	298	296	296	293	289	302	308	320	346

Sources: See Tables 86 & 89.
Note: New housing association tenants include former council tenants transferring to housing associations.

Table 92 Welsh local authority lettings

	1980/81	1981/82	1982/83	1983/84	1984/85	1985/86	1986/87	1987/88	1988/89	1989/90	1990/91	1991/92	1992/93	1993/94
Stock (000s)	297	288	278	265	260	256	258	253	248	238	227	221	217	212
All lettings to new tenants	14,009	13,436	14,864	13,889	15,045	13,896	13,403	13,379	13,071	11,494	11,530	12,030	11,648	12,537
Lettings to homeless	1,531	1,460	1,696	1,597	1,766	2,149	2,054	1,872	2,424	2,429	2,473	2,674	2,676	2,421
Homeless lettings as a % of all lettings	10.9	10.9	11.4	11.5	11.7	15.5	15.3	14.0	18.5	21.1	21.4	22.2	23.0	19.3

Sources: Welsh Housing Statistics, Housing and Construction Statistics.
Notes: Excludes new towns. Stock figures are for the beginning of the financial year.

Table 93 Scottish local authority lettings

	1984/85	1985/86	1986/87	1987/88	1988/89	1989/90	1990/91	1991/92	1992/93	1993/94
New lettings	45,910	45,039	46,720	45,035	47,935	47,086	47,480	44,248	41,234	40,262
Percentage of new lets to homeless	13.6	16.3	15.3	14.3	14.3	16.0	20.0	21.4	23.8	22.7

Source: Scottish Office
Notes: New lettings include waiting list, homeless, National Mobility Scheme and other lettings, but excludes transfers and mutual exchanges.
Figures also include lettings of general needs dwellings owned by other agencies to whose stock the local authority has nomination rights.

Table 94 Northern Ireland Housing Executive lettings and homelessness in Northern Ireland

	1979/80	1980/81	1981/82	1982/83	1983/84	1984/85	1985/86	1986/87	1987/88	1988/89	1989/90	1990/91	1991/92	1992/93	1993/94
Allocations to priority groups	12,043	9,966	10,621	12,824	13,152	12,491	12,417	11,877	10,940	11,357	11,357	11,637	11,170	10,489	10,280
Homelessness:															
presenting											6,675	9,187	10,081	10,099	9,731
accepted A1											3,110	4,404	4,158	4,061	3,971
Placed in temporary accommodation											741	1,849	1,771	1,790	1,865

Source: Department of the Environment for Northern Ireland.
Notes: Allocations to priority groups comprise lettings to new tenants, and exclude transfers. Accepted 'A1' priority need corresponds to acceptance as priority need case elsewhere in the UK. Homeless legislation was only extended to Northern Ireland in April 1989.

Help with housing costs

Table 95 Mortgage interest tax relief

	1980/81	1981/82	1982/83	1983/84	1984/85	1985/86	1986/87	1987/88	1988/89	1989/90	1990/91	1991/92	1992/93	1993/94	1994/95	1995/96
Cost of tax relief (£m) (A)	1,960	2,050	2,150	2,780	3,580	4,750	4,670	4,850	5,400	6,900	7,700	6,100	5,200	4,300	3,500	2,800
Of which in excess of basic rate of income tax (£m)	130	190	170	160	200	260	300	400	350	420	470	0	0	0	0	0
Number of beneficiaries (000s) (B)	5,860	5,850	6,130	7,500	7,800	8,100	8,450	8,750	9,200	9,400	9,600	9,700	9,800	10,000	10,300	10,500
Average tax relief (A/B)	330	350	350	370	460	590	550	550	590	740	820	640	530	430	340	270

Sources: Inland Revenue Statistics, Parliamentary Questions 17/3/93, 25/3/93 and 2/11/93.
Notes: Number of beneficiaries is number of tax units. The 1994/95 and 1995/96 figures are estimates taking account of the successive reductions in the MIRAS rate to 20% & 15%.

Table 96 Mortgage interest tax relief by income band

Income bands	Cost of mortgage tax relief (£ million) (A)							Numbers receiving tax relief (000s) (B)							Average tax relief (£ per annum) (A/B)						
	1988/89	1989/90	1990/91	1991/92	1992/93	1993/94	1994/95	1988/89	1989/90	1990/91	1991/92	1992/93	1993/94	1994/95	1988/89	1989/90	1990/91	1991/92	1992/93	1993/94	1994/95
£0-5,000	270	190	270	260	340	310	250	690	450	490	620	840	840	840	400	420	550	430	410	370	300
£5-10,000	940	970	640	420	520	420	280	1,830	1,660	1,050	850	1,130	1,120	1,050	510	580	610	490	460	380	270
£10-15,000	1,420	1,520	1,520	1,170	1,360	1,050	670	2,560	2,320	2,060	1,920	2,670	2,540	2,080	560	660	740	610	510	410	320
£15-20,000	1,000	1,480	1,670	1,450	1,340	1,050	810	1,710	2,030	2,110	2,180	2,400	2,330	2,260	580	730	800	660	560	450	360
£20-25,000	670	980	1,240	1,120	600	560	510	1,030	1,210	1,530	1,600	1,050	1,220	1,360	650	790	810	700	570	460	380
£25-30,000	380	570	750	590	300	260	360	480	660	850	870	510	570	910	810	860	880	680	590	460	400
£30-40,000	440	650	770	590	370	320	330	460	550	710	850	610	640	800	950	1,180	1,090	690	610	500	400
£40,000 +	380	570	840	500	370	330	290	340	420	600	710	590	640	700	1,100	1,360	1,400	700	630	510	420

Sources: Inland Revenue Statistics, Parliamentary Questions 12/7/93 and 2/11/93.
Note: The numbers receiving relief are defined as the number of tax units. The estimates for 1994/95 take account of the reduction in the MIRAS rate to 20%.

Table 97 Regional mortgage interest tax relief
£ million

	1979/80	1980/81	1981/82	1982/83	1983/84	1984/85	1985/86	1986/87	1987/88	1988/89	1989/90	1990/91	1991/92	1992/93	1993/94
Northern	60	80	70	95	100	140	180	200	210	250	310	350	310	230	190
Yorkshire & Humberside	110	155	150	160	210	260	340	350	360	370	460	510	450	340	350
North West	135	200	180	215	260	330	440	490	510	530	690	770	640	500	450
East Midlands	85	115	110	130	180	230	300	320	330	340	430	480	410	340	350
West Midlands	145	160	190	170	230	280	370	350	360	430	550	620	510	400	390
East Anglia	45	50	60	75	90	130	170	170	180	220	270	300	250	180	170
Greater London	235	280	290	260	400	500	670	620	650	780	980	1,100	710	740	500
Rest of South East	375	555	600	650	740	950	1,270	1,220	1,260	1,350	1,750	1,940	1,510	1,390	1,000
South West	110	140	170	140	230	300	400	380	400	520	660	730	570	480	380
England	1,300	1,735	1,820	1,900	2,440	3,120	4,140	4,100	4,260	4,790	6,100	6,800	5,360	4,600	3,780
+ Wales	45	65	80	80	110	150	200	210	220	180	240	270	230	190	180
+ Scotland	85	125	120	140	190	260	350	300	310	370	470	530	420	340	280
+ Northern Ireland	20	35	30	30	40	50	60	60	60	60	90	100	90	70	60
= United Kingdom	1,450	1,960	2,050	2,150	2,780	3,580	4,750	4,670	4,850	5,400	6,900	7,700	6,100	5,200	4,300

Sources: Answers to Parliamentary Questions 17/3/93 and 29/11/93; Inland Revenue Statistics.
Note: Figures exclude the option mortgage scheme that operated until 1983/84.

Table 98a Subsidies for local authority housing in Great Britain
£ million

	1980/81	1981/82	1982/83	1983/84	1984/85	1985/86	1986/87	1987/88	1988/89	1989/90	1990/91	1991/92	1992/93	1993/94	1994/95	1995/96
England:																
Exchequer subsidy	1,423	881	444	335	381	482	459	445	535	636	1,156	873	508	121	(84)	(226)
+ Rate fund transfers	309	327	252	291	288	258	277	279	309	83	(23)	(21)	(39)	(18)	(21)	(30)
= Total net subsidy	1,732	1,208	696	626	669	740	736	724	844	719	1,133	852	469	103	(105)	(256)
Wales:																
Exchequer subsidy	68	35	10	9	7	10	9	11	12	15	7	(10)	(16)	(37)	(50)	(64)
+ Rate fund transfers	22	12	12	8	5	4	4	8	8	(2)	6	0	0	0	0	0
= Total net subsidy	90	47	22	17	12	14	13	19	20	13	13	(10)	(16)	(37)	(50)	(64)
Scotland:																
Exchequer subsidy	228	162	105	72	67	64	44	42	55	65	58	56	47	36	24	22
+ Rate fund transfers	80	106	125	123	139	98	75	41	25	10	8	(1)	(1)	(2)	(2)	(2)
= Total net subsidy	308	268	230	195	206	162	119	83	80	76	67	55	47	34	23	20
Great Britain:																
Exchequer subsidy	1,719	1,078	559	416	455	556	512	498	602	716	1,221	919	539	120	(110)	(268)
+ Rate fund transfers	411	445	389	422	432	360	356	329	342	93	(9)	(22)	(40)	(20)	(23)	(32)
= Total net subsidy	2,130	1,523	948	838	887	916	868	827	944	809	1,212	897	499	100	(133)	(300)

Sources: See Tables 61, 62, 67, 68 and 74 above. Supplementary information from Department of the Environment, Scottish Office and Welsh Office.
Notes: Figures for transfers between the General Fund and the Housing Revenue Account for the years to 1989/90 are net. Figures for housing subsidy in England and Wales from 1990/91 are for net basic subsidy (positive subsidy entitlements less negative subsidy entitlements).

Table 98b **General subsidies per local authority dwelling**
£ per annum

	1980/81	1981/82	1982/83	1983/84	1984/85	1985/86	1986/87	1987/88	1988/89	1989/90	1990/91	1991/92	1992/93	1993/94	1994/95	1995/96
England:																
Exchequer subsidy	286	179	93	72	84	106	103	102	126	155	286	224	133	32	-23	-63
+ Rate fund transfers	62	66	53	63	63	57	62	64	73	20	-6	-5	-10	-5	-6	-8
= Total net subsidy	348	245	146	135	147	163	165	166	198	175	280	219	123	27	-29	-71
Wales:																
Exchequer subsidy	231	124	36	34	27	40	36	45	52	65	31	-46	-74	-171	-236	-305
+ Rate fund transfers	75	43	43	30	19	16	16	33	34	-9	27	0	0	0	0	0
= Total net subsidy	306	167	79	63	47	55	51	78	86	56	58	-46	-74	-171	-236	-305
Scotland:																
Exchequer subsidy	255	182	119	82	78	75	52	51	68	85	78	77	70	55	38	36
+ Rate fund transfers	89	119	141	141	161	115	89	49	31	13	11	-1	-1	-3	-3	-3
= Total net subsidy	345	301	260	223	239	190	141	100	99	100	90	76	70	52	37	33
Great Britain:																
Exchequer subsidy	279	177	94	72	80	99	92	92	114	140	243	190	115	26	-24	-61
+ Rate fund transfers	67	73	65	73	76	64	64	61	65	18	-2	-5	-9	-4	-5	-7
= Total net subsidy	345	250	160	145	157	163	156	152	178	159	241	186	106	22	-29	-68

Sources: As Table 98a.
Notes: As Table 98a. Average figures per dwelling are calculated by dividing the figures in Table 98a by the average HRA stock figures for the year. In some cases estimated stock figures have been used.

Table 99 Mortgage interest taken into account for income support

	1979	1980	1981	1982	1983	1984	1985	1986	1987	1988	1989	1990	1991	1992	1993	1994
Average mortgage interest:																
£ per week	5.96	10.18	12.18	13.87	11.93	15.18	-	18.96	19.31	18.33	24.18	34.32	44.22	44.03	42.32	38.42
£ per annum (A)	310	529	633	721	620	789	-	986	1,004	953	1,257	1,785	2,299	2,290	2,201	1,998
Number of claimants (000s) (B)	98	134	196	235	242	277	-	356	334	300	281	310	411	499	556	529
Total mortgage interest per annum (£ million) (A x B)	31	71	124	170	150	219	-	351	335	286	353	553	949	1,143	1,222	1,057

Sources: Annual Statistical Enquiries, Parliamentary Question 9/7/91, Income Support Statistics Quarterly Enquiries May 1993 & 1994.
Notes: Figures show mortgage interest liabilities taken into account in calculating eligibility for income support, and in earlier years supplementary benefit. No figures for 1985 are available. Since 1987 the average figure for weekly mortgage interest has been somewhat depressed by the regulation permitting new claimants to claim only 50% of their mortgage costs during the first 16 weeks of their claim.

Table 100 Range of mortgage interest taken into account for income support
Percentage of all new claimant cases

Full weekly interest payment liabilities	1990	1991	1992	1993	1994
£ 0 - £40	36.3	33.7	40.7	57.3	58.4
£40 - £60	21.7	20.9	19.8	19.8	21.0
£60 - £80	14.8	13.1	13.1	10.1	11.3
£80 - £100	7.6	9.2	8.7	6.1	4.7
£100 +	19.5	23.0	17.7	6.7	4.5
Average amount (£ per week)	67.38	71.22	61.18	45.48	41.74

Sources: Annual Statistical Enquiries 1990, 1991 & 1992, Income Support Statistics Quarterly Enquiries May 1993 & 1994.
Note: Figures show the full weekly interest liabilities of new claimant cases where only 50% of the amounts shown are initially eligible for income support assistance.

Help with housing costs

Table 101 Housing benefit - numbers of claimants and average claim in Great Britain

	1979/80	1980/81	1981/82	1982/83	1983/84	1984/85	1985/86	1986/87	1987/88	1988/89	1989/90	1990/91	1991/92	1992/93	1993/94	1994/95
Number of claimants (000s)																
Rent rebates:	1,205	1,330	1,590	3,050	3,735	3,745	3,710	3,720	3,665	3,132	2,923	2,944	2,981	3,053	3,045	2,981
Rent allowances:	220	240	250	260	1,015	1,080	1,150	1,180	1,195	965	1,035	1,044	1,219	1,424	1,619	1,776
Rate Rebates, council tax & community charge benefit:	3,065	3,350	3,700	5,320	7,020	7,230	7,020	7,050	6,875	5,150	5,225	6,898	6,506	6,872	5,526	5,641
Average payments (£ per annum)																
Rent rebates:	199	240	308	306	534	554	606	632	675	824	903	1,030	1,184	1,375	1,505	-
Rent Allowances:	181	199	263	288	528	601	619	811	849	977	1,095	1,323	1,694	1,999	2,268	-
Rate rebates, council tax & community charge benefit:	65	82	101	102	176	178	209	223	243	260	268	319	178	236	317	-

Sources: Parliamentary Questions 10/3/92 & 13/3/92, Social Security Departmental Reports Cms 2213, 2513 & 2813, Social Security Statistics 1991 to 1994.
Notes: From 1983/84 figures include supplementary benefit cases. This accounts for both the substantial increase in numbers and the average benefit payment that year. Rate rebate figures are for the years to 1989/90; community charge benefit figures are for the years 1990/91 to 1992/93 and council tax benefit figures are for 1993/94 onwards. Average benefit payments from 1988/89 onwards are derived from Social Security Statistics; average figures for numbers of claimants from 1988/89 are derived from the DSS Annual Reports; figures for earlier years are derived from the Parliamentary Questions.

Table 102 Supplementary benefit assistance with housing costs in Great Britain

		1978/79	1979/80	1980/81	1981/82	1982/83	1983/84	1984/85
	Local authority tenants:							
	Number of tenants (000s)	1,457	1,420	1,513	1,764	1,980	1,952	2,053
x	Average housing costs (£ per week)	8.00	8.30	10.60	14.70	5.60	1.20	1.20
=	Total housing costs (£ million) (A)	606	613	834	1,348	577	122	128
	Private tenants:							
	Number of tenants (000s)	516	469	473	547	591	548	589
x	Average housing costs (£ per week)	6.50	7.30	8.60	11.30	13.90	1.00	1.10
=	Total housing costs (£ million) (B)	174	178	212	321	427	28	34
	Total costs for all tenants (£ million) (A+B)	781	791	1,045	1,670	1,004	150	162

Source: The Welfare State: Sources of Data on Government Expenditure, Chris Gordon Welfare State Programme Programme Research Note 14, 1988, London School of Economics and Political Science.
Notes: The cost figures are estimates of eligible housing costs that formed part of supplementary benefit payments under the old system. From November 1992 council rents were met under the 'unified' housing benefit scheme, as were private rents from April 1993. Earlier figures include help with rent, general and water rates. Figures after those dates include water rates only. The average figure for council tenants in 1992/93 reflects the switch in systems during the course of the financial year.

Table 103 Housing benefits expenditure and plans for Great Britain
£ million

	1986/87 outturn	1987/88 outturn	1988/89 outturn	1989/90 outturn	1990/91 outturn	1991/92 outturn	1992/93 outturn	1993/94 outturn	1994/95 estimated outturn	1995/96 plans	1996/97 plans	1997/98 plans
Rent rebates [1]:												
England	1,950	2,001	2,144	2,318	2,690	3,256	3,771	4,183	4,433	4,567	4,750	4,900
+ Scotland	263	296	315	364	400	444	490	521	550	545	600	600
+ Wales	134	135	148	156	167	186	212	230	280	296	300	350
+ New Towns	72	74	111	102	87	85	82	86	82	78	100	100
= Total rent rebates	2,419	2,506	2,718	2,940	3,344	3,971	4,555	5,020	5,345	5,486	5,750	5,950
+ Rent allowances	996	1,030	1,055	1,359	1,756	2,404	3,238	4,173	4,908	5,510	6,450	7,350
+ Income support: mortgage costs[2]	351	335	286	353	553	949	1,143	1,222	1,057	1,000	900	900
= Total housing benefits	3,766	3,871	4,059	4,652	5,653	7,324	8,936	10,415	11,310	11,996	13,100	14,200
+ Rate rebate, community charge and council tax benefit	1,635	1,701	1,373	1,520	2,113	1,398	1,685	1,901	2,005	2,039	2,250	2,400
= Total housing & related benefits	5,401	5,572	5,432	6,172	7,766	8,722	10,621	12,316	13,315	14,035	15,350	16,600
Total all social security benefits	44,913	46,697	47,333	50,174	56,453	66,126	75,164	82,398	85,221	87,463	90,900	95,000

Sources: Social Security Departmental Reports, Cms 1914, 2215, 2515 & 2813. Annual Statistical Enquiries etc for Income Support mortgage costs (see Table 99 above).
Notes: 1. Rent rebate figures for England and Wales are gross expenditure, before deducting the contribution to their cost made by rent surpluses - see Tables 62 & 68.
2. Eligible mortgage costs for income support calculation of entitlement. Author's estimates for 1995/96 and subsequent years.

Table 104 **Average housing benefit per recipient in Great Britain**
£ per week

	Housing benefit cases in receipt of income support						Housing benefit cases not in receipt of income support						All housing benefit cases					
	1988	1989	1990	1991	1992	1993	1988	1989	1990	1991	1992	1993	1988	1989	1990	1991	1992	1993
England:																		
Rent rebates	18.61	19.96	22.98	26.76	30.77	33.31	12.54	14.13	16.28	18.88	22.44	24.69	16.26	17.58	20.18	23.35	27.30	29.95
Rent allowances	21.72	25.10	31.28	37.69	43.91	49.41	14.59	15.65	19.07	25.25	29.93	33.45	18.73	21.44	25.86	32.96	39.02	44.34
Scotland:																		
Rent rebates	15.73	17.99	20.39	23.05	25.14	26.47	11.22	12.98	14.26	16.09	18.44	20.16	13.76	15.75	17.71	19.87	22.13	23.79
Rent allowances	24.77	26.81	29.54	34.51	37.64	41.77	13.77	15.06	16.32	21.95	27.62	27.94	19.92	21.61	23.13	29.72	33.72	36.67
Wales:																		
Rent rebates	19.34	21.50	23.26	26.14	29.29	31.04	13.18	15.31	16.56	17.86	21.15	23.64	16.87	18.96	20.37	22.57	25.86	28.12
Rent allowances	19.84	23.18	26.15	32.31	36.94	40.96	13.13	13.06	17.02	24.21	27.43	32.67	17.44	19.17	22.24	29.44	33.80	38.97
Great Britain:																		
Rent rebates	18.16	19.75	22.60	26.16	29.88	32.23	12.33	14.00	15.95	18.37	21.73	23.91	15.85	17.36	19.80	22.76	26.45	28.95
Rent allowances	21.88	25.14	30.88	37.20	43.20	48.58	14.47	15.42	18.72	24.98	29.66	33.05	18.78	21.06	25.45	32.57	38.45	43.61

Source: Social Security Statistics
Notes: All figures based on May in each year. Rent rebates cover local authority and new town tenants. Rent allowances cover housing association and private tenants.

Table 105 Numbers of housing benefit recipients in Great Britain
Thousands

	Housing benefit cases in receipt of income support							Housing benefit cases not in receipt of income support							All housing benefit cases						
	1988	1989	1990	1991	1992	1993	1994	1988	1989	1990	1991	1992	1993	1994	1988	1989	1990	1991	1992	1993	1994
England:																					
Rent rebates	1,515	1,383	1,347	1,324	1,417	1,492	1,518	960	955	964	1,004	1,006	950	919	2,475	2,338	2,311	2,328	2,423	2,442	2,438
Rent allowances	492	481	516	594	748	900	1,007	356	347	411	364	401	419	432	848	828	927	959	1,149	1,319	1,439
All cases	2,007	1,864	1,863	1,918	2,165	2,391	2,525	1,316	1,302	1,375	1,368	1,407	1,369	1,351	3,323	3,166	3,238	3,287	3,572	3,761	3,877
Scotland:																					
Rent rebates	280	264	263	254	254	264	266	216	214	204	212	206	193	187	496	478	467	466	461	458	453
Rent allowances	43	43	44	45	48	54	66	34	34	41	27	31	31	33	77	77	86	72	78	85	99
All cases	323	307	307	299	302	318	332	250	248	245	239	237	224	220	573	555	553	538	539	543	553
Wales:																					
Rent rebates	97	92	86	86	89	93	94	65	64	65	65	65	61	59	161	155	151	151	154	153	153
Rent allowances	28	32	31	35	42	50	57	16	21	24	19	21	22	24	44	53	55	54	63	72	81
All cases	125	124	117	121	131	143	151	81	85	89	84	86	83	83	205	208	206	205	217	225	234
Great Britain:																					
Rent rebates	1,891	1,739	1,696	1,664	1,760	1,849	1,879	1,241	1,233	1,232	1,280	1,277	1,204	1,166	3,132	2,971	2,928	2,945	3,038	3,053	3,044
Rent allowances	563	556	592	674	838	1,004	1,130	406	403	476	411	452	473	489	969	958	1,067	1,085	1,290	1,476	1,619
All cases	2,454	2,295	2,288	2,338	2,598	2,852	3,009	1,647	1,636	1,708	1,691	1,729	1,677	1,655	4,101	3,929	3,995	4,030	4,328	4,529	4,664

Source: Social Security Statistics.
Notes: Figures based on May in each year, except 1994 where figures for February are shown. Sums of component figures may not equal totals due to rounding.

Table 106 **Housing benefit for housing association and private tenants**

Tenure	Numbers of cases				Average weekly rents			Average weekly housing benefit		
	1992 May (000s)	1993 May (000s)	1994 May (000s)	1994 November (000s)	1992 May £	1993 May £	1994 May £	1992 May £	1993 May £	1994 May £
Housing associations	340	412	508	556	35.50	39.90	43.60	32.20	35.80	39.50
Private tenants	952	1,068	1,126	1,146	43.90	49.90	54.20	40.70	46.80	51.10
of which:										
Regulated tenancies	381	339	294	276	-	-	-	-	-	-
De-regulated tenancies	571	729	826	862	-	-	-	-	-	-

Source: Housing Benefit and Council Tax Benefit Summary Statistics, Department of Social Security.
Notes: Separate statistics for housing association tenants receiving housing benefit have only been collected since May 1992. The 1994 totals for the number of private tenants include a small number of 'other' cases that cannot be classed as regulated, deregulated or housing association tenancies. Previously such cases were apportioned to other categories.

Table 107 **Characteristics of housing benefit recipients in Great Britain in 1993**
Thousands

		Aged 60 and over				Aged under 60				
		All aged 60 & over (A)	Retirement pensioners	Receipt other N I benefits	Others over 60	All aged under 60 (B)	Also receiving: Disability Premium	Lone Parent Premium	Unemployment Benefit	Others under 60	All households (A)+(B)
Not in receipt of income support:											
	Rent rebates	838	753	54	31	364	142	67	33	122	1,202
+	Rent allowances	241	216	16	10	232	56	27	62	87	473
+	Total	1,079	969	70	41	596	198	94	95	209	1,675
Also in receipt of income support:											
+	Rent rebates	668	532	58	78	1,175	192	517	22	443	1,843
+	Rent allowances	232	180	18	34	773	88	204	9	472	1,006
=	Total	900	712	76	112	1,948	280	721	31	915	2,849
Of all cases:											
Households with non - dependants											
	Not in receipt of income support	97	80	11	7	69	27	9	8	26	167
	In receipt of income support	106	71	13	22	195	47	56	1	91	301
Capital > £3,000:											
	Rebate cases	139	131	2	6	12	3	1	1	6	150
	Allowance cases	67	62	2	3	7	4	0	0	3	74

Source: Social Security Statistics 1994
Notes: Sums of component figures may not equal totals due to rounding. Aged over 60 cases include benefit units where either claimant or partner is aged 60 or over.

Table 108 Earnings and income levels at which housing benefit entitlement ceases
£ per week

Household type	Earnings & incomes	Rent levels: £30	£40	£50	£60	£70	£80	£90	£100
Single person aged over 25	Gross earnings	113	136	160	183	207	231	254	278
	Net earnings	98	113	128	144	159	175	190	205
Couple aged over 18	Gross earnings	153	177	200	224	248	271	295	319
	Net earnings	129	145	160	175	191	206	222	237
Lone parent with one child aged under 11	Gross earnings	112	185	215	239	262	286	310	333
	Net earnings	102	150	169	185	200	216	231	246
	Net income	155	171	186	202	217	232	248	263
Lone parent with two children aged under 11	Gross earnings	93	165	227	250	274	298	321	345
	Net earnings	87	137	177	192	208	223	239	254
	Net income	171	188	202	218	233	248	263	279
Couple with two children, one aged under 11 and one aged between 11 and 15	Gross earnings	123	202	248	271	295	319	342	366
	Net earnings	109	161	191	206	222	237	252	268
	Net income	179	194	210	225	240	256	271	287
Couple with four children, two aged under 11 and two aged between 11 and 15	Gross earnings	94	172	246	306	330	354	377	401
	Net earnings	88	142	190	229	244	259	275	290
	Net income	218	234	249	264	280	295	311	326

Notes: All figures based on standard 1995/96 tax and benefit rates. Net earnings are net only of income tax and national insurance deductions. Net income figures include child benefit, lone parent benefit and family credit as appropriate. No account is taken of the extra £10 family credit for households working over 30 hours per week, introduced in May 1995, that is disregarded by the housing benefit scheme.

Table 109 Income support and housing benefits
£ million

		1980/81	1981/82	1982/83	1983/84	1984/85	1985/86	1986/87	1987/88	1988/89	1989/90	1990/91	1991/92	1992/93	1993/94	1994/95
	Great Britain:															
	Home-owners	71	124	170	150	219	300	351	335	286	353	553	949	1,143	1,222	1,057
+	Council tenants	841	1,386	1,777	1,980	2,145	2,296	2,419	2,506	2,718	2,940	3,344	3,971	4,555	5,020	5,345
+	Private tenants	183	270	351	536	687	881	996	1,030	1,055	1,359	1,756	2,404	3,238	4,173	4,908
=	Total (A)	1,095	1,780	2,298	2,666	3,051	3,477	3,766	3,871	4,059	4,652	5,653	7,324	8,936	10,415	11,310
	Northern Ireland:															
	Home-owners	-	-	-	-	4	-	7	9	8	11	14	-	18	17	-
+	All tenants	5	10	15	23	77	86	92	98	105	120	134	152	173	195	220
=	Total (B)	7	12	18	26	81	91	99	107	113	131	148	168	191	212	236
	United Kingdom total (A + B)	1,102	1,792	2,316	2,692	3,132	3,568	3,865	3,978	4,172	4,783	5,801	7,492	9,127	10,627	11,546

Sources: Social Security Departmental Reports, Cms 1914, 2213, 2513 & 2813, Northern Ireland Expenditure Plans and Priorities, Cms 1517, 1917, 2216, 2516 & 2816.
DSS Annual Statistical Enquiries, Income Support Statistics Quarterly Enquiries, and Northern Ireland Social Security Statistical Branch.
Notes: Figures for years before 1983/84 include estimates of assistance with rent paid as part of supplementary benefit. Income support and supplementary benefit figures for help with mortgage costs are for eligible mortgage costs taken into account in calculating overall IS/SB entitlement. Mortgage costs data for Northern Ireland is not available for all years; estimates are included in the Northern Ireland and UK total figures.

Help with housing costs

Table 110a Assistance with housing costs for home-owners, council and private tenants
£ million

	1980/81	1981/82	1982/83	1983/84	1984/85	1985/86	1986/87	1987/88	1988/89	1989/90	1990/91	1991/92	1992/93	1993/94	1994/95	1995/96
General subsidies																
Home-owners	1,925	2,020	2,120	2,740	3,530	4,690	4,610	4,790	5,340	6,810	7,600	6,010	5,130	4,240	3,450	2,760
+ Council tenants	2,130	1,523	948	838	887	916	868	827	944	809	1,212	897	499	100	(133)	(300)
= Total	4,055	3,543	3,068	3,578	4,417	5,606	5,478	5,617	6,284	7,619	8,812	6,907	5,629	4,340	3,317	2,460
Means-tested assistance																
Home-owners	71	124	170	150	219	300	351	335	286	353	553	949	1,143	1,222	1,057	1,000
+ Council tenants	841	1,386	1,777	1,980	2,145	2,296	2,419	2,506	2,718	2,940	3,344	3,971	4,555	5,020	5,345	5,486
+ Private tenants	183	270	351	536	687	881	996	1,030	1,055	1,359	1,756	2,404	3,238	4,137	4,908	5,510
= Total	1,095	1,780	2,298	2,666	3,051	3,477	3,766	3,871	4,059	4,652	5,653	7,324	8,936	10,379	11,310	11,996
All forms of assistance																
Home-owners	1,996	2,144	2,290	2,890	3,749	4,990	4,961	5,125	5,626	7,163	8,153	6,959	6,273	5,462	4,507	3,760
+ Council tenants	2,971	2,909	2,725	2,818	3,032	3,212	3,287	3,333	3,662	3,749	4,556	4,868	5,054	5,120	5,212	5,186
+ Private tenants	183	270	351	536	687	881	996	1,030	1,055	1,359	1,756	2,404	3,238	4,137	4,908	5,510
= Total	5,150	5,323	5,366	6,244	7,468	9,083	9,244	9,488	10,343	12,271	14,465	14,231	14,565	14,719	14,627	14,456
Shares of total assistance																
Means-tested	21	33	42	43	41	38	41	41	39	38	39	51	61	71	77	83
Home-owners	39	40	43	46	50	55	54	54	54	58	56	49	43	37	31	26

Sources: See Tables 95, 97, 98a, 99 and 103 above.
Note: All figures are for Great Britain. Figures for means tested assistance to private tenants include housing association tenants.

Table 110b **Assistance with housing costs for home-owners, council and private tenants**
£ million at 1995 prices

	1980/81	1981/82	1982/83	1983/84	1984/85	1985/86	1986/87	1987/88	1988/89	1989/90	1990/91	1991/92	1992/93	1993/94	1994/95	1995/96
General subsidies																
Home-owners	4,339	4,064	3,898	4,844	5,933	7,373	7,033	7,011	7,520	8,877	9,052	6,728	5,507	4,493	3,565	2,760
+ Council tenants	4,801	3,064	1,743	1,481	1,491	1,440	1,324	1,210	1,329	1,055	1,444	1,004	536	106	(137)	(300)
= Total	9,139	7,127	5,641	6,325	7,424	8,813	8,357	8,221	8,850	9,932	10,495	7,732	6,043	4,599	3,427	2,460
Means-tested assistance																
Home-owners	160	249	313	265	368	472	535	490	403	460	659	1,062	1,227	1,295	1,092	1,000
+ Council tenants	1,895	2,788	3,267	3,500	3,605	3,609	3,690	3,668	3,828	3,833	3,983	4,445	4,890	5,320	5,523	5,486
+ Private tenants	412	543	645	948	1,155	1,385	1,519	1,508	1,486	1,772	2,091	2,691	3,476	4,384	5,071	5,510
= Total	2,468	3,581	4,225	4,713	5,128	5,466	5,745	5,666	5,716	6,064	6,733	8,199	9,593	10,999	11,686	11,996
All forms of assistance																
Home-owners	4,499	4,313	4,210	5,109	6,302	7,845	7,568	7,501	7,923	9,338	9,711	7,790	6,734	5,788	4,657	3,660
+ Council tenants	6,696	5,852	5,010	4,982	5,096	5,050	5,015	4,878	5,157	4,887	5,426	5,449	5,425	5,426	5,385	5,186
+ Private tenants	412	543	645	948	1,155	1,385	1,519	1,508	1,486	1,772	2,091	2,691	3,476	4,384	5,071	5,510
= Total	11,607	10,708	9,866	11,038	12,553	14,279	14,102	13,887	14,566	15,996	17,228	15,931	15,635	15,598	15,114	14,456

Sources & Notes: As Table 110a. Cash figures adjusted by the all items Retail Prices Index.